Spatial Models of Parliamentary Voting

This book presents a simple geometric model of voting as a tool to analyze parliamentary roll call data. Each legislator is represented by one point, and each roll call is represented by two points that correspond to the policy consequences of voting Yea or Nay. On every roll call each legislator votes for the closer outcome point, at least probabilistically. These points form a spatial map that summarizes the roll calls. In this sense a spatial map is much like a road map in that it visually depicts the political world of a legislature. The closeness of two legislators on the map shows how similar their voting records are, and the distribution of legislators shows what the dimensions of the space are. These maps can be used to study a wide variety of topics, including how political parties evolve over time, the existence of sophisticated voting, the representation of ethnic minorities in the legislature, constituency interests and legislative behavior, and how an executive influences legislative outcomes.

Keith T. Poole is a professor of political science at the University of California, San Diego. He is the author or coauthor of more than 40 articles as well as the coauthor of *Congress: A Political–Economic History of Roll Call Voting* and *Income Redistribution and the Realignment of American Politics.*

Analytical Methods for Social Research

Analytical Methods for Social Research presents texts on empirical and formal methods for the social sciences. Some series volumes are broad in scope, addressing multiple disciplines; others focus mainly on techniques applied within specific fields, such as political science, sociology, and demography.

Previously published:

Event History Modeling: A Guide for Social Scientists, Janet M. Box-Steffensmeier and Bradford S. Jones

Ecological Inference: New Methodological Strategies, Gary King, Ori Rosen, and Martin A. Tanner

Spatial Models of Parliamentary Voting

Keith T. Poole
University of California, San Diego

CAMBRIDGE
UNIVERSITY PRESS

CAMBRIDGE UNIVERSITY PRESS
Cambridge, New York, Melbourne, Madrid, Cape Town, Singapore, São Paulo

Cambridge University Press
40 West 20th Street, New York, NY 10011-4211, USA

www.cambridge.org
Information on this title: www.cambridge.org/9780521851947

First published 2005

Printed in the United States of America

A catalog record for this publication is available from the British Library.

Library of Congress Cataloging in Publication Data
Poole, Keith T.
Spatial models of parliamentary voting / Keith T. Poole.
    p. cm. – (Analytical methods for social research)
Includes bibliographical references and index.
ISBN 0-521-85194-7 (hardcover) – ISBN 0-521-61747-2 (pbk.)
1. Legislative bodies – Voting – Decision making – Mathematical models.
2. Social choice – Mathematical models. I. Title. II. Series.
JF501.P66   2005
328.3'75 – dc22   2005001003

ISBN-13   978-0-521-85194-7 hardback
ISBN-10   0-521-85194-7 hardback

ISBN-13   978-0-521-61747-5 paperback
ISBN-10   0-521-61747-2 paperback

for Jan

Contents

List of Tables and Figures

Tables

Figures

Preface

This book is the end result of a thirty-year journey that began at the University of Rochester in 1974. In the spring semester of that year I took a course from Richard McKelvey on scaling methods. That course changed my life. Dick showed us how to take lists of numbers and transform them into simple pictures that conveyed meaning. Summarizing data with pictures! It was a revelation – I knew that this was what I wanted to do as a career.

Everything crystallized for me because the previous academic year I had taken a graduate course with Bill Riker on positive political theory where I learned about spatial voting models. After reading Riker and Ordeshook (1973) and Converse (1964), the scaling course with Dick convinced me that the correct way to measure ideology or Conversian belief systems was through the empirical estimation of spatial models of choice.

Dick left Rochester in the fall of 1974 to visit at Carnegie-Mellon for a year, and then he elected to stay at CMU. Partly due to my persistence but mostly due to his being such a nice guy, Dick agreed to chair my dissertation despite the fact that he had left Rochester. I went down to Pittsburgh two times to work with him before I finished up in late 1977. During my first trip, early in 1977, I had an after-dinner conversation with Dick and Peter Ordeshook during which Peter explained the two-space theory that he and Mel Hinich had developed. For me that was the last piece of the puzzle. The two-space theory reconciled classical spatial theory with the low-dimensional spatial maps from the early applications of multidimensional scaling to political choice data.

During my last trip to Pittsburgh in 1977, when I was nearly finished with my dissertation, I remember sitting in a Burger King with Dick – we were into gourmet food – and telling him an idea I had about interest group ratings. He liked the idea, gave me some advice on how to estimate the model I had in mind, and encouraged me to pursue it. That was the source of my first publication, and it got my academic career off the ground. A few years later, in 1981, Dick put in a good word on my behalf when I was being considered for a postdoc at Carnegie-Mellon.

During the 1981–1982 academic year I was a postdoctoral Fellow at the Graduate School of Industrial Administration (GSIA) at Carnegie-Mellon University and had the very good fortune of linking up with Howard Rosenthal. Howard was also interested in ideology because of his in-depth studies of French politics, and he was also very knowledgeable about spatial theory. Very early in 1982 I gave a seminar at GSIA on my early interest group scaling work, and I was somewhat puzzled by the large number of tenured professors (many of whom I did not know well) who came to the talk. I had no idea that it was a stealth job talk. Thanks to Howard's efforts, I was hired at GSIA beginning in the fall of 1982, and our long collaboration began that year.

Howard is a skilled methodologist, and he convinced me that we ought to try modeling congressional roll call voting. Thus, NOMINATE was born in 1982–1983 (Howard invented the acronym – *NOMINA*i *T*hree-*S*tep *E*stimation). In 1985 the NSF began its supercomputing initiative. We applied for and got time on the CYBER 205 supercomputer at Purdue University, and from January 1986 to late 1987 we developed D-NOMINATE.

Howard and I never viewed our NOMINATE work as an end in itself. We were always interested in how the spatial maps could be used to understand U.S. political-economic history. The bulk of our book – *Congress: A Political-Economic History of Roll Call Voting* – is devoted to showing that important episodes in U.S. political and economic history can be better understood by supplementing and/or reinterpreting more traditional analyses with the two-space theory of ideology as measured by the NOMINATE scores.

Unlike my book with Howard, this book is focused on the technical aspects of designing and estimating spatial models of parliamentary voting. However, I adhere to the philosophy that Howard and I stated on many occasions. Estimating spatial maps is easy using existing computer programs. But the maps are worthless unless the user understands both the spatial theory that the computer program embodies and the politics of the legislature that produced the roll calls.

Acknowledgments

There are so many people who have helped me out along the way that it is difficult to know where to begin. I would not have had an academic career if it had not been for the efforts of John Orbell and Bill Mitchell to get me hired at the University of Oregon in the spring of 1978. It was a tough job market back then and I might have ended up as a rich computer programmer in Bellevue, Washington, had I not gotten my foot in the door at the U of O.

At Carnegie-Mellon, Tom Romer, Dennis Epple, Allan Meltzer, Tom Palfrey, John Londregan, Tim Groseclose, Fallaw Sowell, and Steve Spear gave me valuable feedback during the years that NOMINATE and Optimal Classification (OC) were being developed. Just before his untimely death in 1996, my friend Jerry Salancik gave me a set of invaluable comments on my first OC paper. He is sorely missed.

I thank my colleagues at the University of Houston Department of Political Science for hiring me in 2000 to fill the Kenneth L. Lay endowed chair. I have enjoyed being in the Department immensely, and it has been a great place to work. They can be justly proud of the strong traditions of the department that emphasize quality research and teaching. It is no accident that so many great scholars have been faculty members here.

Noah Kaplan, Tim Nokken, and Ernesto Calvo have given me valuable feedback, and they have been great colleagues. Ray Duch has been a great friend (and a great cook), and he helped me out with parts of this book on countless occasions.

Kevin Quinn, Andrew Martin, and Jeff Lewis pushed me to learn R and Bayesian simulation. It turns out that an old dog can learn new tricks, and I have them to thank for that. They also read several of the chapters and gave me detailed comments that improved the presentation of Bayesian simulation and the parametric bootstrap (they can't be blamed for any errors that remain, however).

I spent the 2003–2004 academic year at the Center for Advanced Study in the Behavioral Sciences where most of this book was written. During that stay I had the benefit of numerous very helpful conversations with Simon Jackman. He was unfailingly courteous even when I asked the dumbest questions. Kathleen Much of CASBS read the first six chapters and did an outstanding job of editing the manuscript. Whatever bad English grammar remains is my doing, not hers.

I thank Neal Beck not only for pushing me to write the paper on QN that appeared in *Political Analysis* in 2001, but also for prodding me in a very nice way to keep working on this book and finish it. Although the book is about four years late, he was always patient and I appreciate his support.

During the past five years while I was working on this book Gary Cox has read many versions of the chapters and has given me invaluable feedback. He, Mat McCubbins, and Rod Kiewiet were very early consumers of NOMINATE scores, and all three have been very supportive of my research over the past 15 years. I am very grateful to them for that.

Over the past 13 years I have benefited greatly from innumerable discussions with Nolan McCarty on the topics covered in this book. He helped design and program the personal computer version of W-NOMINATE. It's a closely guarded secret, but he can write FORTRAN with the best.

Larry Rothenberg read all of the chapters more than once (sometimes four times). He is a tough but fair critic, and his advice has been invaluable. This book is much better as a result of his careful reading and advice.

My long-time collaborator Howard Rosenthal read many of the chapters and made many suggestions on how to tighten up the presentation. I expect that our collaboration will continue another 10 years until we both finally retire.

Finally, I dedicate this book to my sweet wife Jan. Her love and support for more than 32 years has been and will always be my center of gravity. I am amazed that she has put up with me for all these years. To me she will always be the beautiful young woman in the flowing flowered tie-dyed dress with the long brown hair. I age but she never does and she never will.

Data and Software

The Web site for this book is http://k7moa.com/Spatial_Models_of_Parliamentary_Voting.htm. There is a separate Web page for each chapter. All the programs and data that are used in each chapter can be downloaded from the corresponding chapter Web page. All the spatial maps shown in this book were done in R, and the R code and data used to make the maps are also posted on the corresponding chapter Web pages. Feel free to contact me via the e-mail address posted on http://k7moa.com if you need help with any of the data or programs.

I will also post problem sets for each chapter to assist those scholars who wish to use this book as part of a college course on scaling. I will be happy to make the answers available to instructors.

CHAPTER 1

Introduction

Overview

In this book I show how to use a simple spatial model of voting as a tool to analyze parliamentary roll call data. Each legislator is represented by one point, and each roll call is represented by two points – one for Yea and one for Nay. On every roll call each legislator votes for the closer outcome point, at least probabilistically. These points form a *spatial map* that summarizes the roll calls. In this sense a spatial map is much like a road map. A spreadsheet that tabulates all the distances between pairs of sizable cities in the U.S. contains the same information as the corresponding map of the U.S., but the spreadsheet gives you no idea what the U.S. looks like.[1] Much like a road map, a spatial map formed from roll calls gives us a way of visualizing the political world of a legislature. The closeness of two legislators on the map shows how similar their voting records are, and the distribution of legislators shows what the dimensions of the space are.

The number of dimensions needed to represent the points is usually small, because legislators typically decide how to vote on the basis of their positions on a small number of underlying evaluative, or *basic*, dimensions. For example, in recent U.S. Congresses, we can easily predict how a "liberal" or a "conservative" will vote on most issues. These basic dimensions structure the roll call votes and are captured by the spatial maps.

In this chapter I develop a simple theory of spatial maps that I call the *basic-space theory of ideology*. In subsequent chapters I use the theory to show how to construct and interpret the spatial maps that reflect it. The theory is based on the work of many scholars in psychology, economics, and political science over the past 50 years and is a parsimonious tool for understanding the construction and interpretation of spatial maps.

---

[1] I borrowed this analogy from Jordan Ellenberg, who used it in an article about my political polarization research with Howard Rosenthal (Ellenberg, 2001).

I begin with some observations on theory and meaning. A spatial map is a picture, and for it to be a summary, it must have a *meaning* for the viewer. That meaning must flow from *a theory about the picture*. In this sense, "a picture is worth a thousand words." My point is simple. Anyone can construct a spatial map using the computer programs I discuss in subsequent chapters. But the maps are worthless unless the user understands both the spatial theory that the computer program embodies and the politics of the legislature that produced the roll calls. A practitioner must be able to stand before an audience of her peers and explain the meaning of the spatial map.

After discussing theory and meaning, the rest of the chapter lays out my theory of spatial maps.

Theory and Meaning

To reiterate, this is a book about the use of pictures to summarize parliamentary roll call data. For the most part these pictures consist of simple geometric representations of the legislators and of the roll calls. For example, members of the left, or liberal, party cluster together on one side of the picture, and members of the right, or conservative, party cluster together on the opposite side of the picture. In this case a glance at the picture by an *experienced* researcher shows what the main sources of conflict are within the parliament and how the roll call voting is structured. By "experienced" I mean that the researcher must understand how the picture was constructed and must understand the political environment of the parliament or legislature. It is the researcher's understanding of the theory about the picture that gives the picture meaning. Without this understanding a person viewing the picture would see just a bunch of dots (or tokens; see Figure 1.2). This would be like someone not trained in physics trying to make sense out of cloud chamber photographs, or someone not trained in electronics trying to make sense out of an ammeter reading of a plate current, and so on.[2]

Although the pictures that are the subject of this book – spatial maps of parliamentary voting – are *not* art, the concept of picture-as-summary is a slippery one that must be used with caution. The boundary line between picture-as-summary and picture-as-art is not as clear as it may appear. For example, consider the most recognized picture in the world – Leonardo da Vinci's painting, *Mona Lisa* (Figure 1.1).[3] Why does this painting seem to

---

[2]Philosophers of science have explored this topic in great depth. Kuhn (1962/1996, pp. 187–191) has a nice discussion of the training of physicists that illustrates the shift in meaning between amateur and specialist.

[3]Leonardo began painting *Mona Lisa* about 1503 and worked on it for many years. Francis I of France bought the portrait but let Leonardo keep it until his death in 1519.

FIGURE 1.1. *Mona Lisa.*

transcend cultures and national boundaries? Is it the finest portrait ever painted? Is it more important than Picasso's *Les Demoiselles d'Avignon*?[4] The answer

---

[4]*Les Demoiselles d'Avignon* was painted in 1907 and is considered a landmark in modern art. It marked the beginning of Picasso's long Cubist period.

of course is obvious – the *smile*. But why the smile? In my opinion Leonardo's genius was, figuratively, to flip a coin and have it land on its edge. He managed to paint a facial expression that is exactly on the cusp between a smile and a frown. Consequently, when we look at the painting, it does not instantly match what we recognize as a smile or a frown. So we attend to it longer than we normally would, and we have to think about it. Hence our fascination.

Not everyone will agree with my interpretation[5] of *Mona Lisa*, but consensus is not my purpose in offering it. Clearly, *Mona Lisa* is not a picture-as-summary for most people. Most people see a beautiful painting of a woman with an ambiguous smile. I see a perceptual trick much like the simple figures used by the Gestalt psychologists. It is high art *and* the work of a great scientific mind. This meaning of the picture for me flows from my theory of the picture.

A Theory of Spatial Maps

Unlike my *Mona Lisa* theory, the basic space theory of ideology underlying the spatial maps of parliamentary voting analyzed in this book is the end result of the work of a large number of scholars. I am deliberately using the word "theory" broadly and loosely for now. In the notion of theory I include: (1) the technical apparatus of the spatial model; (2) a theory of how legislators make decisions; (3) a theory of belief systems (ideology) that is tied to the assumptions of the spatial model and the theory of decision-making; (4) the computer program that embodies (1), (2), and (3) and actually generates the spatial maps; and (5) a substantive understanding of the political system that the parliament or legislature is embedded in. All these are *necessary* for meaning to flow from the spatial map. Simply pushing a matrix of roll call data through a computer program does not itself produce a meaningful picture.

For example, Figure 1.2 is a spatial map of the final passage vote of the landmark 1964 Civil Rights Act in the U.S. Senate.[6] The act was one of the most important roll call votes in U.S. history. It was passed seven months after President John Kennedy was assassinated in November of 1963. In June of 1963 Kennedy introduced his civil rights bill to the nation in a nationally televised address. In a supreme act of leadership, he argued that it was a moral issue

---

[5] For a theory that supports my own, see Livingstone (2002). Her explanation centers on the way an individual's center of gaze on the eyes interacts with peripheral vision to suggest a smile. When an individual then looks directly at the mouth, the smile disappears. My view is that Leonardo deliberately painted the picture the way he did to achieve this effect. For a more traditional interpretation of *Mona Lisa*, see Gombrich (1978, pp. 227–229). He also emphasizes the role of Leonardo the scientist in the construction of *Mona Lisa*.

[6] All the spatial maps in this book were produced in R. The R code and data files for all the spatial maps can be found at the website for this book: http://k7moa.com/Spatial_Models_of_Parliamentary_Voting.htm, under the corresponding chapter links.

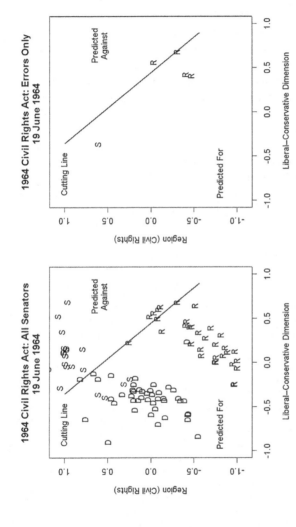

FIGURE 1.2. *Final passage vote on the 1964 Civil Rights Act. Each token corresponds to a senator's ideal point. R stands for Republican, D for Northern Democrat, and S for Southern Democrat. Errors are concentrated near the cutting line. The ideal points and the cutting line are estimates from the DW-NOMINATE model, with a linear time trend in legislator positions. The second dimension is shown unweighted for purposes of clarity.*

that went to the heart of how people treated one another. Discrimination on the basis of skin color was morally wrong, and it must be ended.[7] President Lyndon Johnson in his January 1964 State of the Union address made the civil rights legislation introduced by Kennedy his top legislative priority, and he pushed it through Congress with the help of the Republican and Northern Democratic Congressional leaders.[8]

The spatial map is from DW-NOMINATE (McCarty, Poole, and Rosenthal, 1997; Poole and Rosenthal, 2001). The left panel shows all the senators, and the right panel shows just the five senators who were *errors* in the DW-NOMINATE analysis.[9] Each senator's location in the map is a function of all the roll calls the senator participated in during his/her career. The cutting line is specific to the roll call and divides the senators who are predicted to vote Yea from those who are predicted to vote Nay. The senators who are predicted incorrectly are errors.

Consider just the spatial map of all the senators. The descriptive labels and the relative positions of the party tokens in the map show that a coalition of Republicans and Northern Democrats voted for the act and a coalition of Southern[10] Democrats and a few Republicans voted against the act.[11] The map also shows a clear separation of the Democrats from the Republicans and a sharp division within the Democratic Party. All but four of the Southern Democrats are up near the top of the map.

My analysis of Figure 1.2 so far has not revealed any information that a sophisticated student of American political history would not already know. For me to go any further requires that I say something about the *structure* of the map. I have to explain what the dimensions represent and explain the relative placement of the D, S, and R tokens on the dimensions. These *explanations* of the structure of the map cannot be based on the technical apparatus that

---

[7]"The heart of the question is whether all Americans are to be afforded equal rights and equal opportunities, whether we are going to treat our fellow Americans as we want to be treated. If an American, because his skin is dark, cannot eat lunch in a restaurant open to the public, if he cannot send his children to the best public school available, if he cannot vote for the public officials who represent him, if, in short, he cannot enjoy the full and free life which all of us want, then who among us would be content to have the color of his skin changed and stand in his place?" (John F. Kennedy, 11 June 1963, televised address to the nation.)

[8]See Perlstein (2001) for a thorough account of the events leading up to the passage of the act and its subsequent effect on the 1964 Presidential election.

[9]DW-NOMINATE uses a *weighted Euclidean metric* (see Chapter 4). Figure 1.2 shows the dimensions without the weights for purposes of clarity. If the second-dimension weight of 0.338 were applied to the spatial map, it would squash the configuration down.

[10]Throughout this book the South is defined as the 11 states of the Confederacy plus Kentucky and Oklahoma.

[11]The vote was 73 Yea and 27 Nay. The 67 Democrats who voted split 46 Yea and 21 Nay (Northern Democrats split 43 Yea and 1 Nay; Southern Democrats split 3 Yea and 20 Nay). The 33 Republicans split 27 Yea and 6 Nay.

produced the map. Rather, they must be grounded in the substance of American politics. Furthermore, I have to assume that the reader believes that the technical apparatus that produced the map is reliable and that the reader has a basic understanding of it. Consequently, for me to go further and offer my interpretation of the spatial map of the 1964 Civil Rights Act, I need to outline my theory of spatial maps.

Spatial Models of Voting

The spatial maps used in this book rest on the work of researchers in psychology, economics, and political science. The three fields are equally important to the theory.

In psychology various methods of *multidimensional scaling* (MDS) have been developed during the past 50 years to analyze similarity and preferential choice data. For example, a set of respondents are asked to judge how similar various countries are to each other. MDS methods model these similarities as distances between points representing the countries in a geometric space. These MDS programs are designed to produce a picture-as-summary – literally to summarize a large set of data graphically.[12]

At the same time psychologists were developing MDS, economists and political scientists were developing the spatial theory of voting. In its simplest form the spatial theory of voting can be represented as a map of voters and candidates where the voters vote for the candidate closest to them. In this regard, a spatial map is literally a visual representation of the spatial model of voting. Although Hotelling (1929) and Smithies (1941) are credited with originating the idea, it was the publication of Anthony Downs's *An Economic Theory of Democracy* in 1957 that really established spatial theory as a conceptual tool.

Hotelling studied the logic of the location of a grocery store in a *linear* town – that is, a town strung out along a highway, where all the houses face a single road. It is easy to demonstrate that the optimum location for a grocery store is the *median* of the town (the median minimizes the sum of the walking distances to the store). Hotelling showed that if there are *two* grocery stores, they will locate adjacent to one another. Smithies elaborated this model a bit by introducing elastic demand, so that people at the edges of town might stop shopping at the store if it moved too far to the center (Downs, 1957, p. 117). Hence the stores might not converge at the median of the town.

Downs took the Hotelling–Smithies model of spatial competition of stores and applied it to the competition of political parties. He assumed that voters were distributed over a dimension – for example, government intervention in

---

[12] Two eminent psychometricians, Ingwer Borg and Patrick Groenen, state this very clearly: "The main reason for doing [MDS] is that one wants a graphical display of the structure of the data, one that is much easier to understand than an array of numbers" (Borg and Groenen, 1997, p. vii).

the economy – and that political parties played the role of the stores. He derived a large number of classic results from this simple model. For example, if voters vote for the party closest to them on the dimension, the parties will converge to the median voter. Duncan Black (1948, 1958) had earlier derived a similar result for voting in committees.

Although Downs's work is a brilliant *tour de force*, it did not present spatial theory in a form that was susceptible to empirical testing. No rigorous mathematical structure was presented from which measuring instruments could be designed to test the theory. The needed structure was provided by the work of Otto Davis, Melvin Hinich, and Peter Ordeshook (Davis and Hinich, 1966; Davis, Hinich, and Ordeshook, 1970). By the early 1970s the mathematical structure of spatial theory was largely completed. The dimensions of the space represented issues or policies. Each voter had a position on each issue or policy, and this vector of positions was the voter's *ideal point* in the space. Each voter also had a utility function centered on her ideal point that assigned a utility to each point in the space. The further a point was from the voter's ideal point, the lower the utility. Each candidate also had a position on each issue dimension and therefore was represented as a point in the space. Each voter then voted for the candidate for whom she had the highest utility. In the context of parliamentary voting, the model is exactly the same, only policy outcomes rather than candidates for public office are now the choices.

This early version of the spatial theory of voting did not allow for *error* by voters. That is, voting was deterministic. Voters had ideal points and voted for the candidate closest to them in the policy space. Later, more realistic assumptions about voters' decision rules allowed for probabilistic voting.[13] Nevertheless, this version of spatial theory could at least be investigated empirically.

Psychometrics and Tests of Spatial Theory

In order to test the spatial theory of voting, you need data from voters about how "far" they are from candidates. The first comprehensive test of spatial theory was by Cahoon (1975) and Cahoon, Hinich, and Ordeshook (1976; 1978) using candidate feeling thermometers. Beginning in 1968, feeling thermometers were included in the NES surveys. A feeling thermometer measures how warm or cold a person feels toward the stimulus; the measure ranges from 0 (very cold, unfavorable feeling) to 100 (very warm, favorable feeling), with 50 as a neutral point. In 1968 respondents were asked to give feeling thermometer ratings to the presidential candidates George Wallace, Hubert Humphrey, and Richard Nixon, along with their vice presidential running mates and six other political

---

[13] For example, the standard formulation is to make the probability that a voter chooses the closest candidate a function of both the closeness of the candidate to the voter and a random draw from an error distribution. See McFadden (1976) for a survey of random utility models.

figures.[14] These thermometer scores can be interpreted as distances between the respondent's ideal point and the spatial positions of the candidates. For example, if a respondent gave Humphrey a 100, Nixon a 40, and Wallace a 0, then she was likely to be very close to Humphrey, very far from Wallace, but closer to Nixon than to Wallace.

Cahoon constructed a statistical model of the thermometer scores based on the spatial theory of voting and found that a simple two-dimensional spatial map largely accounted for the observed thermometer scores. His predictions of how the respondents would vote closely matched their actual voting choices.

Figure 1.3 shows a configuration of presidential candidates similar to that estimated by Cahoon. The horizontal dimension is from liberal (on the left) to conservative (on the right), and the vertical dimension is from Democratic (toward the top) to Republican (toward the bottom).

Cahoon was the first to test the spatial theory of voting using thermometer scores, but he was not the first to construct spatial maps from thermometer scores. Herbert Weisberg and Jerrold Rusk (1970) used the MDS procedure developed by Kruskal (1964a,b) to recover a candidate configuration from the candidate-by-candidate correlation matrix computed across the respondents. They did not estimate the respondents' locations.[15]

Although the spatial maps produced by Cahoon and by Weisberg and Rusk are essentially the same and are both pictures-as-summary, they have very different theoretical foundations. The MDS procedures developed by psychologists were intended to help answer questions of importance to psychologists. Namely, given a set of judged similarities between objects (nations, colors, types of crime, emotional states, etc.), researchers could use MDS procedures to uncover underlying psychological dimensions or as a tool to formulate a convincing description of the data. For example, two dimensions – communist–noncommunist and developed–underdeveloped – were found to underlie similarity judgments of nations (Kruskal and Wish, 1978). In contrast, the spatial theory of voting is a *theory of behavior* that states that *if* a set of assumptions holds, *then* voters should behave in a certain way *and* we should observe certain types of outcomes. It is a theory that makes predictions that can be tested.

Although the theoretical foundations are different, as a practical matter the MDS procedures developed by the psychologists are very similar in form to procedures developed to test spatial theory. A full-blown test of spatial theory

---

[14] Besides George Wallace, Hubert Humphrey, and Richard Nixon, the target politicians were Eugene McCarthy, Ronald Reagan, Nelson Rockefeller, Lyndon Johnson, George Romney, Robert Kennedy, Edmund Muskie, Spiro Agnew, and Curtis LeMay. The NES survey was conducted after Robert Kennedy's assassination in June 1968. The assassination obviously affected the ratings Kennedy received.

[15] The 1968 set of thermometer scores has been analyzed by a variety of scaling techniques. See Wang, Schonemann, and Rusk (1975), Rabinowitz (1976), and Poole and Rosenthal (1984a) for examples.

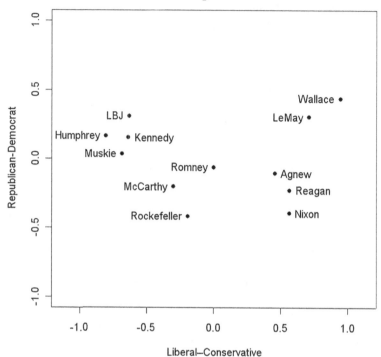

**1968 Candidate Configuration
From Feeling Thermometers**

FIGURE 1.3. *Spatial map of the 1968 presidential candidates. The map was produced by applying nonmetric multidimensional scaling to the candidate-by-candidate Pearson correlation matrix computed from the feeling thermometers.*

like that performed by Cahoon estimates ideal points for the voters and points for the candidates in a spatial map such that the distances between the voters and candidates in the map are as close as possible to the original data. For example, the thermometers range from 0 to 100. Cahoon transformed these into distances by subtracting the thermometer value from 100. Finding points for the voters and points for the candidates that reproduce these distances is known as an *unfolding analysis* in psychology (Coombs, 1964). Techniques to perform unfolding analyses were developed by psychologists in the 1950s and 1960s (Chang and Carroll, 1969; Kruskal, Young, and Seery, 1973), and Cahoon's is also an unfolding methodology. Later Rabinowitz (1976), Poole and Rosenthal (1984a), and Brady (1990) developed unfolding procedures that they applied to thermometer scores.[16]

---

[16]Technically, Brady estimates the *distribution* of the voters rather than their ideal points.

Analyses of roll call data during this period did not attempt to unfold them. Rather, factor analysis and cluster analysis were used to analyze correlation–covariance matrices computed between members across the roll calls (MacRae, 1958, 1970).[17] Similarly, Hoadley (1980) analyzed the emergence of political parties in the early Congresses by computing agreement scores from the roll calls and used Kruskal's MDS procedure to recover configurations of members of Congress. Weisberg (1968), in his analysis of roll call voting, showed that one-dimensional spatial voting would look much like the responses to a classic Guttman scale. But he did not attempt the joint estimation of a spatial map of both the roll calls and legislators.

Why So Few Dimensions? Psychometrics and Multidimensional Scaling

The early tests of spatial theory produced two important puzzles. First, the number of dimensions of the spatial maps appeared to be three or less, and in most applications two dimensions seemed to account adequately for the data. And second, contrary to the predictions of spatial theory, the candidates did not appear to have converged near the median voter or anywhere near the center of the space. This latter problem was later remedied by advances in the theory by a number of scholars.[18] For example, if candidates are motivated by their policy preferences, they may not converge to the center of the space.

With the benefit of hindsight, the finding of low dimensionality should have been no surprise. Low-dimensional maps were a common result of MDS applications in psychology by the early 1970s. For example, the experimental data on the perception of color, perception of sound, similarity of Morse code signals, similarity of nations, relatedness among societal problems (war, poverty, crime, etc.), perceived association of psychological traits (honest, helpful, sincere, tolerant, etc.), and similarity of diseases all fit simple two-dimensional maps.[19]

In addition to low dimensionality, another strong regularity that emerged from the work in psychology was that when people judged the similarity between stimuli or were asked to report preferences for stimuli, they appeared to be using an *exponential response function*. That is, when the actual judged similarities

---

[17] MacRae proposed the model of roll call voting that Howard Rosenthal and I implemented as NOMINATE – namely, ideal points for legislators and two policy outcomes per roll call, one for Yea and one for Nay. But MacRae did not attempt to estimate this unfolding model.

[18] For example, Wittman (1977, 1983), Palfrey (1984), Bernhardt and Ingberman (1985), Calvert (1985), Austen-Smith (1987), Morton (1987), Aldrich and McGinnis (1989), Harrington (1992), and Spector (2000).

[19] See Ekman (1954) and Borg and Groenen (1997) for the color circle example; Shepard (1963) for sound and Morse code examples; Wish (1971) for nations; Wish and Carroll (1974) for societal problems; Rosenberg, Nelson, and Vivekananthan (1968) for traits; and D'Andrade et al. (1972) for disease.

are graphed against some objective measure of similarity, they almost always produce an exponential-like plot (Shepard, 1987). Specifically, if the similarity measure, A, is a number between zero (most similar) and one (least similar), then people tend to report e^{-kA}, where k is a scaling constant. Because people are not perfect judges, when perceptual error is added to Shepard's model the expected value of the response function tends to be *Gaussian* – that is, e^{-kA^2} (Nosofsky, 1986, 1988; Ennis, 1988a, 1988b; Shepard, 1988a; 1988b; Ennis, Palen, and Mullin, 1988).

The fact that the response functions uncovered by psychologists tend to be normal-distribution-like is important because of the general form of the voter's utility function in spatial theory. Most theoretical work on spatial voting models has assumed that the utility function is either quadratic or normal. Empirically, the quadratic utility function is a good approximation to the normal in most applications of spatial voting models (see Chapter 4). Hence, a utility function is not simply a convenient mathematical abstraction. In a choice situation it appears to be capturing a basic type of response to stimulus evaluation. Voters are comparing their ideal point with the choice alternatives, and in spatial theory they choose the alternative that is closest (most similar) to their ideal point.

Other findings from psychology that support low dimensionality are that people are limited in their ability to perceive distinct objects (Miller, 1956) and differing groups of people have a tendency to be drawn into group-against-group hostility (Tajfel, 1981).

Within political science, survey researchers had shown by the late 1960s that most voters did not have highly structured attitudes about politics (Campbell et al., 1960; Nie, Verba, and Petrocik, 1979). Only a small slice of Americans could be said to have *coherent* sets of issue positions. In 1964 Philip Converse published his seminal essay "The Nature of Belief Systems in Mass Publics," which drew heavily on his experience with those surveys. Converse was concerned with the "differences in the nature of belief systems held on the one hand by elite political actors and, on the other, by the masses" (p. 206). Converse defined a belief system as "a configuration of ideas and attitudes in which the elements are bound together by some form of constraint or functional interdependence" (p. 207). Constraint means that issues are interrelated or bundled and that ideology is fundamentally *the knowledge of what goes with what*.[20]

From an observer's point of view, the knowledge of one or two issue positions makes the remaining positions easily predictable.[21] The simplest of all

---

[20] As Hinich and Pollard (1981) point out, it is not necessary that the person influenced by the ideology know *why* what goes with what. Rather, words like "liberal" and "conservative" are best understood as labels that have become attached to certain consistent patterns of political behavior. (See Poole, 1988, for an elaboration of this point.)

[21] Sowell (1987, p. 13) observes that "One of the curious things about political opinions is how often the same people line up on opposite sides of different issues. The issues themselves may have

is the *liberal–moderate–conservative* continuum so familiar to journalists and the political cognoscenti. "The efficiency of such a yardstick in the evaluation of events is quite obvious. Under certain appropriate circumstances, the single word 'conservative' used to describe a piece of proposed legislation can convey a tremendous amount of more specific information about the bill – who probably proposed it and toward what ends, who is likely to resist it . . . its long-term social consequences . . . and . . . how the actor himself should expect to evaluate it" (p. 214). In contemporary American politics the knowledge that a politician opposes raising the minimum wage makes it virtually certain that she opposes universal health care, opposes affirmative action, and so on. In short, that she is a *conservative* and almost certainly a Republican.

Although forty years of empirical work by political scientists have shown that the American public is not *strictly* ideological in that most people do not have coherent belief systems, Americans also are not "ideologically innocent" either (Feldman and Zaller, 1992). Ideological consistency – that is, the degree to which issue positions are generated by a few underlying basic issues, such as liberal–conservative – clearly varies. It is almost certainly a top-down phenomenon. Political elites are more ideologically consistent than the mass public, and it is quite likely that this consistency affects how issues are "packaged" (Hinich and Munger, 1997, Chapter 9). Hence members of national legislatures such as the U.S. Congress should exhibit coherent belief systems.

The Breakthrough: The Two-Space Theory

If the voters have coherent belief systems, then within the spatial theory of voting their issue positions lie on a low-dimensional plane through the issue space, because attitudes across the issues are *constrained*. The presence of constraint means that a voter's positions on a variety of specific issues can be captured by her position on one or two fundamental dimensions such as liberalism–conservatism. The presence of constraint implies *two* spaces – one with a few fundamental dimensions, and a second, high-dimensional space representing all the distinct issues.

For example, suppose there are s fundamental dimensions, p voters, and n issues, where $s < n$. Let $\mathbf{X}$ be the p by s matrix of ideal points of the p voters on the s dimensions, and let $\mathbf{Y}$ be the p by n matrix of voters' ideal points on the n issues. The presence of constraint means that the voters' positions on the fundamental dimensions $\mathbf{X}$ generate all the issue positions $\mathbf{Y}$; that is, $\mathbf{XW} = \mathbf{Y}$, where the s by n matrix $\mathbf{W}$ maps the fundamental dimensions onto the issue

---

no intrinsic connection with each other. They may range from military spending to drug laws to monetary policy to education. Yet the same familiar faces can be found glaring at each other from opposite sides of the political fence, again and again."

dimensions.[22] Under this interpretation, the low-dimensional maps produced by the various scaling procedures discussed above show the low-dimensional space underlying individuals' evaluations (the X *space*) – not the multidimensional issue space (the Y *space*).

This two-space theory was stated as a conjecture by Cahoon, Hinich, and Ordeshook (1976), who dubbed the low-dimensional space a *basic space* and the high-dimensional space an *action space* containing all "contemporary political issues [and] government policies" (Ordeshook, 1976, p. 308).[23] Hinich and his colleagues then developed the theory in detail, including how one space mapped into the other (Hinich and Pollard, 1981; Enelow and Hinich, 1984). They labeled the dimensions of the low-dimensional space the *predictive dimensions*. More generally, these are latent or evaluative dimensions, and in political science work they are commonly referred to as *ideological dimensions* (Hinich and Munger, 1994; 1997). I will refer to these as *basic dimensions* in this book.[24]

The 1964 Civil Rights Act

The basic-space theory of ideology outlined above permits a parsimonious interpretation of the spatial map of the final passage vote of the 1964 Civil Rights Act shown in Figure 1.2. There are two basic dimensions. The primary dimension is indeed the liberal–moderate–conservative dimension epitomized by voting on the fundamental issue of the role of government in the economy. The second dimension captures the conflict over race and civil rights. It emerged during the latter part of the New Deal when, in the wake of the 1936 elections, Northern Democrats heavily outnumbered Southern Democrats in the U.S. Congress. Many of the programs initiated during the subsequent Second New Deal were not to the liking of the South. Voting on minimum wages in 1937 and 1938, followed by voting during World War II on the poll tax and voting rights in the armed forces, helped to split the Democratic Party into two distinct regional wings (Poole and Rosenthal, 1997; McCarty, Poole, and Rosenthal,

---

[22] Alternatively, the issue positions can be viewed as being mapped onto the fundamental dimensions: $X = YW$, where the n by s matrix W maps Y into X. This is almost certainly true of *new* issues (Poole and Rosenthal, 1997, Chapter 5).

[23] Ordeshook (1976) proposed a model with *three* spaces – a common underlying preference space, an action space, and a third space identical to the action space but recording the positions of the candidates. It is not clear that Ordeshook's "common underlying preference space" is of low dimensionality, but in a conversation with me in November 1976, he explicitly outlined in detail the basic-space–action-space model used in this book.

[24] My use of the label "basic dimensions" is also motivated by the fact that Horst (1963) refers to the singular value decomposition of a rectangular matrix as the *basic structure* of a matrix. Roll call matrices are inherently rectangular, and any method that estimates parameters for legislators and parameters for roll calls is performing a form of matrix decomposition. Hence the connection.

1997). Voting in the U.S. Congress became two-dimensional in order to differentiate Northerners from Southerners on civil rights and related votes. With the passage of the 1964 Civil Rights Act, the 1965 Voting Rights Act, and the 1967 Open Housing Act, the second dimension slowly declined in importance, and it is now almost totally absent.

Race-related issues – affirmative action, welfare, Medicaid, subsidized housing, etc. – are now largely questions of *redistribution*. Voting on these issues, along with more symbolic issues like hate-crimes legislation, now take place along the liberal–conservative dimension, and the old split in the Democratic Party between North and South has largely disappeared.[25] Voting in the U.S. Congress is now almost purely one-dimensional – a single dimension accounts for almost 90 percent of roll call voting choices in the 104th through the 107th Congresses – and the two parties are increasingly polarized.[26]

Note that I used both the basic dimensions and the specific issue dimensions to interpret the 1964 Civil Rights Act vote. The basic dimensions cannot be understood unless *all* the roll calls are classified by their substantive content. The overall fit of a set of roll calls with same issue content can be used to determine the extent to which a specific issue dimension is captured by the basic space.

A Road Map to the Rest of This Book

In the next two chapters I develop the geometry of roll call voting. Legislators are represented as points, and the roll calls are represented as lines or planes that pass through the legislators, dividing them into those who vote Yea and those who vote Nay. The configuration of legislator points determines the locations of the roll call lines or planes, and the configuration of roll call lines or planes determines the locations of the legislator points. I consider only the simple spatial model of two outcomes per roll call. I do not consider abstention or multichoice voting, because most existing research is focused on the two choice spatial model. In addition, the geometry of the multichoice model still has not been fully worked out.

Chapter 2 deals with *perfect voting*, that is, voting with no errors by the legislators. Perfect voting allows me to show the inherent limits that the geometry places upon any scaling procedure. For example, in one dimension with perfect voting, the legislators are identified only up to a rank ordering. In more than

---

[25] See Carmines and Stimson (1989) for a brilliant discussion of how race has transformed American party politics since the end of World War II.

[26] Polarization is analyzed by Poole and Rosenthal (1984b; 1997), King (1998), and McCarty, Poole, and Rosenthal (2001).

one dimension, legislators are identified only up to polytopes (regions bounded by cutting lines or planes).

Chapter 3 details a nonparametric method – *optimal classification* (OC) – that is based on the geometry shown in Chapter 2 and is designed to analyze real-world roll call data. OC maximizes the correct classification of legislative choices. At the heart of OC are two algorithms – the *cutting plane procedure* and the *legislative procedure*. Both of these procedures are unique and are very stable. In particular, when the number of legislators is 100 or greater and the number of roll calls is on the order of 500 – typical of national legislatures like the U.S. Senate – then the recovery of the legislators and cutting lines or planes is very precise (Poole, 1997; 2000a;b). OC is a stable building block upon which more complex parametric scaling methods can be constructed.

In Chapter 4, I discuss probabilistic models of parliamentary voting. Error is introduced via the *random utility model*, and the main scaling methods are explained in detail – NOMINATE, quadratic–normal (QN) scaling, and the Bayesian Markov chain Monte Carlo (MCMC) approach. These methods are related to the basic geometry detailed in Chapter 2.

In Chapter 5, I turn to practical issues of estimation of spatial models – how to generate good starting values, how to determine dimensionality, how to interpret the dimensions, and so on, along with some computing tricks I have used over the years that eager readers who want to "roll their own" might find useful. The practicalities discussed in this chapter are the result of 30 years of experimentation in computer code. They are a product of my experience as a builder of computer programs that estimate spatial maps of parliamentary voting. There is usually more than one way to build a mousetrap, and the practical solutions I offer for problems that arise in estimating spatial models are not necessarily unique or my exclusive creation. They have one thing going for them, however: They all work.

In Chapter 6, I show a variety of natural experiments that one can perform using roll call matrices: for example, simple ways to combine roll call data matrices to test whether or not legislators alter their ideal points when they change political parties, when they are in the their last term (the so-called "shirking" phenomenon), when they move from one chamber of a legislature to another chamber, when their geographic districts are redrawn, and so on. Chapter 6 is the applied chapter of this book, and it builds upon Chapters 2 through 5.

I conclude in Chapter 7 with short discussions of two topics. The first is the scientific status of the state of knowledge about geometric representations of human choice and judgment. If science is the observation, identification, description, experimental investigation, and theoretical explanation of natural phenomena, this field – encompassing work in psychology, political science, economics, and other disciplines – is a classic example of scientific progress.

In the final section of Chapter 7, I discuss what I believe to be the significant unsolved problems in the study of geometric models of legislative choice. I believe that these will be solved because so many capable young researchers are now interested in the field. I hope the readers of this book take these as a challenge and strive to solve them.

CHAPTER 2

The Geometry of Parliamentary Roll Call Voting

Overview

In this chapter, I show the geometry of parliamentary roll call voting for the simplest possible spatial model; each legislator is represented as a point and each roll call is represented as *two points* – one corresponding to the policy outcome associated with Yea, and one corresponding to the policy outcome associated with Nay. I do not consider abstention or multichoice spatial models. I assume that legislators vote *sincerely* – that is, they vote for the outcome closest to their ideal point – and that there are no voting errors. Hereafter, I will refer to this simple two-outcome spatial model with no error as *perfect voting*.

In Chapter 1, I outlined a simple theory of spatial maps that I call the basic-space theory of ideology. This theory is a parsimonious tool for understanding the construction and interpretation of spatial maps. The maps are based on a simple Euclidean geometry of points, lines, and planes, and the purpose of this chapter is to show the basics of this geometry.

Understanding this geometry is an essential foundation for realistic models of choice that allow for error. Perfect voting is not a "pie in the sky" assumption. For example, a two-dimensional spatial model correctly classifies over 95 percent of the choices in most legislative sessions during the French Fourth Republic (Rosenthal and Voeten, 2004), and a one-dimensional spatial model correctly classifies over 90 percent of the choices in recent U.S. Houses and Senates.

I will analyze the one-dimensional problem first. After I develop the geometry of perfect voting, I will show how the model can be extended to the analysis of interest group ratings and how it compares to the Rasch model used in educational testing and the pick-any-N model used in marketing and psychometrics. The second half of the chapter will show the geometry in more than one dimension.

The Geometry in One Dimension

Suppose there are p legislators and q roll calls. I assume that each legislator has an ideal point in the policy space, represented by the point X_i with a symmetric single-peaked utility function centered at the ideal point. Figure 2.1 shows the two most common utility functions used in applied work – the normal and the quadratic. The classic normal "bell curve" has the advantage that the utility is always positive and the tails of the distribution asymptote, so that alternatives far away from the ideal point have very small utilities. The quadratic has the advantage of mathematical simplicity.

When error is added to the utility function in order to allow for probabilistic voting – the *random utility* model – the choice of the utility function is important. In particular, the two utility functions have different implications for how extremists vote (see Chapter 4).

With no error and sincere voting, the legislator votes for the closest alternative in the policy space on every roll call, because her utility function is *symmetric*. Let the two policy outcomes corresponding to Yea and Nay on the jth roll call be represented by O_{jy} and O_{jn}, respectively. In most cases it is more convenient to work with the midpoint of the two outcomes:

$$Z_j = \frac{O_{jy} + O_{jn}}{2}.$$

In one dimension Z_j is known as a *cutting point* that divides the Yeas from the Nays. With perfect spatial voting, all the legislators to the left of Z_j vote for one outcome, and all the legislators to the right of Z_j vote for the opposite outcome. To simplify matters, assume that that every legislator to the left of Z_j votes "Yea" and every legislator to the right of Z_j votes "Nay." Fixing the *polarity* of the roll calls so that the left outcome is always Yea does not affect any of the analysis below.

Figure 2.2 shows six evenly spaced legislators along a dimension with five cutting points – one between each pair of adjacent legislators. The five roll calls are shown below the cutting points. With the legislators and cutting points arranged in order from left to right and with Yea always to the left of the cutting point, the pattern of Y's and N's forms a triangle. This pattern of Yeas and Nays is identical to the responses to a classic Guttman scale (Weisberg, 1968). In this regard, the algorithms described below and in Chapter 3 that recover the legislator ideal points and roll call midpoints are quite similar to a Guttman scaling of *dominance* data.[1]

---

[1] Guttman (1944) developed his method to analyze a *cumulative* dimension. For example, a set of subjects is asked a series of questions concerning racial tolerance, and the questions are designed to tap ever-greater levels of tolerance. Therefore, if a subject answers "Yes" to a question tapping an intermediate level of tolerance, he or she should answer "Yes" to all questions tapping lower levels of tolerance. Weisberg (1968) discusses in detail the connection between traditional Guttman scaling and the one-dimensional roll call voting problem.

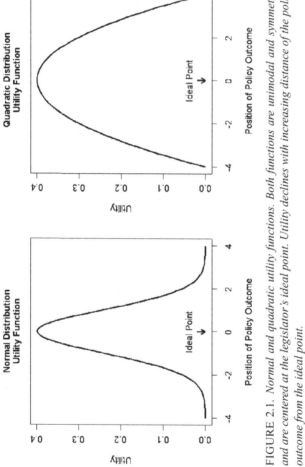

FIGURE 2.1. *Normal and quadratic utility functions. Both functions are unimodal and symmetric and are centered at the legislator's ideal point. Utility declines with increasing distance of the policy outcome from the ideal point.*

20

```
-1---------0--------+1
```

Legislators	X_1	X_2	X_3	X_4	X_5	X_6
Cutting Points	Z_1	Z_2	Z_3	Z_4	Z_5	

1	Y	N	N	N	N	N
2	Y	Y	N	N	N	N
3	Y	Y	Y	N	N	N
4	Y	Y	Y	Y	N	N
5	Y	Y	Y	Y	Y	N

FIGURE 2.2. *Perfect spatial voting in one dimension. The six legislators and five cutting points are evenly spaced along the dimension with one cutting line between each adjacent pair of legislators. The Yea alternative is always on the left.*

As a practical matter, we almost never observe real roll call data with the nice triangle pattern. Instead, we are more likely to see something like the data displayed in Figure 2.3. This is the same data as shown in Figure 2.2, but I have changed the order of the legislators and the roll calls. I have also changed the polarity of roll calls 3 and 5 so that Nay rather than Yea is to the left of the cutting point. The data is also displayed in the conventional manner with the rows as legislators and the columns as roll calls.

With perfect one-dimensional voting, legislator ideal points and roll call cutting points can always be found that exactly reproduce the roll call data. A formal proof of this statement is shown in the appendix to this chapter. Here I will simply show how to recover the legislator and roll call points in one dimension with a simple four-step process.

The first step is to compute an *agreement score* matrix for the legislators. The agreement score between two legislators is simply the proportion of times they vote the same way over all the roll calls. This matrix is shown below the roll call data in Figure 2.3. (The agreement score matrix is symmetric, so I show only the lower triangle in the figure.) For example, legislators Five and Six vote the same way except on roll call 5, where legislator Five votes Nay and legislator Six votes Yea. Hence their agreement score is 4/5, or .8. Similarly, legislators Six and Four vote the same way on roll calls 1, 3, and 2, and opposite each other on roll calls 5 and 4. Therefore their agreement score is 3/5, or .6. This score is in the third row and second column of the matrix.

In general, suppose the legislators are ordered $1, 2, 3, \ldots, p$, from left to right. Let k_1 be the number of cutting points between legislators 1 and 2, k_2 be the number of cutting points between legislators 2 and 3, and so on, with k_{p-1} being the number of cutting points between legislators $p - 1$ and p. Defined in

| | Roll Calls | | | | |
Legislators	1	3	5	4	2
Five	N	Y	N	N	N
Six	N	Y	Y	N	N
Four	N	Y	N	Y	N
One	Y	N	N	Y	Y
Two	N	N	N	Y	Y
Three	N	N	N	Y	N

Agreement Scores

1.0					
.8	1.0				
.8	.6	1.0			
.2	.0	.4	1.0		
.4	.2	.6	.8	1.0	
.6	.4	.8	.6	.8	1.0

Squared Distances

.00					
.04	.00				
.04	.16	.00			
.64	1.00	.36	.00		
.36	.64	.16	.04	.00	
.16	.36	.04	.16	.04	.00

Double-Centered Matrix

.09					
.15	.25				
.03	.05	.01			
-.15	-.25	-.05	.25		
-.09	-.15	-.03	.15	.09	
-.03	-.05	-.01	.05	.03	.01

Legislator Points

$X_5 = .3$
$X_6 = .5$
$X_4 = .1$
$X_1 = -.5$
$X_2 = -.3$
$X_3 = -.1$

FIGURE 2.3. *Recovering the legislator ideal points and cutting points when voting is perfect and one-dimensional. The roll call data are from Figure 2.2. The agreement scores are computed for every pair of legislators. The squared distances are the squares of one minus the corresponding agreement score. The double-centered matrix is computed from the squared distance matrix, and the legislator points are computed from the double-centered matrix.*

this way, the k's will add up to q; that is,

$$q = \sum_{i=1}^{p-1} k_i > 0. \tag{2.1}$$

The agreement score between legislators 1 and 2 is simply $(q - k_1)/q$, because 1 and 2 agree on all roll calls except for those with cutting points between them.

Similarly, the agreement score between legislators 1 and 3 is $(q - k_1 - k_2)/q$ and the agreement score between legislators 2 and 3 is $(q - k_2)/q$. In general, for two legislators X_a and X_b where $a \neq b$, the agreement score is

$$A_{ab} = \frac{q - \sum_{i=a}^{b-1} k_i}{q}. \tag{2.2}$$

For our six-person legislature shown in Figure 2.2, there is only one cutting point between every adjacent pair of legislators, so all the k's are equal to one.

The second step to getting the legislator and roll call points is to convert the agreement score matrix into a matrix of *squared distances*.[2] We do this by simply subtracting the agreement scores from 1 and squaring them. That is,

$$d_{ab}^2 = (1 - A_{ab})^2 = \left[1 - \frac{q - \sum_{i=a}^{b-1} k_i}{q} \right]^2 = \left[\frac{\sum_{i=a}^{b-1} k_i}{q} \right]^2. \tag{2.3}$$

The squared distances are shown to the right of the agreement scores in Figure 2.3. In the appendix to this chapter I prove that with perfect one-dimensional voting, these distances are *exact*. That is, there exists a set of points *on a straight line* that exactly reproduce these distances *and the roll calls* that are used to create the distances. The rank ordering of those points is the same as the rank ordering of the "true" legislator points. In other words, with perfect voting in one dimension, you can recover only a rank ordering. It is impossible to recover an interval scale. I will illustrate this rank ordering property with some examples after I finish showing how to get the legislator points.

The third step is to *double-center* the matrix of squared distances. That is, from each element of the matrix of squared distances subtract the row mean, subtract the column mean, add the matrix mean, and divide by -2. Double-centering the matrix of squared distances produces a cross product matrix of the legislator coordinates (Young and Householder, 1938; Ross and Cliff, 1964). For example, the squared distance between legislator a and legislator b is

$$d_{ab}^2 = \left[\frac{\sum_{i=a}^{b-1} k_i}{q} \right]^2 = (X_a - X_b)^2. \tag{2.4}$$

The mean of row a is

$$\frac{\sum_{i=1}^{p} d_{ai}^2}{p} = X_a^2 - 2X_a \bar{X} + \frac{\sum_{i=1}^{p} X_i^2}{p}$$

---

[2] By distance I mean *Euclidean* distance. The following are the most important properties of Euclidean distances. For any pair of points a and b, we have $d_{aa} = d_{bb} = 0$, $d_{ab} = d_{ba} \geq 0$ – that is, the distance between a point and itself is zero; the distance from a to b is the same as the distance from b to a; and distance must be nonnegative. For any triple of points a, b, and c, we have $d_{ac} \leq d_{ab} + d_{bc}$ (triangle inequality) and $d_{ab}^2 = d_{ac}^2 + d_{bc}^2 - 2d_{ac}d_{bc} \cos\theta$, where θ is the angle between the vector from c to a and the vector from c to b (cosine law).

where $\bar{X}$ is the mean of the p X's. The mean of column b is

$$\frac{\sum_{i=1}^{p} d_{ib}^2}{p} = X_b^2 - 2X_b\bar{X} + \frac{\sum_{i=1}^{p} X_i^2}{p}$$

and the mean of the matrix is

$$\frac{\sum_{i=1}^{p} \sum_{h=1}^{p} d_{ih}^2}{p^2} = \frac{\sum_{h=1}^{p} X_h^2}{p} - 2\bar{X}^2 + \frac{\sum_{i=1}^{p} X_i^2}{p}$$

where $h = 1, \ldots, p$. Subtracting the row and column means and adding the matrix mean cancels all the squared terms, leaving only the cross products. To see this, note that

$$\left\{ \left(X_a^2 - 2X_aX_b + X_b^2\right) - \left(X_a^2 - 2X_a\bar{X} - \frac{\sum_{i=1}^{p} X_i^2}{p}\right) \right.$$
$$\left. - \left(X_b^2 - 2X_b\bar{X} - \frac{\sum_{i=1}^{p} X_i^2}{p}\right) + \left(\frac{\sum_{h=1}^{p} X_h^2}{p} - 2\bar{X}^2 + \frac{\sum_{i=1}^{p} X_i^2}{p}\right) \right\}$$
$$\div (-2) = (X_a - \bar{X})(X_b - \bar{X}).$$

If we adopt the restriction that legislator coordinates must add up to zero – that is, $\bar{X} = 0$ – then the entries of the double-centered matrix are simply X_aX_b for all pairs of legislators. The diagonal terms are simply the legislator coordinates squared; that is, X_a^2.

The final step is to take the square root of a diagonal element of the double-centered matrix and then divide through the corresponding column of the matrix by this square root. Using the first diagonal element produces the legislator coordinates as shown in Figure 2.3. In sum, to get the legislator coordinates:

1. Compute the p by p agreement score matrix
2. Convert the agreement score matrix into a matrix of squared distances
3. Double-center the matrix of squared distances
4. Take the square root of a diagonal element of the double-centered matrix, and divide it through the corresponding column.

Figure 2.3 shows that an interval level set of points is recovered. *It is an artifact of the distribution of cutting points.* For example, if $k_1 > k_2$, then $d_{12} > d_{23}$ even if the true coordinates X_1, X_2, X_3 were evenly spaced. For example, Figure 2.4 repeats the steps shown in Figure 2.3 with exactly the same set of roll calls, only now instead of one roll call cutting point between X_1 and X_2 there are four cutting points between them; that is, $k_1 = 4$, so that $q = 8$. In other words, the first roll call is repeated four times. The agreement score matrix is symmetric, so I show only the lower triangle in Figure 2.4.

With one cutting point between each pair of legislators, the recovered legislator coordinates are evenly spaced: $-.5, -.3 -.1, +.1, +.3, +.5$. Placing three additional cutting points between X_1 and X_2 pushes them apart in the

Agreement Scores

```
1.000
 .875 1.000
 .875  .750 1.000
 .125  .000  .250 1.000
 .625  .500  .750  .500 1.000
 .750  .625  .875  .375  .875 1.000
```

Squared Distances

```
0.000000
0.015625  0.000000
0.015625  0.062525  0.000000
0.765625  1.000000  0.562500  0.000000
0.140625  0.250000  0.062500  0.250000  0.000000
0.062525  0.140625  0.015625  0.390625  0.015625  0.000000
```

Double-Centered Matrix

```
 0.062500
 0.093750  0.140625
 0.031250  0.046875  0.015625
-0.156250 -0.234375 -0.078125  0.390625
-0.031250 -0.046875 -0.015625  0.078125  0.015625
 0.000000  0.000000  0.000000  0.000000  0.000000  0.000000
```

Legislator Points

$$X_5 = .250$$
$$X_6 = .375$$
$$X_4 = .125$$
$$X_1 = -.625$$
$$X_2 = -.125$$
$$X_3 = .000$$

FIGURE 2.4. *Effect of the number of cutting points on the recovery of the legislator ideal points when voting is perfect and one-dimensional. The spacing between adjacent legislators is a function of the number of cutting points between them. No interval scale information can be recovered.*

recovered coordinates: $-.625$, $-.125$, $.000$, $+.125$, $+.250$, $+.375$. But both sets of legislator points produce the same set of roll call votes. With perfect voting the two configurations produce the same voting patterns.

In sum, with perfect one-dimensional voting, the legislator configuration is identified only up to a *weak monotone transformation of the true rank ordering.*

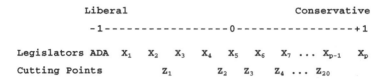

FIGURE 2.5. *Interest group ratings in one dimension with perfect voting. The ADA is to the left of all the legislators, so that its ratings will be weakly monotone with the true rank ordering of the legislators.*

"Weak monotone" means that if there are no cutting points between a pair of legislators (some $k_i = 0$), those legislators will be recovered in the same position – a tied rank – because their voting patterns will be identical. But if there are cutting points between every pair of adjacent legislators, that is, $k_i \geq 1$ for $i = 1, \ldots, p - 1$, then *the true rank ordering is recovered*. Note that the mirror image of the recovered rank ordering is also a solution. Taking the mirror image of the rank ordering and reversing the polarity assigned to each cutting point produces the same roll call votes.

Interest Group Ratings

When an interest group like the Americans for Democratic Action (ADA) issues ratings of members of Congress or members of a state legislature,[3] it typically selects about ten to twenty roll calls that the group views as important and computes a simple agreement score between how its members would have voted and how the legislators actually voted. The ratings are typically reported in the form of percentages, so that they range from 100, indicating a perfect rating, to 0, meaning that the legislator is under the influence of the forces of darkness. For example, if the ADA rating is used as a measure of liberalism, a legislator receiving a rating of 100 is more liberal than a legislator receiving a rating of 90, who in turn is more liberal than someone receiving a rating of 80, and so on. Using rankings in this way, a researcher is implicitly assuming that the interest group is *exterior to the legislators*. That is, she assumes that a member can't be more liberal than the ADA (no one can get a rating of 110).

In the context of the one-dimensional spatial model developed above, the interest group is at the end of the dimension *exterior to the legislators and the cutting points of the roll calls it chooses for its ratings*. An example of this spatial arrangement is shown in Figure 2.5.

Suppose Yea is always the outcome to the left of a midpoint and Nay is the outcome to the right, and there is perfect spatial voting. On the twenty

---

[3] Elizabeth Gerber and Jeff Lewis (2002) have analyzed interest group ratings of the California State Assembly.

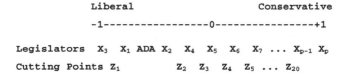

FIGURE 2.6. *Folded interest group ratings in one dimension with perfect voting. The ADA is in the midst of the legislators, so that its ratings will not be monotone with the true rank ordering of the legislators.*

roll calls selected by the ADA, it and legislators X_1 and X_2 would vote Yea, so that legislators X_1 and X_2 would receive ratings of 100. Legislators X_3 and X_4 vote Nay on the first roll call and Yea on the other nineteen, so they would receive a 95 rating. As the number of cutting points between a legislator and the ADA increases, the rating decreases. Because the ADA chooses only twenty roll calls to compute its ratings, the ratings will be very coarse, with many legislators receiving the same rating. This lumping of the ratings is likely to be quite severe at the ends of the dimension, with many legislators receiving 100's and 0's. In addition, not only will the ratings be quite coarse, the example at the end of the previous section shows that the ratings will be very sensitive to the *distribution* of the cutting points (Snyder, 1992; Poole and Rosenthal, 1997). For example, if the cutting points are concentrated near the middle of the distribution of legislators, there will be an abundance of 100 and 0 ratings.

The assumption that legislators cannot be more liberal than the ADA leads to the simple spatial model shown in Figure 2.5, where the interest group is at the end of the dimension exterior to the legislators and the cutting points of the roll calls it chooses for its ratings. This is an *assumption* and should be tested. For example, Figure 2.6 shows a configuration of legislators, cutting points, and the ADA that produces exactly the same ratings as the configuration shown in Figure 2.5. In Figure 2.6 the Yea outcome on the first roll call is now to the right of its cutting point, while the Yea outcome is to the left of the other nineteen cutting points as in Figure 2.5. With perfect spatial voting, the ADA gives ratings of 100 to legislators X_1 and X_2. Legislator X_3 votes Nay on the first roll call and Yea on the other nineteen, so she receives a 95 rating. Legislator X_4 votes Yea on the first roll call, Nay on the second roll call, and Yea on the other eighteen, so she would also receive a 95 rating.

The spatial configurations in Figures 2.5 and 2.6 produce exactly the same ADA ratings. If Figure 2.6 is the true configuration, the ADA ratings are not an accurate measure of liberalism. Legislator X_3 is the most liberal, but she receives a rating lower than legislators X_1 and X_2, who are adjacent to the ADA. Adding to the distortion, legislator X_4, who is towards the interior of the dimension, receives the same rating as the most liberal legislator, X_3.

If Figure 2.6 is the true configuration, then Figure 2.5 is an example of a *folded dimension* (Coombs, 1964, Chapter 5). That is, if the dimension in Figure 2.6 is a string that we can pick up at the position of the ADA, the left end folds back onto the dimension and we get the configuration in Figure 2.5. In order to get the true dimension, the ADA ratings have to be *unfolded*.[4]

To reiterate, when interest group ratings are used as measures of some dimension like liberal–conservative or environmentalism, the implicit assumption is that the interest group is at the end of the dimension exterior to the legislators and the cutting points of the roll calls it chooses for its ratings. This assumption can be tested by treating the interest group as if it were a member of Congress (e.g., Poole and Rosenthal, 1997, ch. 8).

The Rasch Model From Educational Testing

The simple configuration of legislator ideal points and roll call cutting points shown in Figure 2.2 can also be interpreted in an educational testing context. Suppose the dimension corresponds to some latent ability – for example, the ability to solve logical puzzles. Then X_i is the individual test taker's level of ability, and Z_j is the level of difficulty of the test question. Suppose the dimension ranges from low ability (-1) to high ability $(+1)$. In this framework a Y corresponds to "wrong answer" and an N corresponds to "correct answer." X_1 is unable to solve any of the problems, whereas X_6 solves all five of the problems.

The simple item response model developed by Rasch (1961) is mathematically equivalent to the basic spatial model shown in Figure 2.2 if legislators have quadratic utility functions with additive random error. As this will be an important topic in Chapter 4, I will show the relationship here for the simple one-dimensional case with no error. In Chapter 4, I will discuss the multiple-dimension case with error.

In the quadratic utility model, the utility of the ith legislator for the Yea and Nay alternatives is simply the negative of the squared distance from the legislator's ideal point to the outcomes:

$$U_{iy} = -(X_i - O_{jy})^2 \quad \text{and} \quad U_{in} = -(X_i - O_{jn})^2.$$

In the spatial voting model, if $U_{iy} > U_{in}$ the legislator votes Yea. Stated another way, if the difference $U_{iy} - U_{in}$ is positive, the legislator votes Yea.

---

[4]Note that if Figure 2.6 is the true configuration but the ADA chooses no cutting points to its left, its ratings will produce the correct *weak* rank ordering. That is, legislators 1, 2, and 3 will get the same rating.

Algebraically:

$$
\begin{aligned}
U_{iy} - U_{in} &= -(X_i - O_{jy})^2 + (X_i - O_{jn})^2 \\
&= 2X_i O_{jy} - O_{jy}^2 - 2X_i O_{jn} + O_{jn}^2 \\
&= 2X_i(O_{jy} - O_{jn}) - \left(O_{jy}^2 - O_{jn}^2\right) = 2\gamma_j(X_i - Z_j), \quad (2.5)
\end{aligned}
$$

where $\gamma_j = O_{jy} - O_{jn}$ and $2Z_j = O_{jy} + O_{jn}$. With perfect voting the legislator and the chosen outcome are on the same side of the midpoint. Hence,

$$
\begin{aligned}
&\text{if} \quad 2\gamma_j(X_j - Z_j) > 0, \quad \text{vote Yea} \\
&\text{if} \quad 2\gamma_j(X_i - Z_j) < 0, \quad \text{vote Nay.}
\end{aligned} \quad (2.6)
$$

If $O_{jy} > O_{jn}$, this decision rule simplifies to

$$
\begin{aligned}
&\text{if} \quad X_i - Z_j > 0, \quad \text{vote Yea} \\
&\text{if} \quad X_i - Z_j > 0, \quad \text{vote Nay.}
\end{aligned}
$$

The corresponding formulation for the Rasch model is

$$
\begin{aligned}
&\text{if} \quad \beta_j X_i - \alpha_j > 0, \quad \text{correct answer} \\
&\text{if} \quad \beta_j X_i - \alpha_j < 0, \quad \text{wrong answer}
\end{aligned} \quad (2.7)
$$

where β_j is the *item discrimination parameter* and α_j is the *difficulty parameter*. If the test question is clearly stated so that there is no ambiguity, then by convention $\beta_j = 1$. A poorly constructed and ambiguous question would have a β_j near 0. Here α_j is simply the level of difficulty on the latent dimension.

Although the two models look very much alike – especially with $\beta_j = 1$ – they are analytically *very different*. The spatial voting model is a model of *choice* between two alternatives, whereas the testing model is concerned with *ability*.

The Pick-Any-*N* Data Model from Marketing

Pick-any-*N* choice data is used in the marketing field to analyze consumer buy–not-buy choices for a range of products. For example, a set of consumers are asked if they drink a number of soft drinks – "Do you drink Pepsi?" "Do you drink Coke?" "Do you drink Royal Crown Cola?" etc. The consumers simply answer "Yes" or "No." The dimension corresponds to some attribute of the products – for example, level of sweetness. Analytically, in one dimension, this data is equivalent to roll call data if the products are treated as the legislators – the X_i – and the consumers are treated as the roll call midpoints – the Z_j. The consumer approves, would buy, or would use all the products below her location and does not approve, would not buy, or would not use all the products above her location.

In more than one dimension, the consumer is represented as a *vector* and the products are represented by points. This vector is perpendicular to a cutting plane that separates the products the consumer approves from those she does not approve. This geometry is the same as that for the roll call voting problem.

Summary: One-Dimensional Perfect Voting

With perfect one-dimensional roll call voting, legislator ideal points and roll call cutting points can always be found that exactly reproduce the roll call data. But only a rank ordering of the legislators can be recovered. Recovering interval-level information from the perfect one-dimensional roll call data is impossible. In addition, with perfect voting (choice, responses) in one dimension, the roll call voting problem, the educational testing problem, and the pick-any-N data problem are *observationally equivalent*.

The Geometry in More than One Dimension

In one-dimensional perfect roll call voting both the legislators and the roll call midpoints are represented by points – X_i and Z_j, respectively – and a joint rank ordering of the legislators and roll call midpoints can be found that exactly reproduces the roll call votes. In two- or more-dimensional perfect voting a legislator is still represented by a point – the s by 1 vector $\mathbf{X}_i$, where s is the number of dimensions – but a roll call is now represented by a *plane* that is perpendicular to a line joining the Yea and Nay policy points – the s by 1 vectors $\mathbf{O}_{jy}$ and $\mathbf{O}_{jn}$ – and passes through the midpoint, the s by 1 vector $\mathbf{Z}_j$. The *normal vector* to this *cutting plane* is parallel to the line joining the Yea and Nay policy points. Figure 2.7 shows a simple example of twelve legislators in two dimensions.[5]

In Figure 2.7 the legislators are displayed as N's or Y's corresponding to their votes on the hypothetical roll call. The cutting plane divides the legislators who vote Yea from those who vote Nay, and the line joining the Yea and Nay outcomes is parallel to the normal vector. Note that, in the case of perfect voting, the policy points are not identified – any pair of points on a line perpendicular to the plane that are on opposite sides and equidistant from the plane would produce the same pattern of votes. But the cutting plane is identified up to a region of the space that divides the Yeas from the Nays. For example, the cutting line in Figure 2.7 could be rotated slightly in either direction.

Technically, even through I treated legislators as *specific* points in the one-dimensional perfect voting problem, each legislator could be anywhere in the region between the corresponding pair of roll call midpoints. For example, in

---

[5]All the spatial maps in this book were produced in R. The R code and data files for all the spatial maps can be found at the website for this book: http://pooleandrosenthal.com/ Spatial_Models_of_Parliamentary_Voting.htm, under the corresponding chapter link.

Twelve Legislators in Two Dimensions

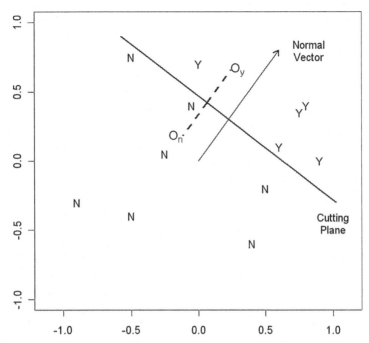

FIGURE 2.7. *Twelve legislators in two dimensions with perfect voting. The legislators are displayed as N's or Y's corresponding to their votes on the hypothetical roll call. The cutting plane divides the legislators who vote Yea from those who vote Nay, and the line joining the Yea and Nay outcomes is parallel to the normal vector.*

Figure 2.2 X_2 could be located anywhere between Z_1 and Z_2. The counterpart to this ideal point ambiguity in more than one dimension is that the legislator can be anywhere in an area (or volume) bounded by a set of cutting lines (or planes). These regions are known as *polytopes*. A two-dimensional polytope is a polygon – an area of a two-dimensional space that is bounded by line segments. A three-dimensional polytope is a polyhedron – a volume of three-dimensional space that is bounded by two-dimensional polygons.

For example, in two dimensions, if various voting coalitions form among the legislators, then the q cutting lines will criss-cross one another in a myriad of directions, creating a very large number of polytopes in the plane (see Figure 2.8 below). Indeed, Coombs (1964, p. 262) shows that q roll calls create a maximum of

$$\sum_{k=0}^{s} \binom{q}{k}$$

polytopes, where s is the number of dimensions. For two dimensions, $1 + q + q(q - 1)/2$ polytopes are possible, with each polytope corresponding to a voting pattern on the q roll calls – e.g., YYNYNYY. . . . If all the possible polytopes are present, I will refer to the corresponding configuration of cutting lines or planes as a *complete Coombs mesh*.

Figure 2.8 shows two simple complete Coombs meshes for five roll calls ($q = 5$) in two dimensions ($s = 2$). The five cutting lines are numbered at the ends, and the Y and N on either side of each cutting line indicate how a legislator on that side of the cutting line should vote. The maximum number of polytopes created by five cutting lines in two dimensions is 16, and each of these 16 polytopes corresponds to a unique vector of votes. To reduce clutter, Figure 2.8 shows only the vectors of votes for six polytopes in each mesh. Note that the polytopes vary considerably in size, from the small triangles and polygons in the middle of the meshes to the larger polytopes at the edges – for example, NYNNN in both meshes. (Technically, the region containing NYNNN in both meshes is not a polytope, because it has no outer boundary.)

In order to produce the maximum number of polytopes for q roll calls in two dimensions, every cutting line must intersect every other cutting line. There will be $[q(q - 1)]/2$ intersection points, and they must be unique for there to be the maximum of $1 + q + q(q - 1)/2$ polytopes. In addition, $[(q - 2)(q - 1)]/2$ of the polytopes will be in the interior of the Coombs mesh, and $2q$ polytopes will be distributed around the edge of the mesh – that is, they will be *open*.[6] For example, the region containing NYNNN in both meshes is open in that there are no more intersection points. The region is infinite. In terms of the coordinate system shown in Figure 2.8, any point with second-dimension coordinate of 0.0 and first-dimension coordinate between -0.5 and $-\infty$ corresponds to NYNNN in both meshes.

With q roll calls there are $q!$ ways to number the roll calls and 2^q polarity possibilities, for a total of $q!2^q$ combinations of polarity and numbering. Given a numbering and polarity of the roll calls and $q(q - 1)/2$ unique intersection points, there are only $1 + q + q(q - 1)/2$ unique patterns of votes corresponding to the $1 + q + q(q - 1)/2$ polytopes. For example, the two meshes in Figure 2.8 have the same numbering of the five roll call cutting lines clockwise around the mesh and the same polarity on each roll call. Consequently, the 10 open polytopes around the edge of the mesh have exactly the same patterns. The

---

[6]Technically, "open" polytope is a contradiction, because a polytope has to be bounded. I use the expression because it is a convenient way to describe the exterior regions. Note that I could make these open polytopes real polytopes by drawing straight lines – chords – at the "edges" of the space. For example, the squares that frame the graphs in Figure 2.8 would work, because all the boundary lines are beyond all the intersections of the cutting lines. In three dimensions the open polytopes can be closed by inserting planes at the edges of the space beyond all the intersections of the cutting planes. Note that these are entirely arbitrary decisions.

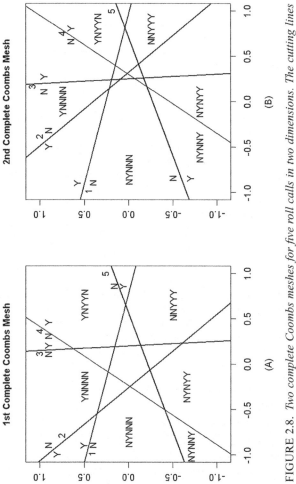

FIGURE 2.8. *Two complete Coombs meshes for five roll calls in two dimensions. The cutting lines are numbered at the ends, and the Y and N on either side indicate how a legislator on that side of the cutting line should vote. The maximum number of polytopes created by five roll calls in two dimensions is 16.*

33

Roll Calls

Legislators	Fig. 2.8 (1st)					Fig. 2.8 (2nd)				
	1	2	3	4	5	1	2	3	4	5
1	Y	Y	N	N	N	Y	Y	N	N	N
2	Y	N	N	N	N	Y	N	N	N	N
3	Y	N	Y	N	N	Y	N	Y	N	N
4	Y	N	Y	Y	N	Y	N	Y	Y	N
5	Y	N	Y	Y	Y	Y	N	Y	Y	Y
6	N	N	Y	Y	Y	N	N	Y	Y	Y
7	N	Y	Y	Y	Y	N	Y	Y	Y	Y
8	N	Y	N	Y	Y	N	Y	N	Y	Y
9	N	Y	N	N	Y	N	Y	N	N	Y
10	N	Y	N	N	N	N	Y	N	N	N
11	N	N	N	N	N	N	N	N	N	N
12	Y	N	N	Y	N	N	N	Y	N	N
13	N	N	Y	Y	N	N	N	Y	Y	N
14	N	N	N	Y	Y	N	Y	Y	Y	N
15	N	Y	N	Y	N	N	Y	N	Y	N
16	N	N	N	Y	N	N	Y	Y	N	N

FIGURE 2.9. *The roll call matrices produced by the complete Coombs meshes shown in Figure 2.8. The first ten rows correspond to the open polytopes clockwise around the meshes, and the last six rows correspond to the six interior polytopes. Three of the six interior polytopes of the two meshes produce different voting patterns.*

6 interior polytopes differ in their patterns because the 10 interior intersection points are arranged differently.

This simple example illustrates the complexity of the perfect-voting problem. Even if the numbering and the polarity of the roll calls are fixed, there are multiple possible arrangements of the $(q-2)(q-1)/2$ interior polytopes, and each arrangement produces a different roll call matrix. For example, Figure 2.9 shows the roll call matrices for the two meshes in Figure 2.8. The first 10 rows correspond to the 10 open polytopes clockwise around the meshes and the last 6 rows correspond to the 6 interior polytopes. Note that 3 of the 6 interior polytopes of the two meshes have the same roll call voting patterns (rows 11, 13, and 15). Hence if there were only 13 legislators with perfect voting on five roll calls in two dimensions and the matrix consisted of rows 1 to 11, 13, and 15, either mesh in Figure 2.8 would result in a perfect solution.

In practice, the number of legislators will be small compared to the number of polytopes, so there will be many empty polytopes. For example, in recent U.S. Senates there have been at least 500 nonunanimous roll calls. With 500 roll calls in two dimensions there are 125,251 polytopes and only 100 senators. This disparity is typical of real-world-size roll call matrices. Most of the polytopes in any estimated mesh will be empty.

Empty polytopes are also required to reproduce the actual Yea-versus-Nay margins on roll calls. For example, every roll call in the first mesh in Figure 2.8 has six polytopes on one side of the cutting line and ten polytopes on the opposite side. Hence if a legislator were assigned to each polytope, all five roll calls would divide $10 - 6$. In contrast, in the second mesh there are five polytopes on one side of the cutting lines for roll calls 1 and 5, and eleven polytopes on the opposite side. If a legislator were assigned to each polytope for the second mesh, the margins of the roll calls – ignoring which side is Yea and which is Nay – would be $11 - 5, 8 - 8, 9 - 7, 8 - 8$, and $11 - 5$.

This simple example makes it clear that the *minimum* number of polytopes on one side of a cutting line is q. For 11 roll calls there are a maximum of 67 polytopes, so that if a legislator were assigned to each polytope, the most lopsided a roll call could be is 56 to 11. In real-world legislative voting very lopsided votes (for example, 99 percent to 1 percent) frequently occur. Consequently, for these to be present in perfect voting, the number of legislators must be much smaller than the number of polytopes, so that there are enough empty polytopes on one side of a roll call cutting line to produce a lopsided vote. For example, in Figure 2.8B, if there were only one legislator on the Yea side of the cutting line for the first roll call and all 11 polytopes on the Nay side of the cutting line contained a single legislator each, the margin would be 11 Nays and 1 Yea.

Adding to the difficulty of the two- or more-dimensional perfect-voting problem is the fact that the number of cutting lines or planes between pairs of legislators cannot be treated as the Euclidean distance between them. In one-dimensional perfect voting the number of cutting points between a pair of legislators could be so treated. Furthermore, if there were three cutting points between legislators A and B and three cutting points between legislators C and D, the points representing A and B would be three units apart and the points representing C and D would also be three units apart. This is not true of two- or more-dimensional perfect voting. For example, Figure 2.10 shows a *symmetric complete* Coombs mesh for 11 roll calls in two dimensions.[7] (The mesh is symmetric in that the normal vectors for the cutting lines are evenly spaced from $\pi/2$ to $-\pi/2$ radians. The mesh is complete in that it produces

---

[7] R code to create and plot a symmetric complete Coombs mesh can be found at the website for this book under the link for this chapter. The program also produces a matrix of roll call votes for the mesh.

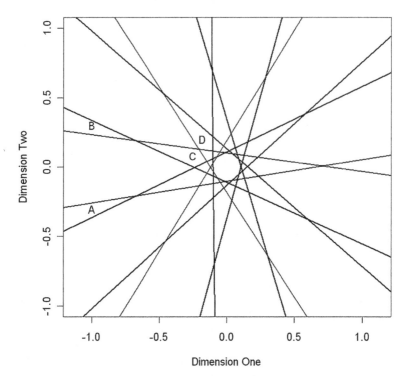

Symmetric Complete Coombs Mesh
11 Roll Calls

FIGURE 2.10. *A symmetric complete Coombs mesh for eleven roll calls in two dimensions. The mesh is symmetric because the normal vectors for the cutting lines are evenly spaced from $\pi/2$ to $-\pi/2$ radians. The numbers of cutting lines between pairs of legislators cannot be treated as Euclidean distances. A and B have two cutting lines between them, and C and D also have two cutting lines between them, but A and B are further apart in the space.*

all the possible polytopes. The meshes in Figure 2.8 are also complete.) The pair of legislators in the open polytopes labeled A and B have two cutting lines between them, and the pair of legislators in the polytopes labeled C and D also have two cutting lines between them. In addition, C is two cutting lines away from A and B. Because the number of cutting lines between pairs of legislators cannot be treated as Euclidean distances, the method used to solve the one-dimensional perfect-voting problem (analyzing the double-centered matrix of squared distances) cannot be used to solve the higher-dimensional problem.

Summary: Perfect Voting in More than One Dimension

In summary, with perfect voting in two or more dimensions a solution can always be found by constructing complete Coombs meshes and searching through them. This procedure would be a computational nightmare, however. For every $q!2^q$ possible combinations of roll call numbering and polarity, there are a myriad of complete Coombs meshes like those shown in Figure 2.8 for two dimensions. Unfortunately, brute force searching is simply not practical. The complete Coombs mesh for 500 roll calls in two dimensions would have 125,251 polytopes, and this number explodes to 20,833,751 in three dimensions. The number of combinations of roll call numbering and polarity is $500!2^{500}$, which is an unimaginably large number on the order of 10^{1000}. Removing the duplicate meshes that differ only by a rigid rotation (see Figure 2.10) only reduces the complexity of the problem by a trivial amount.

Clearly, exhaustive search on large problems is not practical with current computers.[8] It may well be in the future.

The Relationship to the Geometry of Probit and Logit

The complexity of the roll call voting problem in more than one dimension would be greatly simplified if we knew *a priori* the legislator ideal points. The problem would then simplify to finding the cutting planes vis-à-vis the legislator ideal points. In psychometrics this is known as an *external analysis* (Carroll, 1972) or an *external unfolding* (Borg and Groenen, 1997). For example, suppose we are given the configuration of ideal points shown in Figure 2.7 and the corresponding Yeas and Nays for that particular roll call. In an external analysis we take the X_i's as given and we estimate the cutting plane for the roll call. If error is present, the problem of estimating the cutting plane is equivalent to a probit or logit analysis, depending on the assumptions made about the error. To simplify the presentation below, I will continue to assume that voting is perfect even though both probit and logit "blow up" (that is, the maximum likelihood estimator of the parameters does not exist [Silvapulle, 1981]) when there is no error.[9] My aim is to show the geometry of cutting planes between choices. The presence of error affects only the *placement* of the cutting planes. It does not affect the fundamental geometry of the planes themselves. I will discuss the former in Chapter 3. Here I discuss only the geometry itself.

Figure 2.11 shows the same configuration of legislators as Figure 2.7 and illustrates the geometry of a roll call vote in two dimensions. The normal vector

---

[8] A simple FORTRAN program that does an exhaustive search for $p = 10$ and $5 \leq q \leq 10$ is posted on the website for this book under the link for this chapter.

[9] This problem is known as *complete separation* (Silvapulle, 1981; Albert and Anderson, 1984).

Twelve Legislator Example
Normal Vector and Normal Vector Line

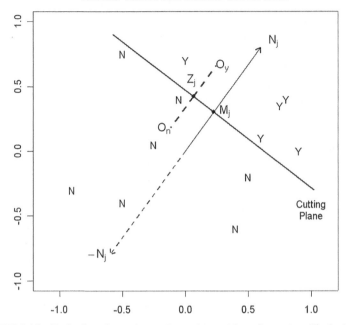

FIGURE 2.11. *Twelve legislators in two dimensions with perfect voting. The legislators are displayed as N's or Y's corresponding to their votes on the hypothetical roll call. The cutting plane divides the legislators who vote Yea from those who vote Nay, and the line joining the Yea and Nay outcomes is parallel to the normal vector. The normal vector is denoted as* $\mathbf{N}_j$, *and its reflection as* $-\mathbf{N}_j$. $\mathbf{Z}_j$ *is the midpoint of the two policy outcomes, and* $\mathbf{M}_j$ *is its projection onto the normal vector line.*

is denoted as $\mathbf{N}_j$, and its *reflection* as $-\mathbf{N}_j$. The normal vector is perpendicular to the cutting plane. The cutting plane in two dimensions is defined by the equation

$$N_{j1}(W_1 - Z_{j1}) + N_{j2}(W_2 - Z_{j2}) = 0$$

where N_{j1} and N_{j2} are the components of the normal vector and (Z_{j1}, Z_{j2}), is the midpoint of the roll call outcomes (see Figure 2.11). Any point (W_1, W_2) that satisfies the equation above lies on the cutting plane. For example, if the normal vector is $(3, -2)$ and the roll call midpoint is $(1, 0)$, this produces the equation

$$3(w_1 - 1) - 2(w_2 - 0) = 3w_1 - 3 - 2w_2 = 3w_1 - 2w_2 - 3 = 0$$

or

$$3w_1 - 2w_2 = 3$$

so that $(0, -3/2), (1/3, -1), (2, 3/2)$, etc., all lie on the plane.

In three dimensions the cutting plane is defined by the equation

$$N_{j1}(W_1 - Z_{j1}) + N_{j2}(W_2 - Z_{j2}) + N_{j3}(W_3 - Z_{j3}) = 0$$

where, as above, any point (W_1, W_2, W_3) that satisfies the equation above lies on the cutting plane. For example, if the normal vector is $(2, -2, 1)$ and the roll call midpoint is $(1, 1, 1)$, this produces the equation

$$2(w_1 - 1) - 2(w_2 - 1) + (w_3 - 1) = 2w_1 - 2w_2 + w_3 - 1 = 0$$

or

$$2w_1 - 2w_2 + w_3 = 1$$

so that $(0, 0, 1)$, $(1, 0, -1)$, $(0, 1, 3)$, etc., all lie on the plane.

For s dimensions the cutting plane is defined by the vector equation

$$\mathbf{N}'_j(\mathbf{W} - \mathbf{Z}_j) = 0 \tag{2.8}$$

where $\mathbf{N}_j, \mathbf{W}$, and $\mathbf{Z}_j$ are s by 1 vectors.

In general, if $\mathbf{W}_A$ and $\mathbf{W}_B$ are both points in the plane, $\mathbf{W}'_A\mathbf{N}_j = \mathbf{W}'_B\mathbf{N} = c_j$, where c_j is a scalar constant. Geometrically, every point in the plane projects onto the same point on the line defined by the normal vector $\mathbf{N}_j$ and its reflection $-\mathbf{N}_j$ (see Figure 2.11). This projection point is

$$\mathbf{M}_j = c_j \frac{\mathbf{N}_j}{\sum_{k=1}^{s} N_{jk}^2}. \tag{2.9}$$

Note that, by construction, $\mathbf{M}'_j\mathbf{N}_j = c_j$. In addition, because the midpoint of the Yea and Nay policy points, $\mathbf{Z}_j$, is on the cutting plane, it also projects to the point $\mathbf{M}_j$. The cutting plane passes through the line formed by the normal vector and its reflection (see Figure 2.11) at the point $\mathbf{M}_j$.

In the case of a simple probit analysis, the cutting plane consists of all possible legislator ideal points such that the probability of the corresponding legislator voting Yea or voting Nay is exactly .5; namely,

$$P(\text{legislator } i \text{ votes Yea}) = P(\text{legislator } i \text{ votes Nay})$$
$$= \Phi\left(\frac{\beta_0 + \beta_1 X_{i1} + \beta_2 X_{i2} + \cdots + \beta_s X_{is}}{\sigma}\right)$$
$$= 1 - \Phi\left(\frac{\beta_0 + \beta_1 X_{i1} + \beta_2 X_{i2} + \cdots + \beta_s X_{is}}{\sigma}\right)$$
$$= \Phi(0) = .5$$

where $\Phi(\cdot)$ is the distribution function for the normal and $X_{i1}, X_{i2}, \ldots, X_{is}$ are legislator i's coordinates on the s dimensions. Because the β's and σ cannot be separately identified, the usual assumption is to set $\sigma = 1$. The equation above reduces to

$$\beta_0 + \beta_1 X_{i1} + \beta_2 X_{i2} + \cdots + \beta_s X_{is} = 0$$

or

$$\beta_1 X_{i1} + \beta_2 X_{i2} + \cdots + \beta_s X_{is} = \mathbf{X}_i' \tilde{\beta} = -\beta_0$$

where $\mathbf{X}_i$ is the s-length vector of legislator coordinates and $\tilde{\beta}$ is an s-length vector of the coefficients $\beta_1, \beta_2, \beta_3, \ldots, \beta_s$. Note that the expression $\mathbf{X}_i' \tilde{\beta} = -\beta_0$ is exactly the same as $\mathbf{W}_i' \mathbf{N}_j = c_j$, which was used above. Namely, set $\mathbf{N}_j = \tilde{\beta}$, and every point in the plane projects onto the point

$$\mathbf{M}_j = -\beta_0 \frac{\tilde{\beta}}{\sum_{k=1}^s \tilde{\beta}_k^2}. \tag{2.10}$$

In other words, in a regular probit context the coefficients on the independent variables form a normal vector to a plane that passes through the point $-\beta_0(\tilde{\beta}/\sum_{k=1}^s \tilde{\beta}_k^2)$.

The simple logit case is identical to probit. The logit probabilities are

$$\frac{e^{\beta_0 + \beta_1 X_{i1} + \beta_2 X_{i2} + \cdots + \beta_s X_{is}}}{1 + e^{\beta_0 + \beta_1 X_{i1} + \beta_2 X_{i2} + \cdots + \beta_s X_{is}}} = \frac{1}{1 + e^{\beta_0 + \beta_1 X_{i1} + \beta_2 X_{i2} + \cdots + \beta_s X_{is}}} = .5.$$

Canceling out the denominator and taking the natural log of both sides yields the same equation as probit:

$$\beta_0 + \beta_1 X_{i1} + \beta_2 X_{i2} + \cdots + \beta_s X_{is} = 0.$$

In both probit and logit, the coefficients on the independent variables form a normal vector to a plane that passes through the point $-\beta_0(\tilde{\beta}/\sum_{k=1}^s \tilde{\beta}_k^2)$.

The cosine of the angle between the normal vectors from probit and logit should be very close to one. That is,

$$|\cos \theta| = \left| \frac{\tilde{\beta}_P' \tilde{\beta}_L}{\|\tilde{\beta}_P\| \|\tilde{\beta}_L\|} \right| \approx 1$$

where θ is the angle between the two normal vectors, and $\|\cdot\|$ is the corresponding norm of the normal vector. Computing $|\cos \theta|$ is a useful check on the two estimation techniques.

Although I am limiting my analysis in this book to the simple spatial model of only two outcomes per roll call, the geometry of more than two choices is a simple extension of the equations above. For example, in ordered probit or ordered logit there is only one normal vector, but there are multiple cutting planes. In multinomial probit or multinomial logit, there are multiple normal vectors. For example, if there are three choices, there are two normal vectors. The cutting planes that divide the choices are easily derived with simple vector geometry.

Conclusion

Understanding the basic geometry of roll call voting is an essential foundation for realistic models of choice that allow for error. Perfect voting is not a pie-in-the-sky assumption. One- and two-dimensional spatial models correctly classify over 95 percent of the choices in many current parliaments. In one dimension with perfect spatial voting only a rank ordering of the legislators can be estimated (see the appendix of this chapter for a proof). As I discuss in Chapter 7, how error *interacts* with the underlying geometry is the most important unsolved *engineering* problem in spatial voting models. For example, in one dimension, how high does the error level have to be so that interval scale information is recovered?

In two or more dimensions, provided there are 50 or so roll calls, the polytopes for most legislators are so small that recovering interval scale information is straightforward simply due to the geometry. However, the lack of a solution to the perfect-voting problem makes it very difficult to determine how the geometry and the level of error interact.

Although there is no simple solution for the perfect-voting problem in more than one dimension, in applied work this is not a serious problem. In Chapter 3, I show a nonparametric method – optimal classification (OC) – that is based upon the geometry shown above and that is designed to analyze real-world roll call data. Monte Carlo tests show that it accurately recovers the legislator ideal points and the roll cutting planes at high levels of error and missing data in one to ten dimensions (Poole, 1997; 2000a; b).[10]

The OC method embodies the geometry shown in this chapter. It can be used not only simply to estimate a configuration that maximizes correct classification, but also as the foundation for parametric statistically based methods of estimating roll call and legislator parameters (the QN procedure discussed in Chapter 4). A nice by-product of its design is that it will almost always find a solution for the perfect-voting problem.

Appendix: Proof that if Voting Is Perfect in One Dimension, then the First Eigenvector Extracted from the Double-Centered Transformed Agreement Score Matrix has the Same Rank Ordering as the True Data

Notation and Definitions

Let the true ideal points of the p legislators be denoted as $\tilde{X}_1, \tilde{X}_2, \ldots, \tilde{X}_p$. Without loss of generality, let the ordering of the true ideal points of the legislators

---

[10] OC can be run in as many dimensions as the user desires. My Monte Carlo work reported in Poole (1997; 2000a;b) used a maximum of ten dimensions. The OC FORTRAN program, along with numerous examples, is posted on the website for this book under the Chapter 3 link.

on the dimension from left to right be

$$\tilde{X}_1 \leq \tilde{X}_2 \leq \tilde{X}_3 \leq \cdots \leq \tilde{X}_p.$$

Let q be the number of *nonunanimous* roll call votes with $q > 0$, and let the cutting point for the jth roll call be Z_j. Voting is *perfect*. That is, all legislators are sincere voters, and all legislators to the left of a cutting point vote for the same alternative and all legislators to right of a cutting point vote for the opposite alternative. For example, if all legislators to the left of Z_j vote Nay, then all legislators to the right of Z_j vote Yea. Without loss of generality we can assume that every legislator to the left of Z_j votes Yea and every legislator to the right of Z_j votes Nay. That is, the *polarity* of the roll call does not affect the analysis below.

Let k_1 be the number of cutting points between legislators 1 and 2, k_2 be the number of cutting points between legislators 2 and 3, and so on, with k_{p-1} being the number of cutting points between legislators $p - 1$ and p. Hence,

$$q = \sum_{i=1}^{p-1} k_i > 0. \tag{A2.1}$$

The *agreement score* between two legislators is the simple proportion of roll calls in which they vote for the same outcome. Hence, the agreement score between legislators 1 and 2 is simply $(q - k_1)/q$, because 1 and 2 agree on all roll calls except for those with cutting points between them. Similarly, the agreement score between legislators 1 and 3 is $(q - k_1 - k_2)/q$, and the agreement score between legislators 2 and 3 is $(q - k_2)/q$. In general, for two legislators X_a and X_b where $a \neq b$, the agreement score is

$$A_{ab} = \frac{q - \sum_{i=a}^{b-1} k_i}{q}. \tag{A2.2}$$

The agreement scores can be treated as Euclidean distances by simply subtracting them from 1. That is,

$$d_{ab} = 1 - A_{ab} = 1 - \frac{q - \sum_{i=a}^{b-1} k_i}{q} = \frac{\sum_{i=a}^{b-1} k_i}{q}. \tag{A2.3}$$

These definitions allow me to state the following theorem:

Theorem: *If voting is perfect in one dimension, then the first eigenvector extracted from the double-centered p by p matrix of squared distances from equation (A2.3) has at least the same weak monotone rank ordering as the legislators.*

Proof: The d's computed from equation (A2.3) satisfy the three axioms of distance: they are nonnegative because by (A2.2) $0 \leq A_{ab} \leq 1$ so that

$0 \le d_{ab} \le 1$; they are symmetric ($d_{ab} = d_{ba}$); and they satisfy the triangle inequality. To see this, consider any triplet of points $X_a < X_b < X_C$. The distances are

$$d_{ab} = \frac{\sum_{i=a}^{b-1} k_i}{q} \quad \text{and} \quad d_{bc} = \frac{\sum_{i=b}^{c-1} k_i}{q} \quad \text{and} \quad d_{ac} = \frac{\sum_{i=a}^{c-1} k_i}{q}.$$

Hence,

$$d_{ac} = d_{ab} + d_{bc}. \tag{A2.4}$$

Because all the triangle "inequalities" are equalities, in Euclidean geometry this implies that X_a, X_b, and X_c all lie on a straight line (Borg and Groenen, 1997, Chapter 18).

Because all the triangle inequalities are equalities and all triplets of points lie on a straight line, the distances computed from (A2.3) can be directly written as distances between points:

$$d_{ab} = \frac{\sum_{i=a}^{b-1} k_i}{q} = |X_a - X_b| \tag{A2.5}$$

where $d_{aa} = 0$. The p by p matrix of squared distances is

$$\mathbf{D} = \begin{bmatrix} 0 & (X_2 - X_1)^2 & \cdots & (X_p - X_1)^2 \\ (X_1 - X_2)^2 & 0 & \cdots & (X_p - X_2)^2 \\ \vdots & \vdots & \ddots & \vdots \\ (X_1 - X_p)^2 & (X_2 - X_p)^2 & \cdots & 0 \end{bmatrix}. \tag{A2.6}$$

To recover the X's, simply double-center $\mathbf{D}$ and perform an eigenvalue–eigenvector decomposition. The first eigenvector is the solution. To see this, let the mean of the jth column of $\mathbf{D}$ be

$$d_{.j}^2 = \frac{\sum_{i=1}^{p} d_{ij}^2}{p} = X_j^2 - 2X_j\bar{X} + \frac{\sum_{i=1}^{p} X_i^2}{p}$$

let the mean of the ith row of $\mathbf{D}$ be

$$d_{i.}^2 = \frac{\sum_{j=1}^{p} d_{ij}^2}{p} = X_i^2 - 2X_i\bar{X} + \frac{\sum_{j=1}^{p} X_j^2}{p}$$

and let the mean of the matrix $\mathbf{D}$ be

$$d_{..}^2 = \frac{\sum_{i=1}^{p} \sum_{j=1}^{p} d_{ij}^2}{p^2} = \frac{\sum_{j=1}^{p} X_j^2}{p} - 2\bar{X}^2 + \frac{\sum_{i=1}^{p} X_i^2}{p}$$

where $\bar{X} = \sum_{i=1}^{p} X_i/p$ is the mean of the X_i.

The matrix **D** is double-centered as follows: from each element subtract the row mean, subtract the column mean, add the matrix mean, and divide by -2; that is,

$$y_{ij} = \frac{d_{ij}^2 - d_{.j}^2 - d_{i.}^2 + d_{..}^2}{-2} = (X_i - \bar{X})(X_j - \bar{X}).$$

This produces the p by p symmetric positive semidefinite matrix **Y**:

$$\mathbf{Y} = \begin{bmatrix} X_1 - \bar{X} \\ X_2 - \bar{X} \\ \vdots \\ X_p - \bar{X} \end{bmatrix} [X_1 - \bar{X} \; X_2 - \bar{X} \ldots X_p - \bar{X}]. \qquad (A2.7)$$

Because **Y** is symmetric with a rank of one, its eigenvalue–eigenvector decomposition is simply

$$\mathbf{Y} = \begin{bmatrix} u_1 \\ u_2 \\ \vdots \\ u_p \end{bmatrix} \lambda_1 [u_1 u_2 \ldots u_p]. \qquad (A2.8)$$

Hence the solution is

$$\begin{bmatrix} X_1 - \bar{X} \\ X_2 - \bar{X} \\ \vdots \\ X_p - \bar{X} \end{bmatrix} = \sqrt{\lambda_1} \begin{bmatrix} u_1 \\ u_2 \\ \vdots \\ u_p \end{bmatrix}.$$

Because, without loss of generality, the origin can be placed at zero, that is, $\bar{X} = 0$, the solution can also be written as

$$\begin{bmatrix} X_1 \\ X_2 \\ \vdots \\ X_p \end{bmatrix} = \sqrt{\lambda_1} \begin{bmatrix} u_1 \\ u_2 \\ \vdots \\ u_p \end{bmatrix}. \qquad (A2.9)$$

The points from (A2.9) *exactly reproduce* the distances in (A2.4), the agreement scores in (A2.2), and the original roll call votes. In addition, note that the mirror image of the points in (A2.9) (a multiplication by -1) also exactly reproduces the original roll call votes. Furthermore, for any pair of true legislator ideal points $\tilde{X}_a$ and $\tilde{X}_b$ with one or more midpoints between them, $\tilde{X}_a < Z_j < \tilde{X}_b$, the recovered legislator ideal points must have the same ordering, $X_a < X_b$. If there are no midpoints between $\tilde{X}_a$ and $\tilde{X}_b$ – that is, their roll call voting pattern is identical – then the recovered legislator ideal points are identical: $X_a = X_b$.

Hence, if there are cutting points between every pair of adjacent legislators, that is, $k_i \geq 1$ for $i = 1, \ldots, p - 1$, then the rank ordering of the recovered ideal points is the same as the true rank ordering. If some of the $k_i = 0$, then the recovered ideal points have a weak monotone transformation of the true rank ordering (in other words, there are ties: some legislators have the same recovered ideal points).

This completes the proof.   **QED**

Discussion

Note that an interval-level set of points is recovered. But *this is an artifact of the distribution of cutting points*. For example, if $k_1 > k_2$, then $d_{12} > d_{23}$ even if the true coordinates $\tilde{X}_1, \tilde{X}_2, \tilde{X}_3$ were evenly spaced. With perfect one-dimensional voting, the legislator configuration is identified only up to a *weak monotone transformation* of the true rank ordering.

The rank ordering can also be recovered directly from the matrix **Y** given in (A2.7) without performing an eigenvalue–eigenvector decomposition. Note that, with the origin at zero, the diagonal elements of **Y** are simply the legislator coordinates squared. The rank ordering can be recovered by taking the square root of the first diagonal element and then dividing through the first row of the matrix. Note that this sets $X_1 > 0$, and the remaining points are identified vis-à-vis X_1.

Within the field of psychometrics the basic result of this theorem is well known. In Guttman scaling a *perfect simplex* is essentially the same as a perfect roll call matrix in one dimension. However, a perfect simplex has a natural polarity – for example, the Yeas are always on the same side of the cutting points. The theorem above is very similar to Schonemann's (1970) solution for the perfect simplex problem. His solution builds upon Guttman's (1954) analysis of the problem. To my knowledge, no one has stated the result in the form that I did above – namely, as the solution to a roll call voting problem.

CHAPTER 3

The Optimal Classification Method

Overview

In this chapter I show a method I developed (Poole 1997; 2000a) that is based on the geometry shown in Chapter 2 and is designed to analyze real-world roll call data. Simply put, I add error to the simple spatial model developed in Chapter 2 and show an estimation method – *optimal classification* (OC) – that maximizes the correct classification of legislative choices. In Chapter 4, I will focus entirely on models that maximize the *probabilities* of legislative choices using the same error framework. I show OC first because it can be used as a very reliable platform on which to build more intricate estimation methods.

At the heart of OC are two algorithms – the *cutting plane procedure* and the *legislative procedure*. Both of these procedures are unique and stable. In particular, Monte Carlo tests show that when the number of legislators is 100 or greater and the number of roll calls is on the order of 500 – typical of national legislatures like the U.S. Senate – then the recovery of the legislators and cutting lines or planes in one to ten dimensions at high levels of error and missing data is very precise (Poole, 1997; 2000a; b). Even with very small data sets, OC produces reliable results.[1] It is a stable building block upon which more complex parametric scaling methods can be constructed.

Within the psychometrics field, the OC scaling method is a *nonmetric unfolding* procedure. It is an "unfolding" in that the roll calls are treated as preferential choice data and parameters for individuals (legislators) and stimuli

---

[1] Poole (1997) is a working paper that reports Monte Carlo tests of OC for one to ten dimensions and a variety of applications that were not published in Poole (2000a). It can be found at http://pooleandrosenthal.com/p22/p22.htm. Poole (2000b) reports additional Monte Carlo results in a refereed but unpublished appendix. This appendix can be found at http://pooleandrosenthal.com/paapp/paapp.htm. The OC program along with numerous examples and further Monte Carlo results for small matrices is posted on the website for this book http://pooleandrosenthal.com/Spatial_Models_of_Parliamentary_Voting.htm under the Chapter 3 link. I will also make OC available in R.

46

(roll calls) are being estimated. It is "nonmetric" in that no assumptions are made about the parametric form of the legislators' "true" preference functions other than that they are symmetric and single-peaked.

Unfolding was developed for the one-dimensional case by Coombs (1950) and generalized to the multidimensional case by Bennett and Hays (1960). The original unfolding model – later dubbed the *ideal-point model* – represented individuals and stimuli as points and was originally developed to analyze rank orderings of stimuli by individuals. Later, Tucker (1960) developed the *vector model* of unfolding, in which the individuals are treated as vectors and the stimuli as points. The vector model is a special case of the unfolding model where the individual's ideal point goes off to infinity (Carroll, 1980; Borg and Groenen, 1997, Chapter 15). This model is much like Guttman scaling in that the individual's utility rises or falls monotonically from the center of the space off to infinity along the individual's vector. The projections of the stimuli onto the individual's vector reproduce the observed rank ordering. The vector model is the basis of the MDPREF program developed by Chang and Carroll (1969).

With respect to the roll call voting problem, the ideal point and vector unfolding models are closely related. If the individuals are treated as roll calls and the roll calls are treated as individuals, then the individual becomes a cutting plane through the space, and the point where the cutting plane passes through the normal (individual) vector is the individual's *threshold*. That is, the individual approves (accepts) the stimuli on one side of the plane and disapproves (does not accept) the stimuli on the other side of the plane. Pick-any-N data, widely used in marketing applications (DeSarbo and Cho, 1989), has this form. For example, respondents are given a list of soda pops and asked whether they drink or do not drink each soda. The soda pops are then displayed as points in a space, and the individuals as cutting lines that divide the soda pops into drink and do not drink.

Psychometricians have largely abandoned the nonmetric approach in the past fifteen years "because they suspected instability and identification problems" and have focused their efforts on probabilistic and metric alternatives.[2]

OC avoids these problems because the cutting plane procedure and the legislative procedure are constructed directly on the underlying geometry. The recovered legislator coordinates are virtually identical to those recovered by parametric procedures (Poole, 2000a) that must make strong assumptions about the interpersonal comparability of individuals' utility and the functional form of the error distribution (e.g., Heckman and Snyder, 1997; Poole and Rosenthal,

---

[2] Personal communication to the author from Willem J. Heiser, 27 March 1998. Some recent examples of probabilistic metric models within the psychometrics tradition are Heiser (1981); DeSarbo and Hoffman (1987); Gifi (1990); Blokland-Vogelesang (1991); Hojo (1994); and Andrich (1995).

1997). In addition, at very low levels of error,[3] OC is stable and is not susceptible to the problems encountered with many parametric procedures (Rosenthal and Voeten, 2004).

To recap the notation used in Chapter 2, each legislator is represented by an ideal point, an s by 1 vector $\mathbf{X}_i$, in the policy space with a symmetric single-peaked utility function centered at the ideal point (see Figure 2.1), and each roll call is represented as two points – one for the Yea policy outcome ($\mathbf{O}_{jy}$), and one for the Nay policy outcome ($\mathbf{O}_{jn}$) (both s by 1 vectors). If there were no error, the legislator would vote *deterministically* – that is, she would always vote for the closest alternative in the policy space. When random error is added to the utility function, the legislator votes *probabilistically* – that is, depending on the random error, sometimes she votes for the closest alternative and sometimes she does not.

I introduce error into a legislator's choice process by using the *random utility model* (McFadden, 1976). In the random utility model a legislator's overall utility for Yea or Nay is the sum of a deterministic utility and a random error. Suppose there are p legislators, q roll calls, and s dimensions indexed by $i = 1, \ldots, p$, $j = 1, \ldots, q$, and $k = 1, \ldots, s$, respectively. Legislator i's utility for the Yea outcome on roll call j is

$$U_{ijy} = u_{ijy} + \varepsilon_{ijy} \qquad (3.1)$$

where u_{ijy} is the deterministic portion of the utility function and ε_{ijy} is the stochastic (random) portion. With all models of this type, as a practical matter, the error term is picking up perceptual error, simple mistakes, and nonspatial sources of utility. I assume that the combination of all these nonspatial effects is purely random.

In Chapter 4, I will discuss probabilistic voting models that are built up from assumptions about the functional forms of the deterministic and stochastic portions of U_{ijy}. In the remainder of this chapter I assume only that legislators utilize a *symmetric single-peaked* utility function and discuss the general problems of (1) estimating a roll call cutting plane that maximizes correct classification given the legislator ideal points, and (2) estimating a legislator ideal point that maximizes correct classification given the cutting planes.

I discuss the one-dimensional maximum classification problem first because the same algorithm can be used to estimate both roll call cutting points and legislator ideal points. In Chapter 2, I show the one-dimensional solution for the roll call voting problem when there is no error. Consequently, in my discussion of the one-dimensional maximum classification algorithm I will

---

[3] This is not as far-fetched as it sounds. Several European parliaments classify at 95 percent or above in one or two dimensions – for example, most legislative sessions during the French Fourth Republic (Rosenthal and Voeten, 2004), recent sessions of the Czech parliament (personal communication from Abdul Noury), and the 1841 English parliament (shown in this chapter courtesy of Cheryl Schonhardt-Bailey).

assume that error is present. In the multidimensional problem, there is (as yet) no solution for the perfect-voting problem. Nevertheless, the cutting plane procedure and legislator procedure that are used by OC in two or more dimensions do an excellent job of solving both the perfect-voting problem and the roll call voting problem with error.

The One-Dimensional Maximum Classification Scaling Problem – The Janice Algorithm

In Chapter 2, I show a solution to the problem of one-dimensional perfect voting; namely, to get the legislator coordinates:

1. Compute the p by p agreement score matrix.
2. Convert the agreement score matrix into a matrix of squared distances.
3. Double-center the matrix of squared distances.
4. Take the square root of a diagonal element of the double-centered matrix, and divide it through the corresponding column.

In the appendix to Chapter 2, I show that the first eigenvector extracted from the double-centered transformed agreement score matrix has the same rank ordering as the true data. This is equivalent to step 4 above. When error is present this method cannot guarantee that the rank ordering of the first eigenvector maximizes correct classification. But the first eigenvector provides excellent starting values for a rank order that can be iteratively improved, by what I call the *Janice algorithm*,[4] to arrive at a rank ordering that almost certainly maximizes correct classification. I will first discuss the case of very low error and then the more general case of higher error.

The Effect of Very Low Error in One Dimension

Suppose the error ε_{ijy} is drawn from some continuous probability distribution with mean μ and variance σ^2, that is,

$$\varepsilon_{ijy} \sim f(\mu, \sigma^2).$$

Suppose σ is very small, that is, suppose σ is an *infinitesimal quantity of the first order*, "that is, a quantity whose higher powers are, for the problem at hand, negligible in comparison to lower powers of [σ]" (Courant and Hilbert, 1937, vol. 1, p. 41). Then on a roll call only the legislators adjacent to and a very tiny distance away from a cutting point will make a voting error. This case is

---

[4]My sweet wife of 32 years (as this is written in August 2004) is Janice Edith Poole. I developed the Janice algorithm in 1978 and the Edith algorithm in early 1979 when I was at the University of Oregon.

```
              -1---------0--------+1

Legislators   X₁  X₂  X₃  X₄  X₅  X₆
Cutpoints         Z₁  Z₂  Z₃  Z₄  Z₅
```

Legislators	X_1	X_2	X_3	X_4	X_5	X_6
Cutpoints		Z_1	Z_2	Z_3	Z_4	Z_5
1	Y	N	N	N	N	N
2	Y	Y	N	N	N	N
3	Y	Y	Y	N	N	N
4	Y	Y	Y	Y	N	N
5	Y	Y	Y	Y	Y	N

Roll Call Matrix

Roll Calls

Legislators	1	2	3	4	5
One	Y	Y	Y	Y	Y
Two	N	Y	Y	Y	Y
Three	N	N	Y	Y	Y
Four	N	N	N	Y	Y
Five	N	N	N	N	Y
Six	N	N	N	N	N

FIGURE 3.1. *Perfect spatial voting in one dimension. The six legislators and five cutting lines are evenly spaced along the dimension, with one cutting line between each adjacent pair of legislators. The Yea alternative is always on the left. The top part of the figure shows the voting along the dimension, and the lower part shows the voting in the form of a roll call matrix.*

observationally indistinguishable from perfect voting. It is shown in Figures 3.1, 3.2, and 3.3.

Figure 3.1 is the same as Figure 2.2 – perfect voting by six legislators on five roll calls with the Yea alternative always on the left. The upper part of the figure shows the voting along the dimension, and the lower part of the figure shows the voting in the form of a roll call matrix. The lower triangle of the roll call matrix is all Nays, and the upper triangle is all Yeas. Now, suppose legislators Three and Four are very close together with the cutting point for the third roll call between them. With very low error, either, neither, or both legislators could make a voting error. Figure 3.2 illustrates the four possibilities.

The first possibility, case (a), shown in the first row of Figure 3.2, is that neither legislator makes an error; that is, for legislator Three $U_{33y} > U_{33n}$, so she

```
Legislators    X₁  X₂  X₃  X₄  X₅  X₆
                         Z₃


Low Noise (a) Y    Y   Y   N   N   N
Low Noise (b) Y    Y   N   N   N   N  (same as RC 2)
Low Noise (c) Y    Y   Y   Y   N   N  (same as RC 4)
Low Noise (d) Y    Y   N   Y   N   N
```

FIGURE 3.2. *Low-noise spatial voting in one dimension on the third roll call from Figure 3.1. Legislators Three and Four are very close together with the cutting point between them. The four rows show the four error possibilities: neither, Three only, Four only, both.*

votes Yea even with the error, and for legislator Four $U_{43n} > U_{43y}$, so he votes Nay even with the error. In case (b) the addition of the error causes legislator Three's utility for Nay to become larger than her utility for Yea – $U_{33y} < U_{33n}$ – so she now votes Nay, and legislator Four still votes Nay even with the error. Note that this produces a roll call vote that is identical to the second one in Figure 3.1.

Similarly, in case (c), the addition of the error changes legislator Four's vote to Yea while it does not affect legislator Three's vote. Note that this produces a roll call vote that is identical to the fourth one in Figure 3.1.

Finally, in case (d), the addition of the error changes the votes of both legislators.

To recap, cases (a), (b), and (c) are identical to roll call votes 3, 2, and 4, respectively. Consequently, the presence of the error would be unknowable. In case (a) nothing changes. In case (b) it would look as if the cutting points for roll calls 2 and 3 were the same, and in case (c) it would look as if the cutting points for roll calls 3 and 4 were the same.

This leaves case (d). As Figure 3.3 shows, however, the presence of the error even in this "obvious" case also would be unknowable, because legislator Three's voting pattern is now identical to Four's in Figure 3.1. That is, simply transposing the rows corresponding to legislators Three and Four as shown in Figure 3.3 produces a perfect voting pattern.

In sum, when the error level is very low, it cannot be detected. The effect will be perhaps to scramble the "true" ordering slightly, but we can never know whether or not that is occurring, because it is observationally indistinguishable from perfect voting.

The Effect of Higher Levels of Error in One Dimension

Suppose the error is large enough so that rows and columns of the simple roll call matrix in Figure 3.1 cannot be swapped (transposed) so as to produce a

	Roll Calls				
Legislators	1	2	3d	4	5
One	Y	Y	Y	Y	Y
Two	N	Y	Y	Y	Y
Three	N	N	N	Y	Y
Four	N	N	Y	Y	Y
Five	N	N	N	N	Y
Six	N	N	N	N	N

Perfect Voting With Four and Three Transposed

	Roll Calls				
Legislators	1	2	3d	4	5
One	Y	Y	Y	Y	Y
Two	N	Y	Y	Y	Y
Four	N	N	Y	Y	Y
Three	N	N	N	Y	Y
Five	N	N	N	N	Y
Six	N	N	N	N	N

FIGURE 3.3. *Low-noise spatial voting in one dimension on the third roll call from Figure 3.1. Case (d) from Figure 3.2, where legislators Three and Four both make errors, is equivalent to perfect voting if the two legislators are transposed as shown in the lower portion of the figure.*

perfect-voting matrix. In this instance, the error will be detected. An example of this is shown in Figures 3.4 and 3.5. In Figure 3.4 the only error is legislator One voting Nay on roll call 3 when she should vote Yea (shown underlined and in italics). Using the four-step method discussed above, Figure 3.4 also shows the agreement score matrix and the first eigenvector extracted from the double-centered transformed agreement score matrix. The ordering of the legislators implied by the eigenvector is

$$X_2 < X_1 < X_3 < X_4 < X_5 < X_6$$

so that the single voting error by legislator One has transposed the order of legislators One and Two. This rank ordering is used in Figure 3.5 to illustrate how the Janice algorithm works.

| | Roll Calls | | | | |
Legislators	1	2	3	4	5
One	Y	Y	*N*	Y	Y
Two	N	Y	Y	Y	Y
Three	N	N	Y	Y	Y
Four	N	N	N	Y	Y
Five	N	N	N	N	Y
Six	N	N	N	N	N

Agreement Scores						First Eigenvector
1.0						$X_1 = -.44512$
.6	1.0					$X_2 = -.48973$
.4	.8	1.0				$X_3 = -.11093$
.6	.6	.8	1.0			$X_4 = .04431$
.4	.4	.6	.8	1.0		$X_5 = .34859$
.2	.2	.4	.6	.8	1.0	$X_6 = .65288$

FIGURE 3.4. *Recovering the legislator ideal points with voting error. The roll call matrix is the same as Figure 3.1, only legislator One votes Nay on roll call 3 when she should vote Yea (shown underlined and in italics). The agreement score matrix and the first eigenvector extracted from the double-centered transformed agreement score matrix are shown below the roll call matrix. Legislators One and Two are transposed in the eigenvector.*

Figure 3.5 shows how the Janice algorithm finds roll call cutting points that maximize correct classification given a rank ordering of legislators. With six legislators there are seven possible rank positions for a roll call cutting point. These are shown as rows in the figure. For example, if the cutting point is placed before the leftmost legislator, in this case $Z_j < X_2$, this would imply if voting was perfect that all the legislators would vote for the alternative to the right of the cutting point – Nay in the upper part of the figure and Yea in the lower part of the figure. Similarly, if the cutting point is located between X_2 and X_1, that is, $X_2 < Z_j < X_1$, then with perfect voting with Yea as the left alternative, legislator Two votes Yea and the other legislators vote Nay, and vice versa if Yea is the right alternative. This configuration is shown in the second row of both parts of Figure 3.5.

The columns on the right side of Figure 3.5 correspond to the five roll calls from Figure 3.4. The row entries in each column show the number of classification errors when the corresponding cutting point is used for that roll call. For example, for roll call 1, if the cutting point is placed furthest to the left, that is, $Z_1 < X_2$, then the result is only one classification error. In terms of the legislator

```
Legislators       X₂ < X₁ < X₃ < X₄ < X₅ < X₆
```

Predicted Patterns of All Possible Rank Positions For a
Roll Call Cutting point Given the Legislator Ordering Above
(Yea on the Left, Nay on the Right)

							Number of Errors On Roll Calls				
							1	2	3	4	5
$Z_j < X_2$	N	N	N	N	N	N	1	2	2	4	5
$X_2 < Z_j < X_1$	Y	N	N	N	N	N	2	1	1	3	4
$X_1 < Z_j < X_3$	Y	Y	N	N	N	N	*1*	*0*	2	2	3
$X_3 < Z_j < X_4$	Y	Y	Y	N	N	N	2	1	*1*	1	2
$X_4 < Z_j < X_5$	Y	Y	Y	Y	N	N	3	2	2	*0*	1
$X_5 < Z_j < X_6$	Y	Y	Y	Y	Y	N	4	3	3	1	*0*
$X_6 < Z_j$	Y	Y	Y	Y	Y	Y	5	4	4	2	1

(Nay on the Left, Yea on the Right)

$Z_j < X_2$	Y	Y	Y	Y	Y	Y	5	4	4	2	1
$X_2 < Z_j < X_1$	N	Y	Y	Y	Y	Y	4	5	5	3	2
$X_1 < Z_j < X_3$	N	N	Y	Y	Y	Y	5	6	4	4	3
$X_3 < Z_j < X_4$	N	N	N	Y	Y	Y	4	5	5	5	4
$X_4 < Z_j < X_5$	N	N	N	N	Y	Y	3	4	4	6	5
$X_5 < Z_j < X_6$	N	N	N	N	N	Y	2	3	3	5	6
$X_6 < Z_j$	N	N	N	N	N	N	1	2	2	4	5

FIGURE 3.5. *The Janice algorithm for roll calls. With six legislators there are seven possible rank positions for a roll call cutting point. These are shown as rows. The upper portion assumes that Yea is on the left, and the lower that Nay is on the left. The columns on the right side of the figure correspond to the five roll calls from Figure 3.4. The row entries in each column show the number of classification errors when the corresponding cutting point is used for that roll call.*

ordering, the pattern of roll call 1 is NYNNNN, so that predicting NNNNNN produces only one classification error – legislator One is predicted to vote Nay, and she actually votes Yea. Similarly, if the cutting point is placed between legislators Two and One, namely, $X_2 < Z_1 < X_1$, then the predicted pattern is YNNNNN. This pattern produces two classification errors – both legislators Two and One are wrongly predicted. Placing the cutting point between legislators One and Three, $X_1 < Z_1 < X_3$, predicts the pattern YYNNNN, which produces only one classification error – legislator Two. Note that up or down the column can increase or decrease the number of errors t one, and that there can be multiple cutting points with the same num, errors.

The classification error cells shown underlined and in italics correspond to the optimal locations of the corresponding cutting points. When there are two or more cutting points that produce the same best correct classification, the rule is to pick the cutting point closest to the center of the legislator rank ordering. For example, for roll call 1, placing the cutting point furthest to the left produces one classification error when the Nay alternative is on the right. Note, however, that placing the cutting point furthest to the right, $X_6 < Z_1$, also produces one classification error if the Yea alternative is on the right. This is a good illustration of the problems encountered with lopsided roll calls in real-world data. Often, placing the cutting point at either end of the dimension with the polarity reversed in each case produces the same number of correct classifications. In both cases, the cutting point predicts a unanimous vote. But if there are *interior* ranks that produce the same number of correct classifications, the Janice algorithm always picks the most interior cutting point (that is, the one closest to the median rank).

The application of the Janice algorithm shown in Figure 3.5 produces the following joint ordering of legislators and cutting points:

$$X_2 < X_1 < Z_1 = Z_2 < X_3 < Z_3 < X_4 < Z_4 < X_5 < Z_5 < X_6.$$

This joint ordering produces two classification errors – legislator Two is predicted to vote Yea on roll call 1 and he actually votes Nay, and legislator One is predicted to vote Yea on roll call 3 and she actually votes Nay.

Figure 3.6 shows how the Janice algorithm finds legislator rank positions that maximize correct classification given a rank ordering of roll call cutting points and the polarity – what alternative is on the left and what alternative is on the right – of each roll call. These are shown as L and R in the figure. Because legislators do not have a polarity per se, Figure 3.6 is simpler than Figure 3.5. With five roll calls there are six possible rank positions for a legislator. These are shown as rows in the figure. For example, if a legislator is placed before the leftmost roll call cutting point, in this case $X_i < Z_1$, then with perfect voting the legislator would vote for the left alternative on every roll call – LLLLL in the first row of the figure. The fact that roll calls 1 and 2 are tied in rank does not present a problem, *because of the fixed polarities*. Placing a legislator at the tied position – $Z_1 = X_i = Z_2$ – would predict the pattern RLLLL or LRLLL. But treating Z_1 as being "before" Z_2 or vice versa for bookkeeping purposes is not a problem. If the polarities of the two roll calls are the same at the tied position, then this sameness of polarity presents no problem for the placement of a legislator rank. For example, if the polarity of roll calls 1 and 2 at the tied position were L, the implied pattern would be LLLLL. But this pattern is the

Roll Calls $Z_1 = Z_2 < Z_3 < Z_4 < Z_5$

Predicted Patterns of All Possible Rank Positions for a
Legislator Given the Cutting Point Ordering Above
(Roll Call Polarity From Figure 3.5)

						Number of Errors On Legislators					
						1	2	3	4	5	6
$X_i < Z_1$	L	L	L	L	L	_1_	1	2	3	4	5
$Z_1 = X_i = Z_2$	R	L	L	L	L	2	_0_	1	2	3	4
$Z_2 < X_i < Z_3$	R	R	L	L	L	3	1	_0_	1	2	3
$Z_3 < X_i < Z_4$	R	R	R	L	L	2	2	1	_0_	1	2
$Z_4 < X_i < Z_5$	R	R	R	R	L	3	3	2	1	_0_	1
$Z_5 < X_i$	R	R	R	R	R	4	4	3	2	1	_0_

FIGURE 3.6. *The Janice algorithm for legislators. Given the rank ordering of the five roll call cutting points and what alternative is on the left and what alternative is on the right of each cutting point (L and R), there are six possible rank positions for a legislator ideal point. These are shown as rows in the figure. The columns on the right correspond to the six legislators. The row entries in each column show the number of classification errors when the corresponding legislator rank position vis-à-vis the roll call cutting points is used.*

same as the first row of the figure, so that $X_i < Z_1$. If the polarity of both roll calls were R at the tied position, the implied pattern would be RRLLL. This pattern is the same as the pattern produced by placing the legislator between the tied pair and roll call 3 – that is, $Z_1 = Z_2 < X_i < Z_3$. In short, in all cases the placement of the legislator is unambiguous.

The columns on the right side of Figure 3.6 correspond to the six legislators. The row entries in each column show the number of classification errors when the corresponding legislator rank position vis-à-vis the roll call cutting points is used. For example, for legislator One, if the rank position is placed furthest to the left, that is, if $X_1 < Z_1$, the result is only one classification error. Legislator One votes YYNYY on roll calls 1 through 5. Given the polarities, this ordering translates into the pattern LLRLL. Hence predicting LLLLL by placing legislator One to the left of all the roll call cutting points produces only one classification error – she is predicted to vote L (or Yea) on roll call 3 when in fact she votes R (or Nay). Similarly, if legislator One's rank is placed at the tied rank position of roll calls 1 and 2, then the predicted pattern is RLLLL, and this produces two classification errors.

The classification error cells shown underlined and in italics correspond to the optimal locations of the corresponding legislators. When there are two or

```
Legislators      X₁ < X₂ < X₃ < X₄ < X₅ < X₆
```

Predicted Patterns of All Possible Rank Positions for a
Roll Call Cutting Point Given the Legislator Ordering Above
(Yea on the Left, Nay on the Right)

							Number of Errors On Roll Calls				
							1	2	3	4	5
$Z_j < X_1$	N	N	N	N	N	N	1	2	2	4	5
$X_1 < Z_j < X_2$	Y	N	N	N	N	N	*0*	1	3	3	4
$X_2 < Z_j < X_3$	Y	Y	N	N	N	N	1	*0*	2	2	3
$X_3 < Z_j < X_4$	Y	Y	Y	N	N	N	2	1	*1*	1	2
$X_4 < Z_j < X_5$	Y	Y	Y	Y	N	N	3	2	2	*0*	1
$X_5 < Z_j < X_6$	Y	Y	Y	Y	Y	N	4	3	3	1	*0*
$X_6 < Z_j$	Y	Y	Y	Y	Y	Y	5	4	4	2	1

(Nay on the Left, Yea on the Right)

$Z_j < X_1$	Y	Y	Y	Y	Y	Y	5	4	4	2	1
$X_1 < Z_j < X_2$	N	Y	Y	Y	Y	Y	6	5	3	3	2
$X_2 < Z_j < X_3$	N	N	Y	Y	Y	Y	5	6	4	4	3
$X_3 < Z_j < X_4$	N	N	N	Y	Y	Y	4	5	5	5	4
$X_4 < Z_j < X_5$	N	N	N	N	Y	Y	3	4	4	6	5
$X_5 < Z_j < X_6$	N	N	N	N	N	Y	2	3	3	5	6
$X_6 < Z_j$	N	N	N	N	N	N	1	2	2	4	5

FIGURE 3.7. *Second iteration of the Janice algorithm for roll calls, using the legislator ordering from Figure 3.6. The layout is the same as Figure 3.5.*

more rank positions that produce the same best correct classification, the rule is to pick the rank position for the legislator that is closest to the median of the roll call cutting point rank ordering.

The application of the Janice algorithm shown in Figure 3.6 produces the following joint ordering of legislators and cutting points:

$$X_1 < Z_1 = Z_2 = X_2 < X_3 < Z_3 < X_4 < Z_4 < X_5 < Z_5 < X_6.$$

This joint ordering produces only one classification error – legislator One is predicted to vote Yea (L) on roll call 3, and she actually votes Nay (R).

Figure 3.7 shows the application of the Janice algorithm to the roll calls using the new rank ordering of the legislators. Figure 3.7 is laid out the same as Figure 3.5. The joint rank order produced by Figure 3.7 is

$$X_1 < Z_1 < X_2 < Z_2 < X_3 < Z_3 < X_4 < Z_4 < X_5 < Z_5 < X_6.$$

This joint ordering produces only one classification error – legislator One is predicted to vote Yea on roll call 3, and she actually votes Nay.

Note that in going from Figure 3.5 to Figure 3.6 and going from Figure 3.6 to Figure 3.7, *the classification error cannot increase.* Holding the rank ordering of the legislators (of the cutting points) fixed, *the Janice algorithm always finds ranks for the cutting points (for the legislators) that maximize correct classification,* because it checks all possible rank positions. For example, in Figure 3.5 the starting estimate of the legislator rank ordering is used to get the first ordering of the cutting points. This first ordering of the cutting points is then used in Figure 3.6 to get a new legislator ordering. As shown in both figures, the Janice algorithm always finds the ranks that maximize correct classification, because it checks all possible rank positions. Hence, the new ordering of the legislators *must* classify them as well as the initial ordering does. A similar reasoning applies to the transition from Figure 3.6 to Figure 3.7.

An attractive feature of the Janice algorithm is its computational efficiency: It is linear in the number of legislators or of roll calls. In Figure 3.5 there are only $2p$ *unique* perfect patterns. Although there are $2p + 2 = 14$ patterns shown in Figure 3.5, the unanimous patterns appear twice for purposes of clarity. Computationally, it is a simple matter to compare each perfect pattern with the actual pattern of votes. This can be done very efficiently by first assuming that the cutting point is to the left of all the legislators as in row 1 of the figure, and then calculating the corresponding number of correct classifications. This computation requires p calculations. Next assume that the cutting point is between the leftmost pair of legislators – X_2 and X_1 in Figure 3.5. To get the number of correct classifications, only one calculation has to be made, because the only change is that the cutting point rank has been moved from the left of the leftmost legislator to between the leftmost pair of legislators. If there is no missing data, the correct classification either increases by 1 or decreases by 1 when the cutting point is moved one rank position in this fashion. For each possible cutting point rank, the correct classification corresponding to the two possible perfect patterns can be calculated (the upper and lower portions of Figure 3.5). With no missing data, the number of correct classifications for a particular rank position for a perfect pattern and its mirror image must always add to p. Therefore, to know the correct classifications for both polarities, only one calculation is required when the cutting point is moved one rank position with no missing data. Hence the total number of calculations required to find the maximum classification cutting point rank *and* its associated polarity is $2p$.

The same reasoning holds for finding the legislator rank that maximizes correct classification given the cutting point ranks. Given the polarity of the roll calls as shown in Figure 3.6, only $2q$ calculations are required to find the maximum classification rank for each legislator.

In sum, the one-dimensional optimal classification method is:

1. Generate starting estimate of the legislator rank ordering.
2. Holding the legislator rank ordering fixed, use the Janice algorithm to find the optimal cutting point ordering.
3. Holding the cutting point ordering fixed, use the Janice algorithm to find the optimal legislator ordering.
4. Go to step 2.

Hereafter, I will refer to steps 2 to 4 as the *Edith algorithm*.[5]

This simple algorithm converges very rapidly to a solution in which the rank ordering of the legislators and the rank ordering of the roll call midpoints reproduce each other. In the example above, we have

Step 1: $X_2 < X_1 < X_3 < X_4 < X_5 < X_6$
Step 2a: $Z_1 = Z_2 < Z_3 < Z_4 < Z_5$
Step 3a: $X_1 < X_2 < X_3 < X_4 < X_5 < X_6$
Step 2b: $Z_1 < Z_2 < Z_3 < Z_4 < Z_5$
Step 3b: $X_1 < X_2 < X_3 < X_4 < X_5 < X_6$
Step 2c: $Z_1 < Z_2 < Z_3 < Z_4 < Z_5$
etc.

The Edith algorithm always converges to a solution in which the two rank orderings reproduce each other. This joint rank ordering of cutting points and legislators is a very strong form of *conditional global maximum*. Technically, if there are multiple sets of parameters (for example, as in this case, parameters corresponding to rows of a matrix and parameters corresponding to columns of a matrix), and every set of parameters is at a global maximum conditioned on the other sets being held fixed, and these sets reproduce each other, then they are at a conditional global maximum. Note that the overall global maximum, by definition, is a conditional global maximum.

The global maximum in principle can be found by checking each of the $p!/2$ unique orderings of the legislators (the division by two removes the mirror image orderings). That is, for every unique ordering of the legislators, use the Janice algorithm to find the optimal rank positions of the cutting points. For small voting bodies of 15 or less, this could actually be done. Future massively parallel supercomputers could possibly bring into reach legislatures the size of the U.S. Senate ($p = 100$) and U.S. House ($p = 435$). Until then, the Edith algorithm will have to do.

An encouraging aspect of the Edith algorithm is that conditional global maxima are quite rare because of the nature of the constraints. Indeed, in the metric similarities problem, conditional global minima are very rare, and *their number declines as the number of parameters increases* (Poole, 1990).

---

[5] See note 4.

Twelve-Legislator Example
Normal Vector and Normal Vector Line

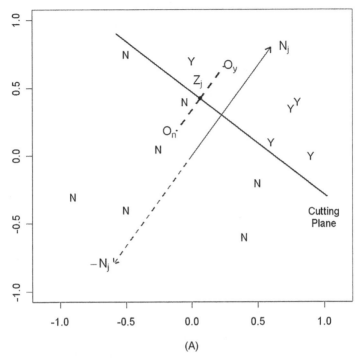

(A)

FIGURE 3.8. *(A) Twelve legislators in two dimensions with perfect voting and normal vector line. The legislators are displayed as N's or Y's corresponding to their votes on the hypothetical roll call. The cutting plane divides the legislators who vote Yea from those who vote Nay, and the line joining the Yea and Nay outcomes is parallel to the normal vector. The normal vector is denoted as $\mathbf{N}_j$, and its reflection as $-\mathbf{N}_j$. The normal vector and its reflection form the normal vector line. (B) Twelve legislators in two dimensions projected onto the normal vector line. The cutting point perfectly classifies the roll call.*

The Multidimensional Maximum Classification Scaling Problem

In two or more dimensions there is as yet no solution for the perfect-voting problem. Indeed, it is difficult to tell whether or not the data is even perfect. What made the one-dimensional perfect-voting problem solvable was the fact that the number of cutting points between a pair of legislators could be converted into a Euclidean distance. In more than one dimension, legislators are identified only up to polytopes, and the distances between these polytopes are not *necessarily* linear in the number of cutting lines or planes between them (see Figure 2.10). A consequence is that error, which is manifest only in the changes of Yeas to

The Optimal Classification Method 61

Twelve-Legislator Example
Points Projected Onto Normal Vector Line

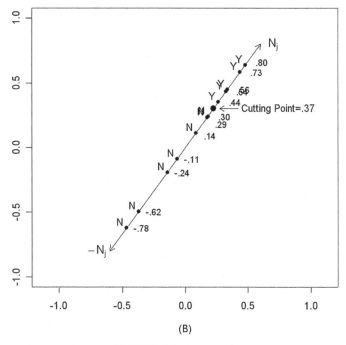

(B)

FIGURE 3.8 *(continued)*

Nays and Nays to Yeas in a legislator's voting pattern, cannot be guaranteed to be symmetric with direction in the space.

These are serious problems, but because the OC method is built directly on the underlying geometry, it can deal with them effectively. Although OC cannot be guaranteed to always find the best possible solution, it will come extremely close in almost all situations.

In the next section I show how to estimate a cutting plane that maximizes correct classification on a roll call, given an estimate of the legislator points. In the following section I show how to find the polytope that maximizes the correct classification of a legislator's choices, given an estimate of the roll call cutting planes.

Estimating a Roll Call Cutting Plane Given the Legislator Ideal Points

Given the legislator ideal points – the p by s matrix $\mathbf{X}$ – and the choices of the legislators on a roll call, the problem is to find a line in two dimensions or a plane in more than two dimensions that divides the legislators into two groups so as to maximize the number of correct classifications. Figure 3.8 shows the basics of the problem in two dimensions.

Panel A of Figure 3.8 is the same as Figure 2.11. It shows the basic geometry of a roll call vote in two dimensions. The normal vector is denoted as $\mathbf{N}_j$, and its *reflection* as $-\mathbf{N}_j$. I impose the constraint that the normal vectors be of unit length, namely;

$$\mathbf{N}_j'\mathbf{N}_j = \sum_{k=1}^{s} N_{jk}^2 = 1. \qquad (3.2)$$

This constraint does not affect the fundamental geometry outlined in Chapter 2. I impose the constraint simply because unit-length normal vectors make the algebra of the problem easier to explain. For example, the normal vector in Figure 3.8 is $\left[\begin{smallmatrix} .6 \\ .8 \end{smallmatrix}\right]$.

I will refer to the line formed by the normal vector and its reflection as the *normal vector line* in my discussion below. The normal vector is perpendicular to the cutting plane that divides the Yeas and Nays. Panel B of Figure 3.8 shows the projection of the legislators onto the normal vector line. Technically, these points are on a line through an s-dimensional space. Because they *are* on a line, however, they can be treated *as* a line. The algebra of the projection is shown in Figure 3.9. I will refer to this line as the *projection line* in my discussion below (these values are also shown in Figure 3.8B).

The upper portion of Figure 3.9 shows the legislator coordinates used in Figure 3.8A and those points projected onto the normal vector line. Note that a legislator's point on the normal vector line can be found by simply drawing a line parallel to the cutting plane down to the normal vector line. Technically, this transformation for an individual legislator is $\mathbf{X}_i'\mathbf{N}_j\mathbf{N}_j'$. Note that it produces a vector of length s, that is, a point in s dimensions.

The lower portion of Figure 3.9 shows the legislator positions on the projection line that is just the normal vector line rigidly rotated to the horizontal so that each legislator is simply a single number along the line. Technically, the legislator values along the projection line are

$$\mathbf{X}_i'\mathbf{N}_j = w_i \qquad (3.3)$$

where w_i is a scalar – that is, a simple number – and not a vector. The spacing of the legislators on the projection line is exactly the same as their spacing on the normal vector line. The reason is straightforward. A legislator's point on the normal vector line is $\mathbf{X}_i'\mathbf{N}_j\mathbf{N}_j'$, or, substituting equation (3.3), $w_i\mathbf{N}_j'$. For two legislators, a and b, the squared distance between them on the projection line is $(w_a - w_b)^2$. The squared distance between them on the normal vector line is

$$\sum_{k=1}^{s}(w_a N_{jk} - w_b N_{jk})^2 = \sum_{k=1}^{s} N_{jk}^2(w_a - w_b)^2$$
$$= (w_a - w_b)^2 \sum_{k=1}^{s} N_{jk}^2 = (w_a - w_b)^2$$

Legislator Points
From Figure 3.8

Legislator Points Projec
Onto Normal Vector Line

$$
\begin{bmatrix}
x_{11} & x_{12} \\
x_{21} & x_{22} \\
x_{31} & x_{32} \\
x_{41} & x_{42} \\
x_{51} & x_{52} \\
x_{61} & x_{62} \\
x_{71} & x_{72} \\
x_{81} & x_{82} \\
x_{91} & x_{92} \\
x_{101} & x_{102} \\
x_{111} & x_{112} \\
x_{121} & x_{122}
\end{bmatrix}
=
\begin{bmatrix}
-.90 & -.30 \\
-.50 & -.40 \\
.40 & -.60 \\
-.25 & .05 \\
.50 & -.20 \\
-.05 & .40 \\
-.50 & .75 \\
.60 & .10 \\
.90 & .00 \\
.00 & .70 \\
.75 & .35 \\
.80 & .40
\end{bmatrix}
\qquad
\begin{bmatrix}
-.468 & -.624 \\
-.372 & -.496 \\
-.144 & -.192 \\
-.066 & -.088 \\
.084 & .112 \\
.174 & .232 \\
.180 & .240 \\
.264 & .352 \\
.324 & .432 \\
.336 & .448 \\
.438 & .584 \\
.480 & .640
\end{bmatrix}
$$

Legislator Values on Projection Line: $X_i'N_j = w_i$

$$
\begin{bmatrix}
w_1 \\
w_2 \\
w_3 \\
w_4 \\
w_5 \\
w_6 \\
w_7 \\
w_8 \\
w_9 \\
w_{10} \\
w_{11} \\
w_{12}
\end{bmatrix}
= XN_j =
\begin{bmatrix}
-.90 & -.30 \\
-.50 & -.40 \\
.40 & -.60 \\
-.25 & .05 \\
.50 & -.20 \\
-.05 & .40 \\
-.50 & .75 \\
.60 & .10 \\
.90 & .00 \\
.00 & .70 \\
.75 & .35 \\
.80 & .40
\end{bmatrix}
\begin{bmatrix}
.6 \\
.8
\end{bmatrix}
=
\begin{bmatrix}
-.78 \\
-.62 \\
-.24 \\
-.11 \\
.14 \\
.29 \\
.30 \\
.44 \\
.54 \\
.56 \\
.73 \\
.80
\end{bmatrix}
$$

FIGURE 3.9. *The twelve legislator points from Figure 3.8 projected onto the normal vector line and the corresponding projection line. The normal vector line is a line through two dimensions, and the projection line is a line in one dimension.*

so that the distance between the legislators on both lines is exactly the same, because the normal vector has unit length [equation (3.2)]. For example, the distance between legislators 11 and 12 in the two projections shown in Figure 3.9 is

$$\sqrt{(.438 - .480)^2 + (.584 - .640)^2} = .07 = |.73 - .80|.$$

Figures 3.8 and 3.9 illustrate the fact that the problem of estimating the roll call cutting plane given the legislator ideal points is equivalent to finding a normal vector, N_j, such that when the legislator points are projected onto the projection line, a cutting point can be found that maximizes the correct classification. Hence the cutting plane problem has two distinct parts. First, given an estimated normal vector, the plane perpendicular to the normal vector that maximizes correct classifications must be found; and second, given an estimated cutting plane, the orientation of the plane in the space must be changed so that a better estimate of the normal vector is found.

The Janice algorithm solves the first problem. To see how, recall from Chapter 2 that a cutting plane in s dimensions is defined by the vector equation

$$\mathbf{N}'_j(\mathbf{W} - \mathbf{Z}_j) = 0 \qquad (3.4)$$

where $\mathbf{N}_j$ is the s by 1 unit-length normal vector, $\mathbf{Z}_j$ is an s by 1 vector that is the midpoint of the Yea and Nay outcome points, and $\mathbf{W}$ is an s by 1 vector that is any point on the surface of the plane. In general, if $\mathbf{W}_A$ and $\mathbf{W}_B$ are both points in the plane, then $\mathbf{W}'_A \mathbf{N}_j = \mathbf{W}'_B \mathbf{N}_j = c_j$, and c_j is a *scalar* not a vector. By definition, the midpoint of the Yea and Nay outcome points projects to c_j; namely,

$$\mathbf{Z}'_j \mathbf{N}_j = c_j. \qquad (3.5)$$

Given the w_i's from equation (3.3), finding the optimal c_j is equivalent to the one-dimensional optimal classification problem for a single roll call shown above. The Janice algorithm will find the optimal position for c_j, given the w_i's, using exactly the same logic displayed in Figures 3.5 and 3.7. Geometrically this is equivalent to moving the cutting plane through the space along the normal vector and counting the correct classifications every time the plane passes through a legislator point.

In this application of the Janice algorithm, real numbers rather than ranks are used. Consider the simple example shown in Figures 3.8 and 3.9. Suppose the cutting point is placed .01 units to the left of legislator One on the projection line – in this case at −.79. With Nay to the right of the cutting point, this placement of the cutting point predicts 12 Nays and 0 Yeas, for five classification errors. With Yea to the right of the cutting point, the prediction is 12 Yeas and 0 Nays, for seven classification errors. Proceeding as in Figure 3.9, placing the cutting point midway between legislators One and Two on the projection line (−.70 in this instance), produces six classification errors with Nay to the right of the cutting point, and six with Yea to the right of the cutting point. Proceeding inward, placing the cutting point between legislators Seven and Eight with Yea to the right of the cutting point, produces perfect classification.

To solve the second part of the cutting plane problem – changing the orientation of the plane in the space to get a better estimate of the normal vector – the cutting plane must be moved through the space in a direction that increases correct classification. This improvement is accomplished by moving the cutting plane toward the legislator points that are classification errors.

Cutting Plane Procedure
Projecting Points onto Cutting Line

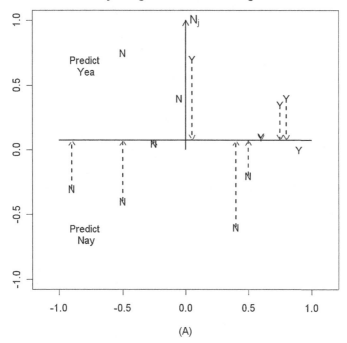

(A)

FIGURE 3.10. *Cutting plane procedure: (A) The twelve legislator points from Figure 3.8 are projected onto a normal vector line that is perpendicular to the first dimension. The dashed arrows show the projections. (B) Three legislators are not correctly classified, so they remain in their original positions. (C) First iteration. The new normal vector is perpendicular to the least squares line through the points from (B).*

To move the cutting plane, a matrix is created by projecting all the *correctly classified* legislator points onto the surface of the current cutting plane while leaving the incorrectly classified legislators at their original positions. In two dimensions this matrix consists of a line of points through the space made up of correctly classified legislators (the current cutting plane) around which is a scattering of points corresponding to the incorrectly classified legislators (see Figure 3.10). Much in the spirit of the classic ordinary least squares regression problem, we can estimate a new cutting plane by simply finding the plane that best fits this set of points using the principle of least squares. The normal vector to this new plane is the new normal vector.

Specifically, a p by s matrix Ψ is constructed as follows: If legislator i is correctly classified, then her point is projected onto the cutting plane, and that point becomes the ith row of Ψ; if legislator i is incorrectly classified, then her

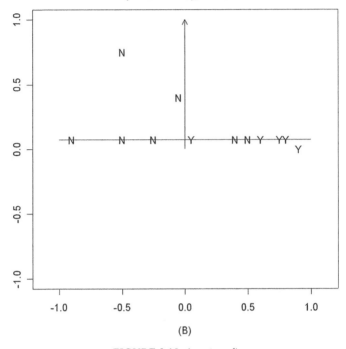

FIGURE 3.10 *(continued)*

point remains at its original position, and that point becomes the ith row of $\boldsymbol{\Psi}$. That is,

$$\boldsymbol{\Psi}_i = \begin{cases} \mathbf{X}_i + (c_j - w_i)\mathbf{N}_j & \text{if correctly classified} \\ \mathbf{X}_i & \text{if incorrectly classified} \end{cases} \tag{3.6}$$

where $\boldsymbol{\Psi}_i$ is an s by 1 vector that is the ith row of $\boldsymbol{\Psi}$. In the correctly classified case, to see that $\boldsymbol{\Psi}_i$ is on the plane, note that, just as in equation (3.5),

$$\mathbf{N}'_j\boldsymbol{\Psi}_i = \mathbf{N}'_j\mathbf{X}_i + (c_j - w_i)\mathbf{N}'_j\mathbf{N}_j = w_i + (c_j - w_i) = c_j$$

because $\mathbf{N}'_j\mathbf{N}_j = 1$.

Figure 3.10A and 3.10B show the projection of the legislator ideal points from Figure 3.8 onto a normal vector that is perpendicular to the first dimension; namely,

$$\mathbf{N}_j = \begin{bmatrix} 0 \\ 1 \end{bmatrix}.$$

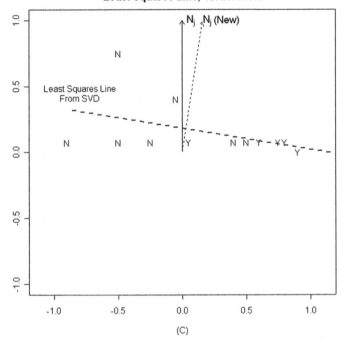

Cutting Plane Procedure
Least Squares Line, 1st Iteration

(C)

FIGURE 3.10 *(continued)*

Three legislators are not on the correct side of the cutting plane – two legislators who actually vote Nay but are predicted to vote Yea, and one legislator who actually votes Yea but is predicted to vote Nay. These three are not projected onto the cutting plane.

It is clear from Figure 3.10A and 3.10B that the cutting plane must rotate clockwise toward the errors for the classification error to be reduced. This rotation is achieved by finding the line through the points in Figure 3.10B that minimizes the sum of the squared distances between the points and the line. The new normal vector is perpendicular to this least squares line, and the new cutting line is found using the Janice algorithm. The new cutting line is parallel to the least squares line.

Figure 3.10C shows the least squares line through the points from Figure 3.10B. Note that the points are projected *orthogonally* onto the least squares line. This should not be confused with the way a simple linear regression line is represented. In OLS one of the dimensions *is the dependent variable* and the projection to the regression line – quite literally the residual – is *parallel* to the dimension representing the dependent variable. In

Legislator Points

Fig. 3.10A		Fig. 3.10B		Means Subtracted	
-.90	-.30	-.90	.075	-1.05	-.0771
-.50	-.40	-.50	.075	-.65	-.0771
.40	-.60	.40	.075	.25	-.0771
-.25	.05	-.25	.075	-.40	-.0771
.50	-.20	.50	.075	.35	-.0771
-.05	.40	-.05	.400	-.20	.2479
-.50	.75	-.50	.750	-.65	.5979
.60	.10	.60	.075	.45	-.0771
.90	.00	.90	.000	.75	-.1521
.05	.70	.05	.075	-.10	-.0771
.75	.35	.75	.075	.60	-.0771
.80	.40	.80	.075	.65	-.0771

Singular Value Decomposition of Ψ*

$$
\begin{bmatrix}
-1.05 & -.0771 \\
-.65 & -.0771 \\
.25 & -.0771 \\
-.40 & -.0771 \\
.35 & -.0771 \\
-.20 & .2479 \\
-.65 & .5979 \\
.45 & -.0771 \\
.75 & -.1521 \\
-.10 & -.0771 \\
.60 & -.0771 \\
.65 & -.0771
\end{bmatrix}
= U\Lambda V' =
\begin{bmatrix}
-.5135 & -.3811 \\
-.3156 & -.2815 \\
.1299 & -.0572 \\
-.1918 & -.2192 \\
.1793 & -.0323 \\
-.1187 & .3345 \\
-.3692 & .7650 \\
.2288 & -.0074 \\
.3833 & -.0489 \\
-.0434 & -.1444 \\
.3031 & .0300 \\
.3278 & .0425
\end{bmatrix}
\begin{bmatrix}
1.9950 & .0 \\
.0 & .6368
\end{bmatrix}
\begin{bmatrix}
.9873 & -.1587 \\
.1587 & .9873
\end{bmatrix}
$$

FIGURE 3.11. *Cutting plane procedure: Numerical values for projections shown in Figure 3.10. The top portion shows the coordinates for the points in Figure 3.10A and 3.10B. The middle and bottom portions show the computations for the least squares line in Figure 3.10C.*

Figure 3.10C there is no dependent variable. Nevertheless, it is a least squares problem.[6]

The normal vector to the least squares line (or plane in more than two dimensions) shown in Figure 3.10C is the new normal vector. The least squares plane is easily estimated. First the means of columns of Ψ are subtracted from the elements of the corresponding columns, and then the *singular value decomposition*

---

[6]This point is discussed in greater detail in a technical appendix to this chapter that can be found on the website for this book under the link for this chapter.

Legislator Values on Least Squares Line (Eckart-Young

Theorem) in Fig. 3.10C

$$
\begin{bmatrix}
-.8615 & .3146 \\
-.4716 & .2520 \\
.4058 & .1110 \\
-.2279 & .2128 \\
.5033 & .0953 \\
-.0838 & .1897 \\
-.5773 & .2690 \\
.6007 & .0796 \\
.9049 & .0308 \\
.0646 & .1658 \\
.7470 & .0561 \\
.7957 & .0483
\end{bmatrix}
=
\begin{bmatrix}
-.5135 & -.3811 \\
-.3156 & -.2815 \\
.1299 & -.0572 \\
-.1918 & -.2192 \\
.1793 & -.0323 \\
-.1187 & .3345 \\
-.3692 & .7650 \\
.2288 & -.0074 \\
.3833 & -.0489 \\
-.0434 & -.1444 \\
.3031 & .0300 \\
.3278 & .0425
\end{bmatrix}
\begin{bmatrix}
1.9950 & .0 \\
.0 & .0
\end{bmatrix}
\begin{bmatrix}
.9873 & -.1587 \\
.1587 & .9873
\end{bmatrix}
+
\begin{bmatrix}
.15 \\
.1521
\end{bmatrix}
$$

FIGURE 3.11 *(continued)*

(SVD) is computed for this mean-centered matrix. In an SVD, a matrix of real numbers is written as the product of two orthogonal matrices and one diagonal matrix. (See the appendix for a discussion of the SVD.) The SVD yields the least squares plane and the new normal vector. Figure 3.11 shows how this calculation is done.

Technically, let μ be the s-length vector of the means of the columns of Ψ, and let J_p be a p by 1 vector of ones. Define Ψ^* as

$$\Psi^* = \Psi - J_p\mu'. \tag{3.7}$$

The top portion of Figure 3.11 shows the original legislator points, the points projected on the initial cutting line in Figure 3.10B, and the points with the coordinate means subtracted. The coordinate means are

$$\mu = \begin{bmatrix} .15 \\ .1521 \end{bmatrix}.$$

The middle portion of Figure 3.11 shows the SVD of Ψ^*, which is

$$\Psi^* = U\Lambda V' \tag{3.8}$$

where U is a p by s orthogonal matrix, V is an s by s orthogonal matrix, and Λ is an s by s diagonal matrix containing the *singular values* in descending order on the diagonal. By definition, $U'U = V'V = I_s$, where I_s is an s by s identity matrix (see appendix).

The bottom portion of Figure 3.11 shows the least squares solution – the dotted line in Figure 3.10C. The line is found by applying the famous Eckart–Young theorem (Eckart and Young, 1936 – see appendix for a formal statement of the theorem) to the points placed at their means – that is, to Ψ^*. The least

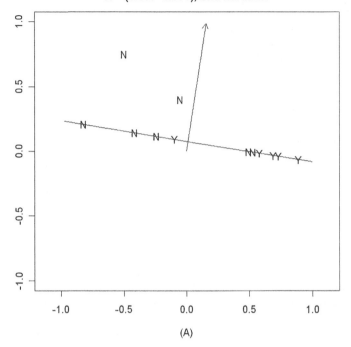

Cutting Plane Procedure
N = (0.157 0.988), 2nd Iteration

(A)

FIGURE 3.12. *Cutting plane procedure: (A) Second iteration. The normal vector is from Figure 3.10C, and the cutting plane is parallel to the least squares line shown in Figures 3.10C and 3.11. Only two classification errors remain. (B) Fifth iteration. Only one classification error remains. (C) Seventh iteration. Perfect classification is achieved.*

squares line is found by inserting a zero in place of the second singular value (the smallest value) in Λ, remultiplying, and then adding the means back to the columns of the reconstructed matrix. That is, let $\Lambda^{\#}$ be the s by s diagonal matrix identical to Λ except for the replacement of the sth singular value by zero (that is, the smallest value); then the estimated line (in two dimensions) or plane (in three or more dimensions) is

$$Y = U\Lambda^{\#}V' + J_p\mu' \qquad (3.9)$$

where the p by s matrix Y will have rank $s - 1$ by construction. In two dimensions, the rows of Y form a line of points as in Figure 3.10C. In three dimensions, the rows of Y are points lying on a two-dimensional plane.

The new normal vector is perpendicular to this least squares line (see Figure 3.10C). By definition, this new normal vector is the sth singular vector (sth column) in V corresponding to the smallest singular value. In this case the

Cutting Plane Procedure
N = (0.492 0.871), 5th Iteration

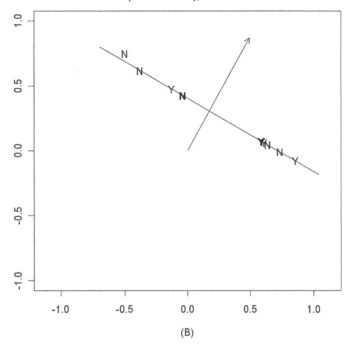

(B)

FIGURE 3.12 *(continued)*

new normal vector is

$$N_j = \begin{bmatrix} .1587 \\ .9873 \end{bmatrix}$$

(recall that **V** is shown as transposed in Figure 3.11), so that for every point
(row) in **Y**, we have $Y_i'N_j = k$, where $k = \mu'N_j$. For example, for the first row
of **Y** in Figure 3.11 this product is

$$Y_1'N_j = -.8615 \times .1587 + .3146 \times .9873 = .1739$$

and

$$\mu'N_j = .15 \times .1587 + .1521 \times .9873 = .1739$$

(there is some rounding error).

Figure 3.12A shows the new normal vector and cutting line. As explained
above, the new cutting line is found with the Janice algorithm, and it is parallel to
the least squares line in Figure 3.10C. Figure 3.12A shows that the cutting plane
must again be rotated clockwise toward the two errors for the classification error
to be reduced. Once again this rotation is achieved by finding the line through the

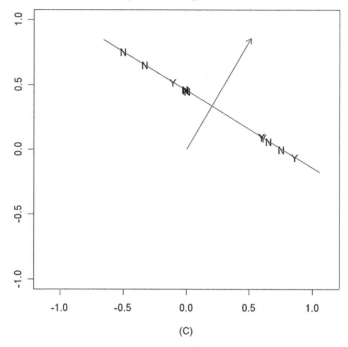

Cutting Plane Procedure
N = (0.514 0.858), 7th Iteration

(C)

FIGURE 3.12 *(continued)*

points in Figure 3.12A that minimizes the sum of the squared distances between the points and the line. The new normal vector is perpendicular to this least squares line, and the new cutting line is found by using the Janice algorithm. This process can be continued until there is no further improvement in classification error. Figure 3.12B shows the process at the 5th iteration, and Figure 3.12C shows the process at the 7th iteration when perfect classification is achieved.

In sum, calculating the optimal $\mathbf{N}_j$ consists of the following steps:

1. Obtain a starting estimate of $\mathbf{N}_j$ (more on the practical aspects of this step in Chapter 5).
2. Calculate the correct classifications associated with $\mathbf{N}_j$.
3. Construct $\mathbf{\Psi}^*$ by using equations (3.6) and (3.7).
4. Perform the SVD $\mathbf{U\Lambda V'}$ of $\mathbf{\Psi}^*$.
5. Use the sth singular vector (sth column) $\mathbf{v}_s$ of $\mathbf{V}$ as the new estimate of $\mathbf{N}_j$.
6. Go to step (2).

In a perfect case like that shown in Figure 3.8, the cutting plane procedure will almost always quickly iterate into the true cutting plane. In an earlier article (Poole, 2000a; b) I report an extensive set of Monte Carlo experiments showing that the cutting plane procedure performs very well.[7] In particular, when error is present, the cutting plane procedure is highly accurate and converges very quickly regardless of the number of dimensions. When there is error, the converged cutting plane may not be the one that maximizes correct classification, because the cutting plane procedure is minimizing the sum of squared distances of the classification errors to the cutting plane. Nevertheless, the converged cutting plane is almost always very close to the optimal cutting plane. This problem is easily dealt with by simply storing the iteration record of the cutting plane procedure and using the normal vector corresponding to the best classification. I have found that this method works very well in practice. The procedure does a good job of correctly classifying the true roll call choices and recovering the true normal vectors in two to ten dimensions – especially at the 15 percent error level, which is the approximate level of the error found in the U.S. Congressional roll call data.[8] Finally, as one would expect, increasing the number of legislators increases the accuracy of the recovery.[9]

Estimating the Legislator Ideal Points Given the Roll Call Cutting Planes

In Chapter 2 I showed that in the geometry of the roll call voting problem legislators are not points; they are polytopes. Given the q cutting lines or planes corresponding to the q normal vectors and given the votes of the ith legislator on the q roll calls, the problem is to find the polytope that maximizes the correct classification. The legislator's ideal point, X_i, is then placed within this polytope. Figure 3.13 shows an example in two dimensions.

---

[7] See note 1.

[8] The first two dimensions estimated by NOMINATE classify about 85 percent of the roll call choices during the period after World War II (Poole and Rosenthal, 1997, Chapter 2). The Monte Carlo tests reported in Poole (1997; 2000a; b) are for one to ten dimensions. In nonsystematic tests in twenty and thirty dimensions I have not found any falloff in the accuracy of the procedure.

[9] The cutting plane procedure is a very efficient method for implementing Manski's maximum score estimator (MSE) for the limited dependent variable (LDV) model (see Manski, 1975, 1985; Manski and Thompson, 1986). In its simplest form the MSE chooses a coefficient vector β to maximize correct classification. Part of the MSE process is very similar to the Janice algorithm. Namely, given a direction, it is easy to find the classification maximum (Manski and Thompson, 1986, pp. 89–90). However, the MSE approach has no method other than exhaustive search to find a better direction through the space (that is, the normal vector).

Intuitively, in terms of the notation developed above, the MSE algorithm consists of two phases. First, given N_j^*, the cutting point, c_j is found. Second, let $N_j^1, N_j^2, N_j^3, \ldots, N_j^{s-1}$, be a set of normal vectors orthogonal to N_j^*. The algorithm then searches along these orthogonal vectors for a better solution than the current one. Unlike the cutting plane procedure that uses equations (3.6) to (3.8) to arrive at a better solution for the normal vector, the MSE algorithm has no systematic criterion for selecting a better search direction (Greene, 1993, pp. 658–659).

**Locating the Legislator NNNYN Polytope
Starting Point**

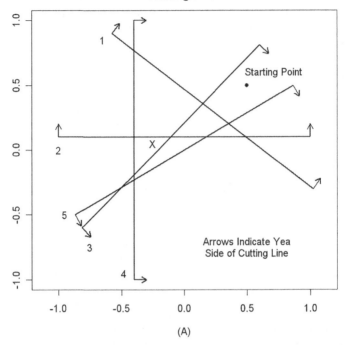

(A)

FIGURE 3.13. *(A) Legislator procedure for five roll calls in two dimensions. There are five cutting lines, each numbered at the end. The arrows indicate the Yea side of the cutting line. The X indicates the NNNYN polytope that corresponds to the legislator's voting pattern. (B) First iteration. The procedure searches along a line through the starting point and an arbitrary point with the same second-dimension coordinate. (C) Second iteration. The procedure searches along a line through the best-fitting point from (B) and an arbitrary point with the same first-dimension coordinate. The line passes through the NNNYN polytope, so that perfect classification is achieved.*

Figure 3.13 shows five cutting lines, each numbered at the end. The arrows at the ends of the cutting lines indicate the Yea side of the cutting line. The five cutting lines produce a complete Coombs mesh, because the number of regions in Figure 3.13 is 16:

$$\sum_{k=0}^{s} \binom{q}{k} = \binom{5}{0} + \binom{5}{1} + \binom{5}{2} = 16.$$

Given a legislator's pattern of votes, in this case NNNYN, the problem is to find the polytope in Figure 3.13 that maximizes the correct classification. In this example the point X is located in the NNNYN polytope corresponding to perfect classification. Suppose the initial estimate of the legislator's coordinates

Locating the Legislator NNNYN Polytope
Search Line 1

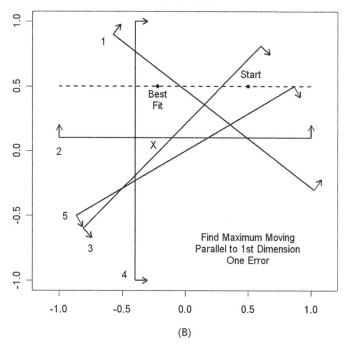

(B)

FIGURE 3.13 *(continued)*

is at the point labeled "starting point" in Figure 3.13A. This initial estimate is in the open polytope YYYYN corresponding to only two correct classifications (roll calls 4 and 5). The problem is to move the point representing the legislator in a direction that increases the number of correct classifications.

A method is shown below for finding the maximum classification point along any arbitrary line passing through the space. This method is used to move the legislator point through the space in a city-block fashion by searching along a line parallel to the first dimension for the polytope that maximizes correct classification. The legislator point is then placed inside the best polytope on the search line. For example, in Figure 3.13B the dotted line through the starting point (from left to right) passes through the polytopes NYNNN, NYNYN, YYNYN, YYYYN (starting polytope), and YYYYY (the open polytope adjacent to the starting polytope). The NYNYN is the best fit, with only one classification error – the legislator is on the wrong side of the cutting line for roll call 2. The best-fit point is placed on the search line midway through the polytope.

The next step is to move the legislator point along a line through this new point but parallel to the second dimension. Again the best polytope is found, and the legislator point is placed inside this polytope on the search line. For example,

Locating the Legislator NNNYN Polytope
Search Line 2

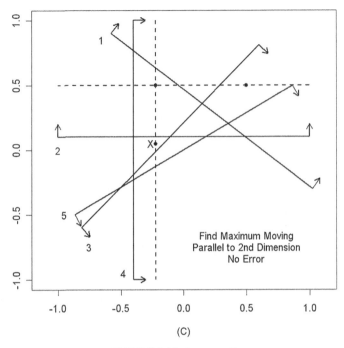

(C)

FIGURE 3.13 *(continued)*

in Figure 3.13C the dotted line through the starting point (from top to bottom) passes through the polytopes YYNYN, NYNYN (current position of legislator point), NNNYN, NNYYN, and NNYYY. The NNNYN polytope is a perfect fit with no classification error, and the legislator is placed at the point *X*.

This process can be repeated as many times as desired. For example, suppose that NNNYN was simply the best fit along the vertical dotted line, but there was still incorrect classification. A line parallel to the first dimension passing through *X* will now be searched. This line will pass through the polytopes NNNNN, NNNYN, NNYYN, NNYYY, and YNYYY.

This city-block-like search procedure always converges to a point inside a polytope for which the coordinates are at a *local maximum* for classification. That is, the point cannot be moved parallel to any dimension and have the correct classifications increase.

The search procedure is constructed as follows. Let $\mathbf{X}_i^{(h)}$ be the initial estimate for legislator i, where h is the iteration number $(1, 2, 3, \ldots)$, and let $\mathbf{X}_i^{(a)}$ be a second point. The problem is to find a new estimate, $\mathbf{X}_i^{(h+1)}$, on the line passing through $\mathbf{X}_i^{(h)}$ and $\mathbf{X}_i^{(a)}$ that is inside a polytope that increases

The Optimal Classification Method

Table 3.1. *Twelve Possible Orderings of Legislator and Cutting Point*

Case	Classification h	a	Limits of α That Correctly Project $x_i^{(h+1)}$
1. $-R < c_j < w_{ij}^{(h)} < w_{ij}^{(a)} < +R$	C[1]	C	$\dfrac{c_j - w_{ij}^{(h)}}{w_{ij}^{(a)} - w_{ij}^{(h)}} < \alpha_j < \dfrac{R - w_{ij}^{(h)}}{w_{ij}^{(a)} - w_{ij}^{(h)}}$
2. $-R < c_j < w_{ij}^{(h)} < w_{ij}^{(a)} < +R$	I	I	$\dfrac{-R - w_{ij}^{(h)}}{w_{ij}^{(a)} - w_{ij}^{(h)}} < \alpha_j < \dfrac{c_j - w_{ij}^{(h)}}{w_{ij}^{(a)} - w_{ij}^{(h)}}$
3. $-R < c_j < w_{ij}^{(a)} < w_{ij}^{(h)} < +R$	C	C	$\dfrac{R - w_{ij}^{(h)}}{w_{ij}^{(a)} - w_{ij}^{(h)}} < \alpha_j < \dfrac{c_j - w_{ij}^{(h)}}{w_{ij}^{(a)} - w_{ij}^{(h)}}$
4. $-R < c_j < w_{ij}^{(a)} < w_{ij}^{(h)} < +R$	I	I	$\dfrac{c_j - w_{ij}^{(h)}}{w_{ij}^{(a)} - w_{ij}^{(h)}} < \alpha_j < \dfrac{-R - w_{ij}^{(h)}}{w_{ij}^{(a)} - w_{ij}^{(h)}}$
5. $-R < w_{ij}^{(h)} < w_{ij}^{(a)} < c_j < +R$	C	C	$\dfrac{-R - w_{ij}^{(h)}}{w_{ij}^{(a)} - w_{ij}^{(h)}} < \alpha_j < \dfrac{c_j - w_{ij}^{(h)}}{w_{ij}^{(a)} - w_{ij}^{(h)}}$
6. $-R < w_{ij}^{(h)} < w_{ij}^{(a)} < c_j < +R$	I	I	$\dfrac{c_j - w_{ij}^{(h)}}{w_{ij}^{(a)} - w_{ij}^{(h)}} < \alpha_j < \dfrac{R - w_{ij}^{(h)}}{w_{ij}^{(a)} - w_{ij}^{(h)}}$
7. $-R < w_{ij}^{(a)} < w_{ij}^{(h)} < c_j < +R$	C	C	$\dfrac{c_j - w_{ij}^{(h)}}{w_{ij}^{(a)} - w_{ij}^{(h)}} < \alpha_j < \dfrac{-R - w_{ij}^{(h)}}{w_{ij}^{(a)} - w_{ij}^{(h)}}$
8. $-R < w_{ij}^{(a)} < w_{ij}^{(h)} < c_j < +R$	I	I	$\dfrac{R - w_{ij}^{(h)}}{w_{ij}^{(a)} - w_{ij}^{(h)}} < \alpha_j < \dfrac{c_j - w_{ij}^{(h)}}{w_{ij}^{(a)} - w_{ij}^{(h)}}$
9. $-R < w_{ij}^{(h)} < c_j < w_{ij}^{(a)} < +R$	C	I	$\dfrac{-R - w_{ij}^{(h)}}{w_{ij}^{(a)} - w_{ij}^{(h)}} < \alpha_j < \dfrac{c_j - w_{ij}^{(h)}}{w_{ij}^{(a)} - w_{ij}^{(h)}}$
10. $-R < w_{ij}^{(h)} < c_j < w_{ij}^{(a)} < +R$	I	C	$\dfrac{c_j - w_{ij}^{(h)}}{w_{ij}^{(a)} - w_{ij}^{(h)}} < \alpha_j < \dfrac{R - w_{ij}^{(h)}}{w_{ij}^{(a)} - w_{ij}^{(h)}}$
11. $-R < w_{ij}^{(a)} < c_j < w_{ij}^{(h)} < +R$	C	I	$\dfrac{R - w_{ij}^{(h)}}{w_{ij}^{(a)} - w_{ij}^{(h)}} < \alpha_j < \dfrac{c_j - w_{ij}^{(h)}}{w_{ij}^{(a)} - w_{ij}^{(h)}}$
12. $-R < w_{ij}^{(a)} < c_j < w_{ij}^{(h)} < +R$	I	C	$\dfrac{c_j - w_{ij}^{(h)}}{w_{ij}^{(a)} - w_{ij}^{(h)}} < \alpha_j < \dfrac{-R - w_{ij}^{(h)}}{w_{ij}^{(a)} - w_{ij}^{(h)}}$

[1] C means correctly classified; I means incorrectly classified.

correct classification as illustrated in Figure 3.13. We find it by analyzing the projections of $\mathbf{X}_i^{(h)}$ and $\mathbf{X}_i^{(a)}$ onto the q normal vectors.

The projection of $\mathbf{X}_i^{(h)}$ onto the jth normal vector is

$$\mathbf{X}_i^{(h)'}\mathbf{N}_j = w_{ij}^{(h)}. \tag{3.10}$$

Similarly, the projection of the second point onto the jth normal vector is $w_{ij}^{(a)}$. These projections correspond to a correct classification on roll call j depending on which side of the cutting point c_j they fall on. There are six possible orderings of $w_{ij}^{(h)}$, $w_{ij}^{(a)}$, and c_j. For each ordering there are two possible classification outcomes, for a total of 12 cases. Table 3.1 shows each case. The R in Table 3.1

is the maximum limit of the dimensions – it is usually set equal to one, so that in two dimensions, the space will be the unit circle.

In case 1, both $\mathbf{X}_i^{(h)}$ and $\mathbf{X}_i^{(a)}$ project to the right of c_j and are on the correct side of the cutting plane for the jth roll call, and they are therefore correctly classified, as indicated by the two classification columns in the middle of the table. Case 2 is the same geometrically, only now $\mathbf{X}_i^{(h)}$ and $\mathbf{X}_i^{(a)}$ are on the wrong side of the cutting plane and are therefore projected as classification errors. Cases 1 to 8 represent no change in classification from moving the legislator point along the line from $\mathbf{X}_i^{(h)}$ to $\mathbf{X}_i^{(a)}$. For $\mathbf{X}_i^{(a)}$ to be an improvement over $\mathbf{X}_i^{(h)}$, the number of cases 10 and 12 must be greater than the number of cases 9 and 11.

Consider the effect of moving $\mathbf{X}_i^{(h)}$ away from $\mathbf{X}_i^{(a)}$. This move has no effect on cases 3–6 or 9–12. Only those cases where $\mathbf{X}_i^{(h)}$ is between $\mathbf{X}_i^{(a)}$ and c_j – cases 1, 2, 7, and 8 – are affected. Depending on how far $\mathbf{X}_i^{(h)}$ is moved away from $\mathbf{X}_i^{(a)}$, case 1 could change to case 10, increasing the error by one; case 2 could change to case 9, decreasing the error by one; case 7 could change to case 12, increasing the error by one; and case 8 could change to case 11, decreasing the error by one. A similar analysis of the effect of moving $\mathbf{X}_i^{(h)}$ towards $\mathbf{X}_i^{(a)}$ can also be done.

More generally, consider the line equation

$$\mathbf{X}_i^{(h+1)} = \mathbf{X}_i^{(h)} + \alpha\left(\mathbf{X}_i^{(a)} - \mathbf{X}_i^{(h)}\right) \qquad (3.11)$$

which, when projected onto the jth normal vector, becomes

$$w_{ij}^{(h+1)} = w_{ij}^{(h)} + \alpha\left(w_{ij}^{(a)} - w_{ij}^{(h)}\right). \qquad (3.12)$$

If $\alpha = 0$, then $\mathbf{X}_i^{(h)} = \mathbf{X}_i^{(h+1)}$ and the legislator point is not moved. If $\alpha > 0$, then $\mathbf{X}_i^{(h)}$ is moved toward $\mathbf{X}_i^{(a)}$, and if $\alpha < 0$, then $\mathbf{X}_i^{(h)}$ is moved away from $\mathbf{X}_i^{(a)}$. For a single roll call, it is easy to solve for α; the resulting values are shown in Table 3.1 for all 12 cases. For example, for case 2, α must be chosen so that the projection of $\mathbf{X}_i^{(h+1)}$, $w_{ij}^{(h+1)}$, is in the region $(-R, c_j)$. Solving for α, we have

$$-R = w_{ij}^{(h)} + \alpha\left(w_{ij}^{(a)} - w_{ij}^{(h)}\right), \qquad \text{so that} \qquad \frac{-R - w_{ij}^{(h)}}{w_{ij}^{(a)} - w_{ij}^{(h)}} < \alpha_j$$

$$c_j = w_{ij}^{(h)} + \alpha\left(w_{ij}^{(a)} - w_{ij}^{(h)}\right), \qquad \text{so that} \qquad \alpha_j < \frac{c_j - w_{ij}^{(h)}}{w_{ij}^{(a)} - w_{ij}^{(h)}}.$$

Given $\mathbf{X}_i^{(h)}$ and $\mathbf{X}_i^{(a)}$, Table 3.1 can be used to find the limits of α for each roll call. Let the upper and lower limits for the jth roll call be U_{ij} and L_{ij}, respectively. The correct classification associated with $\mathbf{X}_i^{(h)}$ can be obtained by setting $\alpha = 0$ and counting the number of roll calls for which $0 \in (L_{ij}, U_{ij})$.

Similarly, the correct classification associated with $\mathbf{X}_i^{(a)}$ is obtained by setting $\alpha = 1$ and counting the number of roll calls for which $1 \in (L_{ij}, U_{ij})$. In general, define

$$\delta_{ij} = \begin{cases} 0 & \text{if} \quad \alpha \notin (L_{ij}, U_{ij}) \\ 1 & \text{if} \quad \alpha \in (L_{ij}, U_{ij}). \end{cases}$$

Then the correct classification is simply

$$\delta(\alpha) = \sum_{j=1}^{q} \delta_{ij}. \tag{3.13}$$

The α that maximizes $\delta(\alpha)$, the number of correct classifications, can be calculated in a simple manner. First, compute the L_{ij} and U_{ij} for each roll call. Second, rank order the L_{ij} and U_{ij}, and use the Janice algorithm to calculate the optimal α. Here the L_{ij} play the role of Yea and the U_{ij} play the role of Nay. For example, if there exists an α that results in perfect classification, the ordering of L's and U's will look like (dropping the i subscript to reduce clutter, and numbering left to right for convenience)

$$L_1 < L_2 < L_3 < \cdots < L_q < U_1 < U_2 < U_3 < \cdots < U_q$$

– that is, all the L_j will be less than all the U_j, so that with $\alpha \in (L_q, U_1)$ there is perfect classification, $\delta(\alpha) = q$.

For example, using the configuration shown in Figure 3.13, the starting point $(h = 1)$ $\mathbf{X}_i^{(1)}$ is placed at $(.5, .5)$, that is,

$$\begin{bmatrix} x_{11}^{(1)} \\ x_{12}^{(1)} \end{bmatrix} = \begin{bmatrix} .5 \\ .5 \end{bmatrix}$$

and the second point $\mathbf{X}_i^{(a)}$ is placed on the dotted line; specifically,

$$\begin{bmatrix} x_{11}^{(a)} \\ x_{12}^{(a)} \end{bmatrix} = \begin{bmatrix} .01 \\ .5 \end{bmatrix}.$$

The resulting rank order of the upper and lower limits is

$$L_4 < L_5 < L_3 < L_1 < U_4 < U_3 < U_5 < U_1.$$

Numerically,

$$-1.020 < -0.747 < 0.433 < 1.105 < 1.837 < 2.887 < 3.335 < 5.782.$$

For the first roll call,

$$w_{11}^{(h)} = [.5 \ .5] \begin{bmatrix} .6 \\ .8 \end{bmatrix} = .7, \quad w_{11}^{(a)} = [.01 \ .5] \begin{bmatrix} .6 \\ .8 \end{bmatrix} = .406, \quad \text{and} \quad c_j = .375$$

so that $c_j < w_{11}^{(a)} < w_{11}^{(h)}$. The hypothetical legislator votes Nay on the first roll call. But both $\mathbf{X}_i^{(h)}$ and $\mathbf{X}_i^{(a)}$ are on the Yea side of the cutting line (see

Figure 3.13B), so that $w_{11}^{(h)}$ and $w_{11}^{(a)}$ are both incorrect classifications in Table 3.1. This is an example of case 4. Using R = 1, the upper and lower limits are

$$\frac{-1 - 0.7}{0.406 - 0.7} = 5.782 \quad \text{and} \quad \frac{0.375 - 0.7}{0.406 - 0.7} = 1.105.$$

Note that L_2 and U_2 do not appear in the ordering. This happens because the normal vector for the second roll call is $[\begin{smallmatrix} .0 \\ 1.0 \end{smallmatrix}]$, so that $w_{i2}^{(h)} = w_{i2}^{(a)}$. In other words, if the line through $\mathbf{X}_i^{(h)}$ and $\mathbf{X}_i^{(a)}$ is parallel to a cutting line, then $w_{ij}^{(a)} - w_{ij}^{(h)}$, which is used in Table 3.1 to find α_j, is equal to zero. This is not a problem, because when the line through $\mathbf{X}_i^{(h)}$ and $\mathbf{X}_i^{(a)}$ is parallel to a cutting line, the classification on the corresponding roll call is the same no matter where on the line $\mathbf{X}_i^{(h+1)}$ is located.

The rank ordering above is a perfect pattern, but there is still one classification error, because both $\mathbf{X}_i^{(h)}$ and $\mathbf{X}_i^{(a)}$ are on the Yea side of the cutting line for the second roll call and it was *omitted* from the rank ordering. Consequently, the point resulting from using $\alpha \in (L_1 = 1.105, U_4 = 1.837)$, namely $\mathbf{X}_i^{(2)}$, the best-fit point in Figure 3.13B, has one classification error with four correct classifications. (In practice, α is set equal to the midpoint; in this case, $(L_1 + U_4)/2 = 1.4711$ [there is rounding error].) When we use equation (3.11), the best-fit point is

$$\begin{bmatrix} .5 \\ .5 \end{bmatrix} + 1.4711 \left(\begin{bmatrix} .01 \\ .5 \end{bmatrix} - \begin{bmatrix} .5 \\ .5 \end{bmatrix} \right) = \begin{bmatrix} -.221 \\ .5 \end{bmatrix}.$$

For the second iteration, $h = 2$, the starting estimate is

$$\begin{bmatrix} \mathbf{x}_{11}^{(2)} \\ \mathbf{x}_{12}^{(2)} \end{bmatrix} = \begin{bmatrix} -.221 \\ .5 \end{bmatrix}$$

and the second point is

$$\begin{bmatrix} \mathbf{x}_{11}^{(a)} \\ \mathbf{x}_{12}^{(a)} \end{bmatrix} = \begin{bmatrix} -.221 \\ .01 \end{bmatrix}.$$

This produces the rank ordering

$$L_3 < L_5 < L_1 < L_2 < U_3 < U_5 < U_2 < U_1.$$

L_4 and U_4 are missing because the classification line is parallel to the cutting line for roll call 4 (see Figure 3.13C). The rank ordering is again a perfect pattern with $\alpha \in (L_2, U_3)$, and there are no classification errors, because $\mathbf{X}_i^{(2)}$ and $\mathbf{X}_i^{(a)}$ are both on the correct side of the cutting line for roll call 4.

Numerically the value for α is .9272. Using equation (3.11), the solution is

$$\begin{bmatrix} -.221 \\ .5 \end{bmatrix} + .9272 \left(\begin{bmatrix} -.221 \\ .01 \end{bmatrix} - \begin{bmatrix} -.221 \\ .5 \end{bmatrix} \right) = \begin{bmatrix} -.221 \\ .046 \end{bmatrix}$$

which is point X in Figure 3.13C.

To recap, the search for the $\mathbf{X}_i$ that maximizes correct classification is conducted in a city-block-like manner. In the first iteration, the search is along a line through the starting point $\mathbf{X}_i^{(1)}$ and the second point $\mathbf{X}_i^{(a)}$, with all but the first-dimension coordinates in $\mathbf{X}_i^{(1)}$ and $\mathbf{X}_i^{(a)}$ set equal to each other, so that they lie on a line parallel to the first dimension. In the second iteration, the first-dimension coordinates are all set equal to the value corresponding to the optimal first-dimension value, and the 3rd-, 4th-, ..., sth-dimension coordinates in $\mathbf{X}_i^{(2)}$ and $\mathbf{X}_i^{(a)}$ are set equal to one another so that the points lie on a line parallel to the second dimension. In the third iteration, the first- and second-dimension coordinates are set equal to the optimal values from the first and second iterations, respectively, and the 4th-, 5th-, ..., sth-dimension coordinates in $\mathbf{X}_i^{(3)}$ and $\mathbf{X}_i^{(a)}$ are set equal to one another so that the points lie on a line parallel to the third dimension. This process continues in the same fashion through the sth dimension. Since the search for the optimal $\mathbf{X}_i$ is being done city-block-wise, dimensions 1 to s can now be searched again.

In sum, calculating the optimal $\mathbf{X}_i$ consists of the following steps: Obtain a realistic starting estimate, $\mathbf{X}_i^{(1)}$ (see Chapter 5).

1. Set $\mathbf{X}_i^{(a)'} = [0.01, X_{i2}^{(1)}, X_{i3}^{(1)}, X_{i4}^{(1)}, X_{i5}^{(1)}, \dots, X_{is}^{(1)}]$; find optimal α and $\mathbf{X}_i^{(2)} = \mathbf{X}_i^{(1)} + \alpha(\mathbf{X}_i^{(a)} - \mathbf{X}_i^{(1)})$.

2. Set $\mathbf{X}_i^{(a)'} = [X_{i1}^{(2)}, 0.01, X_{i3}^{(1)}, X_{i4}^{(1)}, X_{i5}^{(1)}, \dots, X_{is}^{(1)}]$; find optimal α and $\mathbf{X}_i^{(3)} = \mathbf{X}_i^{(2)} + \alpha(\mathbf{X}_i^{(a)} - \mathbf{X}_i^{(2)})$.

3. Set $\mathbf{X}_i^{(a)'} = [X_{i1}^{(2)}, X_{i2}^{(3)}, 0.01, X_{i4}^{(1)}, X_{i5}^{(1)}, \dots, X_{is}^{(1)}]$; find optimal α and $\mathbf{X}_i^{(4)} = \mathbf{X}_i^{(3)} + \alpha(\mathbf{X}_i^{(a)} - \mathbf{X}_i^{(3)})$.

4. Set $\mathbf{X}_i^{(a)'} = [X_{i1}^{(2)}, X_{i2}^{(3)}, X_{i3}^{(4)}, 0.01, X_{i5}^{(1)}, \dots, X_{is}^{(1)}]$; find optimal α and $\mathbf{X}_i^{(5)} = \mathbf{X}_i^{(4)} + \alpha(\mathbf{X}_i^{(a)} - \mathbf{X}_i^{(4)})$.

$\vdots$

$s+1$. Set $\mathbf{X}_i^{(a)'} = [X_{i1}^{(2)}, X_{i2}^{(3)}, X_{i3}^{(4)}, X_{i4}^{(5)}, \dots, X_{is-1}^{(s)}, 0.01]$; find optimal α and $\mathbf{X}_i^{(s+1)} = \mathbf{X}_i^{(s)} + \alpha(\mathbf{X}_i^{(a)} - \mathbf{X}_i^{(s)})$

$s+2$. Go to step 2.

Note that classification error can never increase from one step to the next. This is true because setting $\alpha = 0$ preserves the current value of the classification. This process converges quickly (usually less than 10 iterations through steps 2 to $s + 1$ above) to a vector of coordinates that is a local maximum in terms of classification. That is, it converges to a point such that $\alpha = 0$ for all s dimensions.

In practice, the starting estimate $\mathbf{X}_i^{(h)}$ and the second point $\mathbf{X}_i^{(a)}$ can be placed anywhere within the s-dimensional space. The search does not have to be parallel to any dimension – it can be done along any line through the space. Although the search process does not have to be done by moving city-block-wise through the space, I found through a considerable amount of experimentation that it is the most efficient way to proceed.

To guard against bad local maxima ($\alpha = 0$ in s orthogonal directions), multiple starting points for the $\mathbf{X}_i^{(1)}$'s are used. If different solutions are found (which are rare and almost always close together), the lines joining the unique local maxima are searched for the best solution. After considerable experimentation, I found that three starting points worked very well in practice. One starting point is from the eigenvalue–eigenvector decomposition of the double-centered agreement score matrix (see Chapter 2), and the other two are randomly generated.

Elsewhere (Poole 1997; 2000a; b) I show extensive Monte Carlo studies of the legislator procedure using perfect data as well as data with error.[10] With perfect data the legislator procedure almost always finds the legislator polytope that perfectly classifies the legislator's choices. When error is present, the recovery of the legislator points is very good. Not surprisingly, as the number of cutting planes increases with the error level held fixed, the precision of the recovery of the legislators increases dramatically.

Overall OC Algorithm

The OC algorithm consists of three phases:

1. Generate starting values for the legislators, the $\mathbf{X}_i$'s, from an eigenvalue–eigenvector decomposition of the legislator-by-legislator agreement score matrix.
2. Given the $\mathbf{X}_i$'s, find the optimal estimates of the normal vectors, the $\mathbf{N}_j$'s.
3. Given the $\mathbf{N}_j$'s, find the optimal estimates of the $\mathbf{X}_i$'s.
4. Go to step 2.

With error in one dimension, steps 2 to 4 are the Edith algorithm. In two or more dimensions, step 2 is the cutting plane procedure and step 3 is the legislator procedure. I have reported (Poole 1997; 2000a; b) an extensive set of Monte Carlo experiments applying the OC algorithm to perfect data and data

---

[10]See note 1.

with error in one to ten dimensions.[11] With perfect data I found that the algorithm works well regardless of the number of dimensions. OC also works well when the dimensions are not equally salient. For example, in two dimensions if 85 percent of the cutting lines are nearly parallel to the second dimension, the legislator configuration is recovered with reasonable precision. In real-world applications where noise is present, however, such data will look as if it fitted a one-dimensional model. Consequently, there is no substitute for the researcher's substantive understanding of the data.

Given the history of other multidimensional scaling techniques, most empirical applications of OC will be to data matrices with missing entries, and the estimated configurations will be in three or fewer dimensions. Missing data presents no problem for the algorithm. In the cutting plane procedure it simply means that the total number of legislators may vary from vote to vote. In the legislator procedure it simply means that the number of cutting lines may vary from legislator to legislator. Handling missing data requires a little bookkeeping, but it has no effect on the algorithm. OC works very well with and without error at high levels of missing data.

An example of a two-dimensional OC scaling is shown in Figure 3.14. The spatial map is from an OC scaling of the 1841–1847 British House of Commons. There were 590 members from England and 186 roll calls between 1841 and 1847.[12] To be included in the scaling a legislator had to vote at least 20 times. The number of members scaled was 503, and all 186 roll calls were included. The total number of entries in the matrix was 93,558 (503 × 186), and the number of Yea and Nay choices was 40,641, so that 56.6 percent of the matrix was missing data. The percentage correctly predicted by the estimated configuration of legislator ideal points and cutting lines was 95.2 percent (38,710 of 40,641).[13]

Figure 3.14 is a spatial map of the roll call for the first reading of the landmark repeal of the Corn Laws by the British House of Commons in 1846. The repeal of the Corn Laws was a product of a number of factors. The industrialization of Britain and the steady increase in exports created a strong economic base of support for repeal purely on economic grounds. Adding to the

---

[11] See note 1.

[12] The roll call matrix is courtesy of Cheryl Schonhardt-Bailey (2003; 2004). She excluded Irish, Welsh, and Scottish MPs, since she was unable to get equivalent data on constituency interests for her project. "There were more than 186 roll call votes during the parliament, but an historian, W. O. Aydelotte, who originally coded the votes, included only the relevant divisions. Aydelotte biased his sample towards those divisions that were relatively well-attended (i.e., in which 200 or more MPs participated) and were, in Aydelotte's judgment, important and relevant to key problems of the day. Most MPs failed to attend most of the divisions, as many of these were private bills of no concern to anyone but a particular member or two" (personal communication, Cheryl Schonhardt-Bailey, 20 August 2004).

[13] The APRE (see Chapter 5) was 0.841. A one-dimensional rank ordering correctly classifies 92.2 percent of the 40,641 choices with an APRE of 0.738.

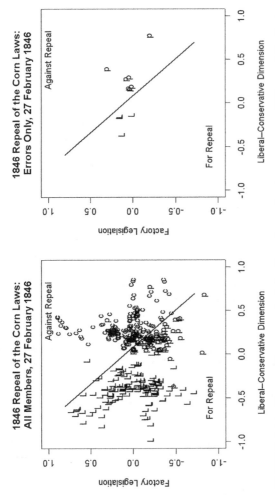

FIGURE 3.14. *First reading, repeal of the Corn Laws. L tokens represent Whigs and Radicals, p tokens represent Peelite conservatives, and c tokens represent conservatives. The left panel shows the 430 English members of the House of Commons who voted on the motion and were included in the OC scaling, and the right panel shows the 12 members who were errors. The errors are all near the cutting line for the roll call. The correct classification was 95.2 percent.*

support for repeal was the general sense of many in the aristocracy that its power would be imperiled if the Corn Laws were not repealed. Ending the agricultural tariffs would lower the price of food for the working classes and stave off more radical demands for reform. Prime Minister Sir Robert Peel was able to convince a substantial number of conservatives that repeal was necessary. "Peel characterized repeal as a means to preserve the traditional institutions of the British government – and, in particular, the aristocracy" (Schonhardt-Bailey, 2004, Chapter 11, p. 4).

The repeal was passed by a coalition of Whigs, Radicals (both shown with L tokens), and a minority of the Conservatives (the P tokens are the Peelite conservatives; the C tokens are the non-Peelite conservatives). The left panel shows the 430 members who voted on the motion and were included in the OC scaling, and the right panel shows the 12 members who were predicted incorrectly. The labeling of the dimensions is from a comprehensive analysis by Cheryl Schonhardt-Bailey (2003; 2004).

Conclusion

OC is a general nonparametric unfolding technique for maximizing the correct classification of binary preferential choice data. The motivation for and the primary focus of OC is parliamentary roll call voting data, but the procedures that implement the unfolding can also be applied to a variety of other problems. In particular, the cutting plane procedure avoids the pitfalls of probit and logit when they are applied to roll calls on which there is perfect classification.

Although neither the cutting plane nor the legislative procedure can be formally shown to converge to the global classification maximum, Monte Carlo tests reported by Poole (1997; 2000a; b) show that both in fact work very well in practice. In the presence of error, the cutting plane procedure almost certainly passes through or very near to the classification maximum, and the maximum can be recovered from the iteration record. The legislative procedure is guaranteed to converge to a very strong local maximum – that is, a local maximum for which the point cannot be moved in any orthogonal direction and have the correct classifications increase. When the two procedures are used together in an alternating framework to analyze binary choice matrices in one to ten dimensions, their performance is excellent. The Monte Carlo tests (Poole, 1997; 2000a; b) are testimony to this fact.

In Chapter 4 I discuss probabilistic models of parliamentary voting. Error is introduced via the random utility model discussed earlier in this chapter, and the main scaling methods are explained in detail – NOMINATE, quadratic–normal (QN) scaling, and the Bayesian Markov chain Monte Carlo (MCMC) approach. These methods are in turn related to the basic geometry detailed in Chapter 2.

Appendix: Two Matrix Decomposition Theorems

The following two well-known matrix decomposition theorems are an important part of the scaling programs discussed in this book. Theorem I states that every *rectangular* matrix of real numbers can be written as the product of two orthogonal matrices and one diagonal matrix. This is known as *singular value decomposition*. Theorem I was stated by Eckart and Young (1936) in their famous paper, but they did not provide a proof. The first proof was given by Johnson (1963). Horst (1963) refers to the decomposition shown in Theorem I as the *basic structure* of a matrix and discusses the mechanics of matrix decomposition in detail in his Chapters 17 and 18. A more recent treatment can be found in Chapters 1 and 2 of Lawson and Hanson (1974).

Theorem II – the famous Eckart–Young theorem – solves the general least squares problem of approximating one matrix by another of lower rank. Geometrically, suppose the matrix is a set of p points in an n-dimensional space and we wish to find the best two-dimensional plane through the p points such that the distances from the points to the surface of the plane are minimized. Technically, let $\mathbf{A}$ be a p by n matrix of rank 15, and let $\mathbf{B}$ be a p by n matrix of rank 2. Given $\mathbf{A}$, the problem is to find the matrix $\mathbf{B}$ such that $\sum_{i=1}^{p} \sum_{j=1}^{n} (a_{ij} - b_{ij})^2$ is minimized.

Theorem II was never explicitly stated by Eckart and Young. Rather, they use two theorems from linear algebra (Theorem I was the first) and a very clever argument to show the truth of their result. Later, Keller (1962) independently rediscovered the Eckart–Young result (Theorem II).

Theorem I (Singular Value Decomposition)

Let $\mathbf{A}$ be a p by n matrix of real elements (not all zeros) with $p \geq n$. Then there is a p by p orthogonal matrix $\mathbf{U}$, an n by n orthogonal matrix $\mathbf{V}$, and a p by n matrix $\mathbf{\Lambda}$ such that

$$\mathbf{A} = \mathbf{U}\mathbf{\Lambda}\mathbf{V}' \quad \text{and} \quad \mathbf{U}'\mathbf{A}\mathbf{V} = \mathbf{\Lambda}$$

where

$$\mathbf{\Lambda} = \left[\frac{\mathbf{\Lambda}_n}{\mathbf{0}} \right]$$

and $\mathbf{U}'\mathbf{U} = \mathbf{U}\mathbf{U}' = \mathbf{I}_p, \mathbf{V}'\mathbf{V} = \mathbf{V}\mathbf{V}' = \mathbf{I}_n$, where $\mathbf{I}_p$ and $\mathbf{I}_n$ are p by p and n by n identity matrices, respectively. $\mathbf{\Lambda}_n$ is an n by n diagonal matrix, and $\mathbf{0}$ is a $p - n$ by n matrix of zeros. The diagonal entries of $\mathbf{\Lambda}_n$ are nonnegative with exactly s entries strictly positive ($s \leq n$).

Theorem II (Eckart and Young)

Given a p by n matrix $\mathbf{A}$ of rank $r \leq n \leq p$, and its SVD $\mathbf{U}\mathbf{\Lambda}\mathbf{V}'$, with the singular values arranged in decreasing sequence

$$\lambda_1 \geq \lambda_2 \geq \lambda_3 \geq \cdots \geq \lambda_n \geq 0,$$

then there exists a p by n matrix $\mathbf{B}$ of rank $s \leq r$ that minimizes the sum of the squared error between the elements of $\mathbf{A}$ and the corresponding elements of $\mathbf{B}$ when

$$\mathbf{B} = \mathbf{U}\mathbf{\Lambda}_s\mathbf{V}'$$

where the diagonal elements of $\mathbf{\Lambda}_s$ are

$$\lambda_1 \geq \lambda_2 \geq \lambda_3 \geq \cdots \geq \lambda_s > \lambda_{s+1} = \lambda_{s+2} = \cdots = \lambda_n = 0.$$

Theorem I states that every real matrix can be written as the product of two orthogonal matrices and one diagonal matrix. Theorem II states that the least squares approximation in s dimensions of a matrix $\mathbf{A}$ can be found by replacing the smallest $n - s$ roots of $\mathbf{\Lambda}$ with zeros and remultiplying $\mathbf{U}\mathbf{\Lambda}\mathbf{V}'$.

Because the lower $p - n$ rows of $\mathbf{\Lambda}$ are all zeros, it is convenient to discard them and work only with the n by n diagonal matrix $\mathbf{\Lambda}_n$. In addition, the $p - n$ eigenvectors in $\mathbf{U}$ corresponding to the $p - n$ lower rows of $\mathbf{\Lambda}$ may also be discarded. With these deletions of redundant rows and columns, $\mathbf{U}$ is a p by n matrix, $\mathbf{\Lambda}$ is an n by n diagonal matrix, and $\mathbf{V}$ is an n by n matrix. Hence $\mathbf{U}'\mathbf{U} = \mathbf{V}'\mathbf{V} = \mathbf{V}\mathbf{V}' = \mathbf{I}_n$. A decomposition according to Theorem I will be assumed to be in this form.

CHAPTER 4

Probabilistic Spatial Models of Parliamentary Voting

Overview

Several probabilistic models of legislative voting have been developed during the past 30 years. In my discussion of the optimal classification (OC) method in Chapter 3, I assumed only that legislators used a symmetric single-peaked utility function. I did not make any assumptions about the functional form of the error distribution or the functional form of the deterministic utility function. OC is simply a nonparametric scaling method that maximizes correct classifications. The downside to OC is that it is difficult to do any meaningful statistical inference beyond straightforward Monte Carlo testing (Poole, 1997; 2000a;b). Determining the statistical properties of OC is an unsolved problem.

Below I make explicit assumptions about the functional form of both the deterministic utility function and the error distribution. These assumptions have consequences – there is no free lunch with probabilistic voting models. Estimation of these models is complicated, and the statistical issues are especially thorny and not fully resolved. The good news is that, despite these drawbacks, the major probabilistic methods produce essentially the same spatial maps for large legislatures (50 or more legislators). This is important from a scientific standpoint, because it means that the basic geometric model of choice that underlies all the estimation methods produces meaningful results.

The major probabilistic models of parliamentary voting are based on the *random utility model* developed by McFadden (1976). In the random utility model, a legislator's overall utility for voting Yea is the sum of a deterministic utility and a random error. The same is true for the utility of voting Nay. To recap the discussion in Chapter 3, suppose there are p legislators, q roll calls, and s dimensions indexed by $i = 1, \ldots, p$, $j = 1, \ldots, q$, and $k = 1, \ldots, s$, respectively. Legislator i's utility for the Yea outcome on roll call j is

$$U_{ijy} = u_{ijy} + \varepsilon_{ijy} \qquad (4.1)$$

where u_{ijy} is the *deterministic* portion of the utility function and ε_{ijy} is the *stochastic*, or *random*, portion. Recall from Chapter 3 that if there is no error, then the legislator votes Yea if $U_{ijy} > U_{ijn}$. Equivalently, if the difference $U_{ijy} - U_{ijn}$ is positive, the legislator votes Yea. With random error the utility difference is

$$U_{ijy} - U_{ijn} = u_{ijy} - u_{ijn} + \varepsilon_{ijy} - \varepsilon_{ijn}$$

so that the legislator votes Yea if

$$u_{ijy} - u_{ijn} > \varepsilon_{ijn} - \varepsilon_{ijy}.$$

That is, the legislator votes Yea if the difference in the deterministic utilities is greater than the difference between the two random errors. Because the errors are unobserved, we must make an assumption about the error distribution from which they are drawn. Armed with that assumption, we can calculate the *probability* that the legislator will vote Yea. That is,

$$P(\text{Legislator } i \text{ Votes Yea}) = P(U_{ijy} - U_{ijn} > 0)$$
$$= P(\varepsilon_{ijn} - \varepsilon_{ijy} < u_{ijy} - u_{ijn})$$
$$P(\text{Legislator } i \text{ Votes Nay}) = P(U_{ijy} - U_{ijn} < 0)$$
$$= P(\varepsilon_{ijn} - \varepsilon_{ijy} > u_{ijy} - u_{ijn})$$

so that $P(\text{Yea}) + P(\text{Nay}) = 1$.[1]

In the next two sections I discuss the functional form of the deterministic portion of the utility function followed by the stochastic portion. These two sections are followed by a discussion of the estimation of the NOMINATE (nominal three-step estimation) (Poole and Rosenthal, 1985; 1991; 1997) and quadratic–normal (Poole, 2001) models. This leads into a discussion of the thorny statistical issues alluded to above, namely, parameter proliferation and the consistency of the estimated parameters, and the problem of obtaining the standard errors of the parameters.

The Deterministic Portion of the Utility Function

The two most common deterministic utility functions used in applied work are the normal and the quadratic. The classic normal "bell curve" has the advantage that the utility is always positive, there is decreasing marginal loss, and the utility asymptotes to a fixed value (usually zero). In contrast, the quadratic function has an increasing marginal loss, and the utility becomes infinitely negative as the distance becomes large (see Figure 2.1).

---

[1] Technically I am assuming that the error distribution is *continuous*. Consequently, I do not have to worry about the case where $P(U_{ijy} - U_{ijn}) = 0$.

Howard Rosenthal and I based our NOMINATE model on the normal distribution utility function. We decided to use the normal distribution rather than the quadratic because we felt that the normal distribution is a more realistic model of choice behavior.[2] The normal distribution concentrates the utility near the individual's ideal point, with tails that quickly approach zero as the choices become more and more distant. Choices out in the tails beyond two standard deviations all have near-zero utility.

Normally distributed utility is therefore an excellent model for the phenomena of alienation and indifference. Alienation occurs when a person is faced with a set of choices that are all very distant from her ideal point and on the same side of the space. For example, if she is a moderate liberal and faced with two choices, both of which have conservative outcomes well to her right, she may abstain because of alienation. Similarly, extremist political groups see big differences between themselves and regard all mainstream political parties as "capitalist tools" or "socialist fools," depending on which end of the spectrum they are looking inward from.

Indifference occurs when the individual is faced with a set of choices that "bracket" her in the space. For example, if she is a moderate conservative and she is faced with two choices, one with a very conservative outcome and another with a very liberal outcome, her utility from either outcome is very low because they are under opposite tails of her utility function, and so she may abstain.

In the U.S. Congress most legislators place a high premium on *not* abstaining, because avoiding a vote is often used against them in the next election. Consequently, a legislator's choice in a setting where she is indifferent because of either alienation or indifference may be driven by the stochastic portion of the utility function because the deterministic utility is so tiny. When better multi-choice spatial models of legislative voting are implemented and applied to legislatures where there is policy-related abstention, I expect that the normal utility model will show an unambiguous advantage over the quadratic.

I will discuss the normal distribution utility function first, then the quadratic, and then how the two differ in the estimation of the roll call outcomes.

---

[2] Recall from Chapter 1 that a strong regularity emerged from the work in psychology on multidimensional scaling: When people judged the similarity between stimuli or were asked to report preferences for stimuli, they appeared to be using an *exponential response function*. That is, when the actual judged similarities are graphed against some objective measure of similarity, they almost always produce an exponential-like plot (Shepard, 1987). Specifically, if the similarity measure A is a number between zero (most similar) and one (least similar), people tend to report e^{-kA}, where k is a scaling constant. Because people are not perfect judges, when perceptual error is added to Shepard's model, the expected value of the response function is *Gaussian* – that is, e^{-kA^2} (Nosofsky, 1986, 1988; Ennis, 1988a, 1988b; Shepard, 1988a; 1988b; Ennis, Palen, and Mullen, 1988). See Chapter 7 for a more detailed discussion of the implications of these results for geometric models of choice in political science.

With the normal distribution utility model, legislator i's utility for the Yea outcome on roll call j is

$$u_{ijy} = \beta \exp\left(-\frac{1}{2}\sum_{k=1}^{s} w_k d_{ijky}^2\right) \tag{4.2}$$

where d_{ijky}^2 is the squared distance of the ith legislator to the Yea outcome on the kth dimension;

$$d_{ijky}^2 = (X_{ik} - O_{jky})^2;$$

the w_k are salience weights ($w_k > 0$); and because there is no natural metric, β "adjusts" for the overall noise level and is proportional to the variance of the error distribution. The w_k allow the indifference curves of the utility function to be ellipses rather than circles.

The difference between the deterministic utilities is

$$u_{ijy} - u_{ijn} = \beta \left\{ \exp\left(-\frac{1}{2}\sum_{k=1}^{s} w_k d_{ijky}^2\right) - \exp\left(-\frac{1}{2}\sum_{k=1}^{s} w_k d_{ijkn}^2\right) \right\}. \tag{4.3}$$

This rather ungainly equation does not lend itself to any further simplification. But, although it looks complex, computationally it is not difficult to work with.

With the quadratic distribution utility model, legislator i's utility for the Yea outcome on roll call j is just

$$u_{ijy} = -d_{ijy}^2 = -\sum_{k=1}^{s} (X_{ik} - O_{jky})^2. \tag{4.4}$$

Unlike the normal distribution utility function, the quadratic utility function simplifies nicely. The difference between the deterministic quadratic utilities is

$$u_{ijy} - u_{ijn}$$

$$= -\sum_{k=1}^{s}(X_{ik} - O_{jky})^2 - \sum_{k=1}^{s}(X_{ik} - O_{jkn})^2$$

$$= -\sum_{k=1}^{s}X_{ik}^2 + 2\sum_{k=1}^{s}X_{ik}O_{jky} - \sum_{k=1}^{s}O_{jky}^2 + \sum_{k=1}^{s}X_{ik}^2$$

$$\quad - 2\sum_{k=1}^{s}X_{ik}O_{jkn} + \sum_{k=1}^{s}O_{jkn}^2$$

$$= -2\sum_{k=1}^{s}X_{ik}(O_{jkn} - O_{jky}) + \sum_{k=1}^{s}(O_{jkn} - O_{jky})(O_{jkn} + O_{jky}). \tag{4.5}$$

The two terms in equation (4.5) are a sum of cross products and a sum of squared outcome locations. The cross product term of equation (4.5) is the foundation for the *directional theory of voting* developed by George Rabinowitz. By separating the two terms in a multivariate framework, it is possible to nest both a directional theory of choice and a *proximity* (distance-based) theory of choice (i.e., the traditional spatial model) in a single framework. Namely, in a regression-like analysis, separate coefficients can be estimated for the two terms (Rabinowitz and Macdonald, 1989; Platt, Poole, and Rosenthal 1992; Merrill and Grofman, 1999).[3] If the two coefficients are equal, a proximity model of choice is appropriate. If the coefficient on the cross product term is large relative to the coefficient on the squared term, it supports the directional model of choice. Platt, Poole, and Rosenthal (1992) applied this model to roll call voting in the 92nd to the 99th U.S. Houses and found that the directional theory can be unambiguously rejected in favor of the traditional spatial model. When we use both a quadratic utility framework with the terms separated as shown above, and the normal utility framework where the squared distances in the exponent of the utility function are broken into a sum of cross products and a sum of squares, the resulting coefficients are almost exactly equal in all cases.[4]

Returning to equation (4.5), note that the s by 1 vector

$$\mathbf{O}_{jn} - \mathbf{O}_{jy} = \begin{bmatrix} O_{j1n} - O_{j1y} \\ O_{j2n} - O_{j2y} \\ \vdots \\ O_{jsn} - O_{jsy} \end{bmatrix}$$

is equal to a constant times the normal vector $\mathbf{N}_j$, because the line joining the outcome points $\mathbf{O}_{jn}$ and $\mathbf{O}_{jy}$ is parallel to the normal vector. Therefore, subtracting $\mathbf{O}_{jy}$ from both points produces a vector that is simply a constant times the normal vector (see Figure 4.1):

$$\gamma_j \mathbf{N}_j = \mathbf{O}_{jn} - \mathbf{O}_{jy} \qquad (4.6)$$

---

[3] The nesting idea was the product of a conversation between George Rabinowitz and Howard Rosenthal at a conference held at Carnegie-Mellon University in 1987. Merrill and Grofman (1999, Chapters 1–3) elaborate on this framework and show how the classical Downsian model and the directional model can be combined in a unified model that can be empirically tested. Their bottom-line findings are that voter choice appears to be a *mix* of directional and proximity components and that this mix varies with the type of candidate (challenger or incumbent). The key empirical result is that voters appear to respond to candidates offering policies in their direction but reject those candidates distant from themselves.

[4] There is a large literature on (and considerable controversy about) the directional versus the proximity (traditional spatial theory of voting) model of choice in mass publics. For example, see Lewis and King (1999) and Macdonald, Rabinowitz, and Listhaug (2001) and the citations therein. The most comprehensive analysis of the two models is by Merrill and Grofman (1999) .

Vector Difference of Outcome Coordinates

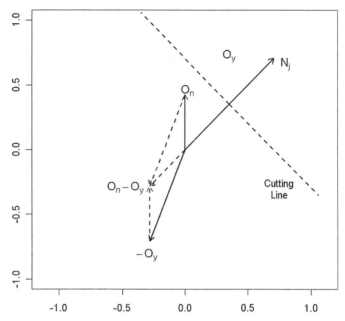

FIGURE 4.1. *The vector difference of the outcome coordinates is equal to a constant times the normal vector.*

where

$$
\gamma_j = \begin{cases} \left[\displaystyle\sum_{k=1}^{s} (O_{jkn} - O_{jky})^2 \right]^{\frac{1}{2}} & \text{if } \mathbf{O}'_{jn}\mathbf{N}_j > \mathbf{O}'_{jy}\mathbf{N}_j \\[2ex] -\left[\displaystyle\sum_{k=1}^{s} (O_{jkn} - O_{jky})^2 \right]^{\frac{1}{2}} & \text{if } \mathbf{O}'_{jn}\mathbf{N}_j < \mathbf{O}'_{jy}\mathbf{N}_j. \end{cases}
$$

Here γ_j is the *directional distance* between the Yea and Nay outcomes in the space.[5]

The s by 1 vector

$$
\mathbf{O}_{jn} + \mathbf{O}_{jy} = \begin{bmatrix} O_{j1n} + O_{j1y} \\ O_{j2n} + O_{j2y} \\ \vdots \\ O_{jsn} + O_{jsy} \end{bmatrix}
$$

---

[5]"Directional distance" as it is used in this chapter is not to be confused with the directional utility model. By directional distance I mean only that it is *signed*.

divided by 2 is simply the s by 1 vector of midpoints for the Yea and Nay outcomes for roll call j. That is,

$$\mathbf{Z}_j = \frac{\mathbf{O}_{jn} + \mathbf{O}_{jy}}{2}.$$

This allows equation (4.5) to be rewritten as the vector equation

$$u_{ijy} - u_{ijn} = 2\gamma_j(\mathbf{Z}'_j\mathbf{N}_j - \mathbf{X}'_i\mathbf{N}_j) = 2\gamma_j(c_j - w_i) \qquad (4.7)$$

where w_i is the projection of the ith legislator's ideal point onto the line defined by the normal vector $\mathbf{N}_j$ and its reflection $-\mathbf{N}_j$ (see Figure 3.8), and c_j is the projection of the midpoint of the roll call outcomes onto that line. If the legislator votes Yea and she is on the same side of the cutting plane as the Yea outcome, then from equation (4.7),

if $\gamma_j > 0$ and $w_i < c_j$ or if $\gamma_j < 0$ and $w_i > c_j,$ then $u_{ijy} > u_{ijn}.$

In one dimension, $\mathbf{N}_j$ can be set equal to 1, and $\gamma_j = O_{jn} - O_{jy}$. Hence, equation (4.7) becomes simply $2(O_{jn} - O_{jy})(c_j - x_i) = 2\gamma_j(x_i - c_j).$[6]

In more than one dimension only the cutting line and the distance between the two outcome points are identified in the quadratic utility model; that is, the directional distance γ_j, the normal vector $\mathbf{N}_j$, and the projection of the midpoint $\mathbf{Z}_j$ on the normal vector, c_j. Although it appears that the number of parameters for a roll call is $s + 2$, given the fact that the normal vector has unit length, that is, $\mathbf{N}'_j\mathbf{N}_j = 1$, the normal vector is completely determined by the $s - 1$ angles of the vector from the coordinate axes, so that the actual number of parameters is $s + 1$. In a polar coordinate system the $s - 1$ angles produce s coordinates provided that the vector is of fixed length. For example, in two dimensions the normal vector can always be written as

$$\begin{bmatrix} \cos\theta \\ \sin\theta \end{bmatrix}$$

where θ is the angle of the vector from the horizontal axis and $0 \leq \theta \leq 2\pi$; in three dimensions the normal vector can always be written as

$$\begin{bmatrix} \sin\varphi\cos\theta \\ \sin\varphi\sin\theta \\ \cos\varphi \end{bmatrix}$$

---

[6]Except for an added "valence" dimension, this model is identical to the one-dimensional model developed by Londregan (2000a, pp. 40–41). Specifically, in Londregan's notation, $g = (O_{jn} - O_{jy})$, $m = (O_{jn} + O_{jy})/2$, $x_v = x_i$, and $z = O_{jy}$ or O_{jn}, depending upon which is the *proposal* (the opposite alternative is the status quo). The utility function used by Londregan is

$$U(z, q \mid x_v) = -\frac{1}{2}(z - x_v)^2 + \alpha q.$$

The αq picks up a "valence" element of policy.

Identification of Outcome Coordinates

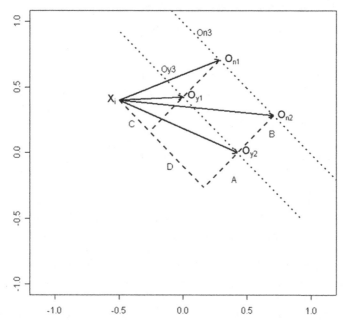

FIGURE 4.2. *Identification of the outcome coordinates. The outcome coordinates are identified only up to parallel tracks through the space when the quadratic utility model is used.*

where θ is the angle in the plane of the first and second dimensions, $0 \le \theta \le 2\pi$, and φ is the angle from the third dimension to the plane, $0 \le \varphi \le \pi$.

In sum, in the quadratic utility model each roll call is determined by $s + 1$ parameters: γ_j, c_j, and the $s - 1$ angles. As a practical matter, however, it is easier simply to estimate the normal vector $\mathbf{N}_j$ directly rather than parameterize the problem in terms of the underlying angles, because techniques similar to the cutting plane procedure in Chapter 3 are easy to implement in probabilistic voting problems.

In more than one dimension the fact that each roll call is determined by only $s + 1$ parameters means that the outcome coordinates are identified only up to *parallel tracks through the space*. Figure 4.2 shows the geometry.

Figure 4.2 shows one legislator, $\mathbf{X}_i$, and her distances to two pairs of outcomes (the vectors in the figure). The parallel dotted lines pass through the two pairs of outcomes. By the Pythagorean theorem, the squared distance between $\mathbf{X}_i$ and $\mathbf{O}_{y1}$ is $C^2 + A^2$ (see the indicated line segments in the figure). Similarly, the squared distance between $\mathbf{X}_i$ and $\mathbf{O}_{n1}$ is $C^2 + (A + B)^2$. Therefore,

$$u_{iy} - u_{in} = -d_{iy}^2 + d_{in}^2 = -(C^2 + A^2) + [C^2 + (A + B)^2] = 2AB + B^2.$$

Similarly, the squared distance between $\mathbf{X}_i$ and $\mathbf{O}_{y2}$ is $(C + D)^2 + A^2$, and the squared distance between $\mathbf{X}_i$ and $\mathbf{O}_{n2}$ is $(C + D)^2 + (A + B)^2$. Therefore,

$$u_{iy} - u_{in} = -d_{iy}^2 + d_{in}^2 = -[(C + D)^2 + A^2] + [(C + D)^2 + (A + B)^2]$$
$$= 2AB + B^2.$$

In sum, in more than one dimension the outcome coordinates in the quadratic utility model are identified only up to the parallel tracks shown in Figure 4.2. The disadvantage is that the outcome points can never be definitively estimated. The advantage is the simplicity of the geometry. With the exception of the signed distance parameter γ_j, the geometry of the quadratic utility function is identical to that shown in Chapter 2, and the OC method shown in Chapter 3 can be used as a basis for estimating the probabilistic model.

In contrast, in the normal distribution utility function the outcome coordinates are identified, but the price is $2s$ parameters – the two outcome points $\mathbf{O}_{jn}$ and $\mathbf{O}_{jy}$. Holding the distance between the two outcomes fixed as in Figure 4.2, $u_{iy} - u_{in}$ will vary as the outcomes are moved up and down the tracks, and it is a maximum when the outcomes are located at $\mathbf{O}_{y3}$ and $\mathbf{O}_{n3}$. This identification is due to the nonlinearity of the utility difference. For any legislator, with the distance between the two outcomes held fixed, the utility difference is maximized when the legislator's ideal point and the outcomes lie on a line parallel to the normal vector for the roll call cutting plane. In the example shown in Figure 4.2, the utility difference equation (4.3) for the $\mathbf{O}_{y3}$ and $\mathbf{O}_{n3}$ outcome points is

$$u_{iy} - u_{in} = e^{-A^2} - e^{-(A+B)^2} = e^{-A^2}\left(1 - e^{-(2AB+B^2)}\right).$$

The utility difference for the $\mathbf{O}_{y1}$ and $\mathbf{O}_{n1}$ outcome points is

$$u_{iy} - u_{in} = e^{-(A^2+C^2)} - e^{-[C^2+(A+B)^2]} = e^{-(A^2+C^2)}\left(1 - e^{-(2AB+B^2)}\right).$$

Now, because $e^{-A^2} > e^{-(A^2+C^2)}$, the legislator's utility difference is always maximized when her ideal point and the outcomes lie on a line parallel to the normal vector.

Not every legislator can be on the line running through the outcome points. Consequently, *if we hold the distance between the outcomes fixed*, the outcomes will be positioned on the tracks so that the total of the utility differences of all the legislators vis-à-vis their chosen outcomes is maximized. In contrast, the total of the utility differences of all the legislators in the quadratic model is the same regardless of the location of the outcome points on the tracks.

Another crucial difference between the two utility functions is how they are affected by an increase in the distance between the two outcomes. Note that as the distance B in Figure 4.2 increases, the quadratic utility difference for $\mathbf{X}_i$ increases monotonically. That is, if $B \to \infty$, then $A \to \infty$ and $2AB + B^2 \to \infty$. However, for the normal utility difference, if $B \to \infty$, then $A \to \infty$ and $e^{-A^2} \to 0$ and $e^{-(A^2+B^2)} \to 0$, so that the utility difference goes to zero. This

Utility Difference Normal Model vs.
Distance Between Outcomes

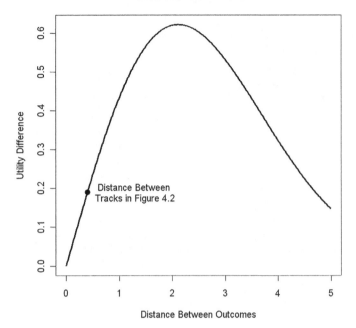

FIGURE 4.3. *Utility difference for the normal distribution deterministic utility function versus the distance between the policy outcomes. In contrast with the quadratic utility model, the distance between the tracks does not explode when there is perfect voting on the roll call.*

means that for the normal utility model the distance between the two outcomes cannot *explode* – that is, there is a value beyond which the utility difference (and the probability of the choice) begins to decline. This fact is illustrated in Figure 4.3.

Figure 4.3 shows the effect of increasing the distance between $\mathbf{O}_{y3}$ and $\mathbf{O}_{n3}$ in Figure 4.2 from 0 to 5 with legislator $\mathbf{X}_i$ held fixed. The distance between the tracks in Figure 4.2 is 0.4, and the corresponding utility difference is about 0.19. The utility difference peaks at a distance of 2.12 with a value of 0.623 and then declines thereafter.

The Stochastic Portion of the Utility Function

When we turn to the stochastic portion of the utility function stated in equation (4.1) above, three probability distributions have been used to model the error: the normal (Ladha, 1991; McCarty, Poole, and Rosenthal, 1997; Londregan, 2000a; Jackman, 2000a; Poole, 2001), uniform (Heckman and Snyder, 1997), and logit (Poole and Rosenthal, 1985; 1991; 1997). The normal is clearly the best from both a theoretical and a behavioral standpoint.

From a statistical standpoint, the random errors associated with the Yea and Nay choices should be a *random sample* (i.e., a set of independent and identically distributed random variables) from a known distribution. If ε_{ijn} and ε_{ijy} are a random sample from a known distribution, then the probability distribution of the difference between the two random errors, $\varepsilon_{ijn} - \varepsilon_{ijy}$, is usually easy to derive. From a behavioral standpoint, it seems sensible to assume that the distributions of ε_{ijn} and ε_{ijy} are *symmetric and unimodal* and that ε_{ijn} and ε_{ijy} are uncorrelated. The normal distribution is the only one of the three distributions to satisfy all these criteria. To illustrate, assume that ε_{ijn} and ε_{ijy} are drawn (a random sample of size two) from a normal distribution with mean zero and variance one-half. The difference between the two errors has a standard normal distribution; that is,

$$\varepsilon_{ijn} - \varepsilon_{ijy} \sim N(0,1)$$

and the distribution of the difference between the overall utilities is

$$U_{ijy} - U_{ijn} \sim N(u_{ijy} - u_{ijn}, 1).$$

Hence the probability that legislator i votes Yea on the jth roll call can be rewritten as

$$P_{ijy} = P(U_{ijy} > U_{ijn}) = P(\varepsilon_{ijn} - \varepsilon_{ijy} < u_{ijy} - u_{ujn})$$
$$= \Phi[u_{ijy} - u_{ijn}]. \tag{4.8}$$

Heckman and Snyder (1997) assume that $\varepsilon_{ijn} - \varepsilon_{ijy}$ has a uniform distribution. This is an extremely problematic assumption, because ε_{ijn} and ε_{ijy} *cannot be a random sample*. Heckman and Snyder (1997) acknowledge that no distribution exists such that the probability distribution of the difference between two random draws has a uniform distribution. For example, if ε_{ijn} and ε_{ijy} are drawn from a uniform distribution, then the distribution of their difference will be triangle-shaped. Assuming that $\varepsilon_{ijn} - \varepsilon_{ijy}$ has a uniform distribution enables Heckman and Snyder to develop a linear probability model, but the price for this simplicity is that they have no intuitive basis for a behavioral model.

Poole and Rosenthal (1985, 1991, 1997) assume that ε_{ijn} and ε_{ijy} are a random sample from the log of the inverse exponential distribution[7]; that is,

$$f(\varepsilon) = e^{-\varepsilon}e^{-e^{-\varepsilon}}, \qquad \text{where } -\infty < \varepsilon < +\infty.$$

[7]When NOMINATE was developed in 1982–1983, computer time, disk space, and memory were scarce resources. Howard Rosenthal and I opted for the logit rather than the normal distribution because logit-based probabilities are *formulas* and were faster to compute. This is no longer an important issue (see Chapter 5 for the practicalities of scaling program design).

Dhrymes (1978, pp. 340–352) shows that the distribution of $\varepsilon_{ijn} - \varepsilon_{ijy}$ is

$$f(z) = \frac{e^{-z}}{(1 + e^{-z})^2}, \qquad \text{where } z = \varepsilon_{ijn} - \varepsilon_{ijy} \text{ and } -\infty < z < +\infty.$$

This is the logit distribution.

The log of the inverse exponential distribution and the logit distribution are unimodal but not symmetric. Neither distribution is terribly skewed, however, and the distribution function of the logit distribution is reasonably close to the normal distribution function. Namely, integrating $f(z)$ from $-\infty$ to $u_{ijy} - u_{ijn}$ yields the probability that the legislator votes Yea:

$$
\begin{aligned}
P_{ijy} = P(U_{ijy} > U_{ijn}) &= P(\varepsilon_{ijn} - \varepsilon_{ijy} < u_{ijy} - u_{ijn}) \\
&= \int_{-\infty}^{u_{ijn} - u_{ijy}} \frac{e^{-z}}{(1 + e^{-z})^2} \, dz = \frac{e^{u_{ijy}}}{e^{u_{ijy}} + e^{u_{ijn}}}.
\end{aligned}
\tag{4.9}
$$

The probabilistic models summarized by equations (4.8) and (4.9) implicitly assume that the underlying error variance is homoskedastic – that is, it is constant across legislators and across roll calls. A more realistic assumption is that the error variance varies across the roll call votes and across the legislators. In reality, however, for the roll calls it is impossible to distinguish between the underlying unknown error variance and the distance between the Yea and Nay alternatives (Ladha, 1991; Poole and Rosenthal, 1997; Londregan, 2000a). The intuition behind this statement is straightforward. As the distance between the Yea and Nay alternatives increases, it becomes easier for legislators to distinguish between the two policy outcomes, and so they are much less likely to make a voting error. Conversely, if the Yea and Nay alternatives are very close together, then the utility difference is small and it is more likely that voting errors occur.

Increasing (decreasing) the distance is equivalent to decreasing (increasing) the variance of the underlying error. For example, for the quadratic utility model with normally distributed error, the probability of the observed choice is

$$\Phi[2\gamma_j(c_j - w_i)] \tag{4.10}$$

where $2\gamma_j(c_j - w_i) > 0$ if the legislator is on the same side of the cutting plane as the policy outcome she voted for (this is picked up by the signed distance term, γ_j). If all the legislators are correctly classified, then $|\gamma_j| \to \infty$ and $\Phi[2\gamma_j(c_j - w_i)] \to 1$ for all legislators. This situation is equivalent to setting the signed distance term to a constant and writing the probability of the observed choice in the more traditional way:

$$\Phi\left[\frac{2\gamma_j(c_j - w_i)}{\sigma_j}\right]$$

where σ_j^2 is the roll call specific variance, that is,

$$\varepsilon_{ijn} - \varepsilon_{ijy} \sim N\left(0, \sigma_j^2\right).$$

Clearly, as $\sigma \to 0$ the probabilities on the jth roll call all go to one.

For the normal utility model the probability of voting Yea is

$$\Phi\left[\beta\left\{\exp\left(-\frac{1}{2}\sum_{k=1}^{s} w_k d_{ijky}^2\right) - \exp\left(-\frac{1}{2}\sum_{k=1}^{s} w_k d_{ijkn}^2\right)\right\}\right]. \quad (4.11)$$

Here the interaction of the distance between the two outcomes and the error variance for the roll call is not as clear-cut, but it is still there. As I explained above, if the roll call cutting plane perfectly classifies the legislators, then in the normal utility model the distance between the two outcome points will grow large – typically both outcomes are outside the space spanned by the legislators – but will not explode. Note that if the overall noise parameter β were allowed to vary across roll calls – that is, if there were q β_j's – then these β_j's would be roll-call-specific variances; that is, $\beta_j = 1/\sigma_j$. Howard Rosenthal and I experimented with this model in some depth in the 1980s. We concluded that even though the distance between the outcome coordinates did not explode, the interaction between the β_j's and the distances was such that estimates of the β_j's were not reliable.

In sum, the roll-call-specific error variances are picked up by the distance between the two outcome points in both the quadratic and normal utility models.

Legislator-specific variance is another matter. In principle, it can be disentangled. For the quadratic utility model the probability of the observed choice is

$$\Phi\left[\frac{2\gamma_j(c_j - w_i)}{\sigma_i}\right] \quad (4.12)$$

where σ_i^2 is the legislator-specific variance, that is,

$$\varepsilon_{ijn} - \varepsilon_{ijy} \sim N\left(0, \sigma_i^2\right).$$

Because each γ_j is estimated with respect to the p legislators and each σ_i is estimated with respect to the q roll calls, in principle the two sets of parameters do not have an interaction problem like that between γ_j and σ_j. But because they enter equation (4.12) as a *ratio*, the γ_j's and σ_i's are identified only up to a multiplicative positive constant. That is, for any $k > 0$,

$$\frac{2\gamma_j(c_j - w_i)}{\sigma_i} = \frac{2k\gamma_j(c_j - w_i)}{k\sigma_i}.$$

In practice this identification problem is not a serious concern, because we are primarily interested in how noisy legislators are *relative* to one another. The model shown in equation (4.12) is the basis of the *quadratic–normal* (QN) scaling program (Poole, 2001). I will discuss it in more detail later in this chapter.

Legislator-specific variance can also be estimated in the normal utility model. The probability of the observed choice is

$$\Phi\left[\frac{\exp\left(-\frac{1}{2}\sum_{k=1}^{s}w_k d_{ijky}^2\right) - \exp\left(-\frac{1}{2}\sum_{k=1}^{s}w_k d_{ijkn}^2\right)}{\sigma_i}\right]. \quad (4.13)$$

In this formulation the overall noise parameter β is unnecessary, because its effect will be picked up by the p σ_j's. This model has never been developed in computer code, and it awaits an adventurous researcher.[8]

Estimation of Probabilistic Spatial Voting Models

In classical statistical inference we assume that we know the type of distribution (normal, Poisson, Bernoulli, etc.) from which our random sample is drawn, and on the basis of that random sample we must infer the values of the *parameters* of the distribution. This is parametric estimation. Within this classical framework, I assume that the distribution of the difference between the utility for Yea and the utility for Nay for the ith legislator on the jth roll call is normally distributed with constant variance; that is,

$$U_{ijy} - U_{ijn} \sim N(u_{ijy} - u_{ijn}, \sigma^2). \quad (4.14)$$

The parameters to be estimated on the basis of a random sample from this distribution are the ps legislator coordinates X_{ik}, the $2qs$ roll call outcome parameters O_{jky} and O_{jkn}, and the utility function parameters β and/or the s w_k's. The approach I take is classical maximum likelihood; that is, I attempt to find parameter values that maximize the likelihood of actually observing the roll call data. Technically, the likelihood function is

$$L = \prod_{i=1}^{p}\prod_{j=1}^{q}\prod_{\tau=1}^{2} P_{ij\tau}^{C_{ij\tau}} \quad (4.15)$$

where τ is the index for Yea and Nay, $P_{ij\tau}$ is the probability of voting for choice τ as given by equations (4.10) to (4.13), and $C_{ij\tau} = 1$ if the legislator's actual choice is τ and zero otherwise. It is standard practice to work with the natural

---

[8]This could probably be done by adding another step to the NOMINATE framework similar to the design of QN. Namely, with all other parameters held fixed, estimate the p σ_i's as a separate step.

log of the likelihood function:

$$L = \sum_{i=1}^{p}\sum_{j=1}^{q}\sum_{\tau=1}^{2} C_{ij\tau} \ln P_{ij\tau}. \tag{4.16}$$

In the conventional approach, the maximum of equation (4.16) is found by taking the first derivatives of the log of the likelihood function with respect to all the parameters, setting the first derivatives equal to zero, and then solving the set of equations for the parameter values. The matrix of second derivatives is also computed to ensure that the solution is indeed a maximum.

This conventional approach does not work well, for two reasons: the number of parameters that must be estimated, and the necessity for constraints on the parameter values.

Even for relatively small legislatures, the number of parameters that must be estimated is very large. For example, a typical recent U.S. Senate has 100 senators casting 500 or more roll call votes. In two dimensions, about 2,200 parameters would have to be estimated simultaneously. Using standard maximization methods would require repeated inversions of matrices of 2,200 by 2,200. Even with modern computers this is a formidable undertaking, and there is good reason to believe that the approach would not work very well in any event. For one thing, how the level of error interacts with the underlying geometry is not yet clearly understood (see Chapter 7). Without knowing this relationship we cannot be certain about the interval scale information that is being recovered by the scaling program and how this affects the matrix of second derivatives. There may be hidden linearities that we do not yet understand. Empirically, a matrix of this size it is very likely to be singular because of "accidental" linear combinations of rows or columns.

The second reason the conventional approach does not work is that constraints must be placed on the legislators and roll calls. For example, if the error level is low and some extreme legislators always vote for the liberal or the conservative outcome on every roll call, their ideal point cannot be identified beyond the fact that they are at the edge of the space. A similar problem crops up for perfect roll calls and for lopsided noisy roll calls. In all three cases the parameters must not be allowed to take on absurd values, so that the estimated parameters are *not* at the maximum of the log-likelihood function.

The approach that Howard Rosenthal and I developed, which we dubbed NOMINATE, solves the estimation problem by dividing the parameters into three sets and estimating each set separately with the other two held fixed. Given reasonable starting values for the legislator ideal points, we can estimate the roll call parameters *given* these ideal points. Similarly, *given* estimates of the roll call parameters, we can obtain better estimates of the ideal points. The third set is the utility function parameters, which are estimated *given* both the legislator ideal points and the roll call outcome points. NOMINATE cycles through the three sets until they reproduce each other.[9] That is, at convergence each set is reproduced by the other two – the parameters no longer change.

The quadratic–normal (QN) scaling method uses a quadratic deterministic utility function and normally distributed error. It is based on OC, and it also solves the estimation problem by dividing the parameters into three sets and cycling through them until the three reproduce each other. The parameters are identical to OC with the addition of the signed distances and legislator-specific variances.

The NOMINATE (Normal–Normal) Model

In our book, Howard Rosenthal and I (Poole and Rosenthal, 1997) detail the original D-NOMINATE and W-NOMINATE algorithms that assumed that error followed the logit model shown in equation (4.9). When we began our work in late 1982, we used the logit model because of computer speed and memory limitations. Calculating logit probabilities was easier and faster because the logit probability is given by a formula. In contrast, in the older computers normal probabilities were calculated by a machine subroutine that used a power series approximation (see Chapter 5).[10]

When NSF announced the supercomputer initiative in the summer of 1985, we were granted time on the Cyber 205 vector supercomputer at Purdue University to develop NOMINATE further. The architecture of the Cyber 205 (its use of vector pipelines – now in all the latest Intel CPUs) and the programming language (VECTOR FORTRAN) that was implemented on it were ideally suited to large discrete choice problems.[11] Consequently, we were able to estimate *dynamic* multidimensional spatial models, and we developed D-NOMINATE from 1986 to 1988.

The original NOMINATE was a one-dimensional program, and it was rewritten by Nolan McCarty in 1991–1992 to analyze more than one dimension.

---

[9] The structure of NOMINATE was inspired by the work of the psychometricians who developed nonmetric multidimensional scaling (Shepard, 1962a,b; Kruskal, 1964a,b) and individual-differences scaling methods (Carroll and Chang, 1970). These scaling methods all used an alternating structure to estimate their models.

[10] In early 1983, even with the logit model it took several hours on a state-of-the-art DEC VAX to analyze a single Senate roll call matrix. To analyze a U. S. House matrix with about 500 roll calls required that we run the program overnight in the batch queue. This took at least 7–9 hours of CPU time.

[11] VECTOR FORTRAN allowed the declaration of *bit vectors*. Because a legislator's vote on a particular roll call is either Yea, Nay, or Abstain, the legislator's choice required only two bits of memory storage on the Cyber 205. The appropriate entry in one bit vector was set to TRUE if the legislator voted Yea. Similarly, the appropriate entry in a second bit vector was set to TRUE if the legislator voted Nay. A logical comparison of the two vectors was used to find abstention. Because bit vectors permitted storing 64 individual roll call votes in just two words of memory, the large memory of the Cyber 205 could be used very efficiently.

This version of NOMINATE became known as W-NOMINATE. The "W" stands for "weighted," because it uses the weighted distance model shown in equation (4.3). The weights allowed for elliptical indifference curves for the utility function, rather than circles.

By the mid-1990s personal computers became powerful enough in processing speed and memory that it became feasible to implement a dynamic multidimensional spatial model on personal computers. DW-NOMINATE is based on normally distributed errors rather than logit errors, and it uses the W-NOMINATE weighted distance model (McCarty, Poole, and Rosenthal, 1997). DW-NOMINATE is structured to analyze any number of Congresses and can be applied to a single Congress. Consequently, I will focus on DW-NOMINATE in my discussion below, rather than the older algorithms.

Although DW-NOMINATE, like D-NOMINATE, was designed to deal with the U.S. House and Senate, it can be used to analyze any voting body that meets in multiple sessions over time: U.S. state legislatures, the United Nations, the European Parliament, and so on. Below I use the term "parliamentary session" to refer to any distinct session of a voting body. In the U.S. context this would be one Congress: a two-year period.

Let T be the number of parliamentary sessions (indexed by $t = 1, \ldots, T$); s denote the number of policy dimensions ($k = 1, \ldots, s$); p_t denote the number of legislators in parliamentary session t ($i = 1, \ldots, p_t$); q_t denote the number of roll call votes in parliamentary session t ($j = 1, \ldots, q_t$); and T_i denote the number of parliamentary sessions in which legislator i served ($t = 1, \ldots, T_i$). To allow for spatial movement over time, the legislator ideal points are treated as being polynomial functions of time; namely, legislator i's coordinate on dimension k at time t is given by

$$X_{ikt} = \chi_{ik0} + \chi_{ik1}T_{t1} + \chi_{ik2}T_{t2} + \cdots + \chi_{ikv}T_{tv} \qquad (4.17)$$

where v is the degree of the polynomial, the χ's are the coefficients of the polynomial, and the time-specific terms – the T's – are Legendre polynomials.[12] Specifically, the first three terms of a Legendre polynomial representation of time are

$$T_{t1} = -1 + (t - 1)\frac{2}{T_i - 1}$$

$$T_{t2} = \frac{3T_{t1}^2 - 1}{2}, \qquad t = 1, \ldots, T_i \qquad (4.18)$$

$$T_{t3} = \frac{5T_{t1}^3 - 3T_{t1}}{2}.$$

---

[12]Mel Hinich suggested this idea to us in 1986. See Hinich and Roll (1981) for an example of their use in a financial economics model.

Legendre polynomials have the nice property of being orthogonal on the interval $[-1, +1]$. This is convenient because DW-NOMINATE scales the legislators and roll call midpoints to be in the unit hypersphere (more on this below). The orthogonality of the Legendre polynomials is a continuous property, but even with discrete data the linear and quadratic terms will be orthogonal. If ordinary powers of time were used instead, that is, t, t^2, t^3, and so on, these would be *correlated*. For example, suppose a legislator serves in five parliamentary sessions. Then her ideal point in two dimensions using a *cubic* model ($v = 3$) can be written as the matrix product

$$
\begin{bmatrix}
1 & -1 & 1 & -1 \\
1 & -.5 & -.125 & .4375 \\
1 & 0 & -.5 & 0 \\
1 & .5 & -.125 & -.4375 \\
1 & 1 & 1 & 1
\end{bmatrix}
\begin{bmatrix}
\chi_{i10} & \chi_{i20} \\
\chi_{i11} & \chi_{i21} \\
\chi_{i12} & \chi_{i22} \\
\chi_{i13} & \chi_{i23}
\end{bmatrix}
=
\begin{bmatrix}
X_{i11} & X_{i21} \\
X_{i12} & X_{i22} \\
X_{i13} & X_{i23} \\
X_{i14} & X_{i24} \\
X_{i15} & X_{i25}
\end{bmatrix}
$$

or

$$\mathbf{T}\chi_i = \mathbf{X}_{iT}. \tag{4.19}$$

If only one parliamentary session is being estimated, the legislator ideal points are simply

$$
\mathbf{X}_i =
\begin{bmatrix}
X_{i1} \\
X_{i2} \\
\vdots \\
X_{is}
\end{bmatrix}
$$

as before.

The two roll call outcome points associated with Yea and Nay on the kth dimension at time t can be written in terms of their midpoint and the distance between them; namely,

$$
\begin{aligned}
O_{jkyt} &= Z_{jkt} - \delta_{jkt} \\
O_{jknt} &= Z_{jkt} + \delta_{jkt}
\end{aligned}
\tag{4.20}
$$

where the midpoint is

$$Z_{jknt} = \frac{O_{jkyt} + O_{jknt}}{2}$$

and δ_{jkt} is *half* the signed distance between the Yea and Nay points on the kth dimension (note that δ_{jkt} can be negative); that is,

$$\delta_{jkt} = \frac{O_{jkyt} - O_{jknt}}{2}. \tag{4.21}$$

Recall that by Figure 1 and equation (4.6), the s by 1 vector $\boldsymbol{\delta}_{jt}$ is equal to a constant times the normal vector for the roll call; that is,

$$\kappa \mathbf{N}_j = \boldsymbol{\delta}_{jt}$$

so that

$$c_j = \frac{1}{\kappa} \mathbf{Z}'_{jt} \boldsymbol{\delta}_{jt}.$$

This shows that the basic underlying geometry is reflected in equations (4.20) and (4.21).

The distance of legislator i to the Yea outcome on the kth dimension for roll call j at time t is

$$d^2_{ijkyt} = (X_{ikt} - O_{jkyt})^2.$$

Legislator i's utility for the Yea outcome on roll call j at time t is

$$U_{ijyt} = u_{ijyt} + \varepsilon_{ijyt} = \beta \exp\left(-\frac{1}{2}\sum_{k=1}^{s} w_k^2 d^2_{ijkyt}\right) + \varepsilon_{ijyt} \qquad (4.22)$$

where u_{ijyt} is the deterministic portion of the utility function, ε_{ijyt} is the stochastic portion, and w_k are the salience weights. Because the stochastic portion of the utility function is normally distributed with constant variance, β is proportional to $1/\sigma^2$, where

$$\varepsilon \sim N(0, \sigma^2).$$

Hence the probability that legislator i votes Yea on the jth roll call at time t is the same as equation (4.11) except for the time subscript; specifically,

$$P_{ijyt} = P(U_{ijyt} > U_{ijnt}) = P(\varepsilon_{ijnt} - \varepsilon_{ijyt} < u_{ijyt} - u_{ijnt}) = \Phi(u_{ijyt} - u_{ijnt})$$

$$= \Phi\left[\beta\left\{\exp\left(-\frac{1}{2}\sum_{k=1}^{s} w_k d^2_{ijkyt}\right) - \exp\left(-\frac{1}{2}\sum_{k=1}^{s} w_k d^2_{ijknt}\right)\right\}\right].$$

$$(4.23)$$

The natural log of the likelihood function is

$$L = \sum_{t=1}^{T}\sum_{i=1}^{p_t}\sum_{j=1}^{q_t}\sum_{\tau=1}^{2} C_{ij\tau t} \ln P_{ij\tau t} \qquad (4.24)$$

where τ is the index for Yea and Nay, $P_{ij\tau t}$ is the probability of voting for choice τ as given by equation (4.23), and $C_{ij\tau t} = 1$ if the legislator's actual choice is τ, and 0 otherwise.

The total number of parameters to be estimated is at most

$$2s\sum_{t=1}^{T} q_t + sp(v + 1) + s$$

where $2s \sum_{t=1}^{T} q_t$ is the number of roll call parameters, $sp(v + 1)$ is the *maximum possible* number of legislator parameters – that is, all p legislators serve in at least $v + 1$ parliamentary sessions, so that the $v + 1$ χ_{ik}'s can be estimated – and s is the total number of parameters $\beta, w_2, \ldots, w_s$ (the weight on the first dimension can be set equal to 1). In practice v is usually 0 (the *constant model* where the legislator's ideal point is the same in every parliamentary session in which she serves) or 1 (the *linear model* in which legislators are allowed to follow a straight line trajectory through the space over time). In our original D-NOMINATE work, Howard Rosenthal and I found that the linear model in two dimensions was the best combination of explanatory power and number of parameters (Poole and Rosenthal, 1991, 1997).

Because the roll calls are nominal data – just Yeas, Nays, and not voting – the spatial model outlined above has no natural metric. Some metric must be chosen. The metric used by DW-NOMINATE is to confine the *constant point of the legislator* [that is, the s by 1 vector χ_{i0} of the s polynomials defined by equation (4.17)] and the midpoints of the roll call outcomes – the $\mathbf{Z}_j$'s – to be within a unit hypersphere. These constraints are similar to those that Howard Rosenthal and I used in D-NOMINATE (Poole and Rosenthal, 1997, Appendix A).

The unit hypersphere constraint has the nice consequence that the normal vectors – the $\mathbf{N}_j$, which are part of the underlying geometry – have the same length as the radius of the space. This is computationally convenient, but not necessary. It just makes estimation easier. Note that confining the constant term of the legislator's polynomials to be within the unit hypersphere means that it is possible for extreme legislators with large time trends to go somewhat outside the boundaries. This is not a serious problem in practice, because the roll call midpoints are confined within the unit hypersphere, so that the legislator coordinates do not explode – that is, legislators who always vote for the liberal, or for the conservative, outcome on every roll call do not have ideal points in outer space.

The parameters of the model are estimated in the following three-step process:

Step 0: Generate starting estimates for the legislator ideal points X_{ik} and the roll call parameters – the Z_{jkt} and δ_{jkt}.

Step 1: Estimate the utility function parameters $\beta, w_2, \ldots, w_s$ with the legislator and roll call parameters held fixed.

Step 2: Estimate the roll call parameters – the Z_{jkt} and δ_{jkt} – with the legislator and utility function parameters held fixed.

Step 3: Estimate the legislator ideal points – the χ_{ik0} through χ_{ikv} – with the roll call and utility parameters held fixed.

Go to step 1.

I will discuss each step in turn.

Step 0 is in many respects the most important. Because the likelihood function is nonlinear, half the battle is in the starting estimates of the parameters. If the number of parliamentary sessions is small, the best method of obtaining starting values for the legislator ideal points is the method outlined in Chapter 2. First, compute the p by p agreement score matrix; second, convert the agreement score matrix into a matrix of squared distances; third, double-center the matrix of squared distances; and finally, perform an eigenvalue–eigenvector decomposition of the double-centered matrix. The s-dimensional starting values are

$$\tilde{\mathbf{X}} = \eta \mathbf{U}_s \qquad (4.25)$$

where $\tilde{\mathbf{X}}$ is the p by s matrix of legislator starting coordinates; $\mathbf{U}$ is the p by s matrix of eigenvectors from the decomposition of the double-centered matrix such that $\mathbf{U}'\mathbf{U} = \mathbf{I}_s$, where $\mathbf{I}_s$ is an s by s identity matrix; and η is a positive constant that is an *inflation factor* that scales the starting coordinates so that the legislator who is farthest from the origin lies on the rim of the unit hypersphere. I will discuss the practical aspects of equation (4.25) in detail in Chapter 5, including how to deal with missing data – that is, two members who do not overlap, so no agreement score can be computed – and how to decide on the number of dimensions to estimate.

These starting estimates for the legislators produce a single ideal point for each legislator; that is, the constant model, $v = 0$, is assumed initially in order to get the overall estimation started. At step 3 this constraint is relaxed and the parameters χ_{ik0} through χ_{ikv} are estimated. The starting estimates for the legislators are constrained to lie within the unit hypersphere.

Given the starting estimates of the legislators, we can use the cutting plane procedure discussed in detail in Chapter 3 to get starting values for the roll call parameters. In particular, the cutting plane procedure produces estimates for the normal vectors (the $\mathbf{N}_j$'s) and the midpoints of the two outcomes (the $\mathbf{Z}_j$'s). The initial values of the (half) distances between the two outcomes, the δ_{jt}'s, can be set to 0.5 and equation (4.20) used to get the starting values for the two outcomes. These starting values are on the normal vector line for each roll call. This process produces legislators and roll call midpoints that all meet the unit hypersphere constraint.

In step 1 we estimate the s utility function parameters, holding the legislator ideal points and roll call parameters fixed. The easiest way to do this is to set β equal to a reasonable value that can be found experimentally. (In recent DW-NOMINATE scalings of various sets of contiguous U.S. Congresses this value has been around 5.0.) Because it is very rare to estimate more than three dimensions, the second- and third-dimension weights – w_2 and w_3 – are easily found through a simple grid search over the unit square.

In step 2 the roll call parameters are estimated with all other parameters held fixed. Because everything is held fixed, the $2s$ parameters Z_{jkt} and δ_{jkt} for each roll call affect the log-likelihood only through the votes of the legislators on that roll call. The likelihood for the jth roll call is therefore independent of the other roll calls. Technically, the second derivatives of the roll call parameters with respect to each other are all zero. This makes it fairly easy to get estimates of the $2s$ parameters using standard gradient methods.

For example, the BHHH algorithm developed by Berndt, Hall, Hall, and Hausman (1974) is a very simple computational approach to the problem. Let θ_j be the $2s$ by 1 vector of parameters for the jth roll call, g_{ij} be the $2s$ by 1 vector of the first derivatives of L from equation (4.24) for the ith legislator on the jth roll call, and Ω_j be the $2s$ by $2s$ matrix that is the sum of the outer products of the g_{ij}; that is,

$$\Omega_j = \sum_{i=1}^{p} g_{ij} g_{ij}'.$$

The update (hill-climbing) formula for the parameters of the jth roll call is

$$\theta_{j(\text{new})} = \theta_{j(\text{old})} + \alpha \Omega_j^{-1} g_{ij} \qquad (4.26)$$

where α is the step size for the gradient. In normal circumstances at convergence, the matrix Ω_j will closely approximate the *negative* of the matrix of second derivatives (the Hessian matrix). Consequently, at convergence, the diagonal of the inverse of Ω_j yields the variances of the parameters.

If the midpoint of the roll call wanders outside the unit hypersphere, it is constrained to lie on the rim. Technically, if this constraint is invoked, it means that *the log-likelihood is not necessarily at a maximum*. As a practical matter, however, this is usually not much of a problem, because roll calls that end up with their midpoints on the rim of the space are usually very lopsided, with more than 90 percent of the legislators in the majority. Consequently, the roll call will appear to fit well because most of the legislators are being correctly classified, and the roll call will tend to have a high log-likelihood.

In step 3 the parameters for the legislator ideal points – the χ_{ik0} through χ_{ikv} – are estimated with the roll call and utility parameters held fixed. Here we have sv parameters to estimate using the legislator's entire voting history. In terms of the BHHH framework, let θ_i be the sv by 1 vector of parameters for the ith legislator, let g_{ijt} be the sv by 1 vector of the first derivatives of L from equation (4.24) for the ith legislator on the jth roll call at time t, and let Ω_i be the sv by sv matrix that is the sum of the outer products of the g_{ijt}; that is,

$$\Omega_i = \sum_{t=1}^{T_i} \sum_{j=1}^{q_t} g_{ijt} g_{ijt}'.$$

The update (hill-climbing) formula for the parameters of the ith legislator is

$$\theta_{i(\text{new})} = \theta_{i(\text{old})} + \alpha\Omega_i^{-1}\mathbf{g}_{ijt}. \tag{4.27}$$

If the constant point for the legislator $-\chi_{i0}$ – wanders outside the unit hypersphere, it is constrained to lie on the rim. Again, as with the roll call midpoint constraint, *the log-likelihood is not necessarily at a maximum*. As a practical matter, however, this is usually not much of a problem either, because legislators near the rim of the space are the most ideologically rigid members, and they tend to fit the model very well. The log-likelihood is usually very high for these legislators.

The three steps outlined above are repeated until the log-likelihood stops improving. At that point all the sets of parameters are reproducing each other. Within the roll call and legislator steps, each roll call or legislator is estimated while all the remaining parameters are held fixed. The maximum of the likelihood function is found for the parameters being estimated, conditioned on all the remaining parameters being held fixed. The algorithm always moves uphill in a city-block-like fashion. At convergence, every parameter is at a maximum, conditioned on all the remaining parameters being held fixed and conditioned on the unit hypersphere constraint. Convergence to the true global maximum cannot be guaranteed, but the *conditional* global maximum that the algorithm reaches is almost certainly close to the overall global maximum.

The Quadratic–Normal (QN) Model

The multidimensional quadratic utility model (QN) is based on the geometry shown in Chapter 2 and uses the optimal classification (OC) method discussed in depth in Chapter 3 as its foundation. I developed QN in 1999 when I realized that the geometry of the quadratic utility model was identical to the geometry in OC. All that was required to make the leap to a probabilistic model was the signed distance parameter γ_j and, optionally, the legislator-specific variance σ_i^2.

QN is not a dynamic program. It is designed to analyze a single legislative session, although, in principle, legislator ideal points could be estimated using the DW-NOMINATE framework outlined above.

To recap equation (4.12), the probability of the observed choice of the ith legislator on the jth roll call is

$$\Phi\left[\frac{2\gamma_j(c_j - w_i)}{\sigma_i}\right]$$

and the log-likelihood is given by equation (4.16):

$$L = \sum_{i=1}^{p}\sum_{j=1}^{q}\sum_{\tau=1}^{2} C_{ij\tau}\ln P_{ij\tau}.$$

The total number of parameters to be estimated is

$$q(s + 2) + p(s + 1).$$

For each roll call, $\mathbf{N}_j$, γ_j, and c_j are estimated for a total of $q(s + 2)$ parameters, and for each legislator, $\mathbf{X}_i$ and σ_i are estimated for a total of $p(s + 1)$. As I explained above, technically, because $\mathbf{N}_j$ is a unit-length vector, it is identified by the $s - 1$ angles. But it is much easier to work directly with the normal vector than with the angles, and furthermore, the unit-length constraint is in reality a "parameter" in terms of its implementation in computer code. Consequently, I will assume $s + 2$ rather than $s + 1$ parameters per roll call.

QN also uses the unit hypersphere constraint. The legislator ideal points (the $\mathbf{X}_i$'s) and the projected roll call midpoints (the c_j's) are constrained to lie within the unit hypersphere. In addition, in the event of a perfect roll call, the signed distance is not allowed to explode. I impose the constraint that the signed distance must be less than 10 units in absolute value: $|\gamma_j| < 10$. This has no real effect on the estimation, because the corresponding probabilities of the legislators are essentially 1.0. A similar constraint is imposed on the σ_i's, but it is very rarely invoked, because perfect voting by legislators almost never occurs, and when it does, it is because a legislator votes only 20 times or so.

The parameters of the QN model are estimated in the following four-step process:

Step 0: Generate starting estimates for the legislator ideal points X_{ik}, the normal vectors N_{jk}, and the projected roll call midpoints c_j.

Step 1a: Estimate the signed distance parameters (the γ_j) with the legislator ideal points, variances, and roll call normal vectors and projected midpoints held fixed.

Step 1b: Estimate the legislator variance parameters (the σ_j) with the legislator ideal points and roll call parameters held fixed.

Go to step 1a until convergence.

Step 2: Estimate the legislator ideal points (the X_{ik}) with the legislator variances and roll call parameters held fixed.

Step 3: Estimate the projected roll call midpoints (the c_j) with the normal vectors, signed distances, and legislator parameters held fixed.

Step 4: Estimate the normal vectors (the N_{jk}) with the projected midpoints, signed distances, and legislator parameters held fixed.

Go to step 1a.

I will discuss each step in turn.

Step 0 is very similar to that of DW-NOMINATE. Initial values for the legislator ideal points are produced from an eigenvalue–eigenvector decomposition of the double-centered matrix of transformed agreement scores. This produces the p by s matrix of legislator starting coordinates, $\tilde{\mathbf{X}}$, shown in equation (4.25).

This initial matrix is then used as the starting coordinates for OC. OC is then run to convergence to produce the starting values of the legislator coordinates, the normal vectors, and the projected roll call midpoints. This process produces excellent starting values for the parameters, because the geometry of QN is identical to that of OC.

In step 1 the signed distances and the legislator variances are estimated in two substeps. This estimation is possible because, as I noted above, for each choice, γ_j and σ_i enter as the *ratio* $2\gamma_j/\sigma_i$. Given this fact, a simple way to start the process is to set all the σ_i equal to 1 and estimate the γ_j's with a simple grid search. With all the other parameters held fixed, the maximum log-likelihood of each of the γ_j's is easily found. Given these γ_j's, the σ_i's are also estimated with a simple grid search. With all the other parameters held fixed, the maximum log-likelihood of each of the σ_i's is also easily found. This process continues until there is no meaningful improvement in the log-likelihood. In practice, this takes no more than three repetitions.

In step 2 new legislator ideal points, the $\mathbf{X}_i$'s, are estimated within the BHHH framework discussed above. Specifically, let θ_i be the s by 1 vector of parameters for the ith legislator, $\mathbf{g}_{ij}$ be the s by 1 vector of the first derivatives of L from equation (4.16) for the ith legislator on the jth roll call, and Ω_i be the s by s matrix that is the sum of the outer products of $\mathbf{g}_{ij}$; that is,

$$\Omega_i = \sum_{j=1}^{q} \mathbf{g}_{ij}\mathbf{g}_{ij}'.$$

The update (hill-climbing) formula for the parameters of the ith legislator is

$$\theta_{i(\text{new})} = \theta_{i(\text{old})} + \alpha\Omega_i^{-1}\mathbf{g}_{ij}.$$

If the legislator's ideal point wanders outside the unit hypersphere, it is constrained to lie on the rim. Again, as with DW-NOMINATE, this means that the log-likelihood is not necessarily at a maximum, but this is not a serious problem, because this type of legislator is almost always very ideologically rigid and has a very high log-likelihood.

In step 3 the projected roll call midpoints, the c_j, are estimated with all other parameters held fixed. They are easily estimated through a simple grid search, because they must lie on the normal vector line between -1 and $+1$.

In step 4 we estimate new normal vectors, the $\mathbf{N}_j$, using standard gradient techniques with the constraints that $\mathbf{N}_j'\mathbf{N}_j = 1$ and that $\mathbf{Z}_j = c_j\mathbf{N}_j$. In other words, the point defined by the end of the normal vector is moved along the surface of the unit hypersphere with the position of the projected midpoint held fixed on the normal vector as it is moved. Geometrically, this is equivalent to moving the cutting plane rigidly through the space as its normal vector is moved. All other parameters are held fixed. A variant of the BHHH method outlined above is used to find the new normal vectors. The unit length constraint for the normal vector is imposed at every step, so that the log-likelihood is computed on the surface of the unit hypersphere.

In one dimension, given a joint rank ordering of the legislators and roll call midpoints from the classification algorithm, step 4 is not necessary and the legislator coordinates in step 2 can be found through a simple grid search. In practice only three overall passes through steps 1 to 4 are required for the QN algorithm to converge.

An attractive feature of the QN model is that *if the ideal points were known*, the roll call parameters could be estimated by probit regression rather than steps 3 and 4. A probit specification is logically consistent with the assumptions of the ideal point estimator. For example, in a probit regression of a particular roll call vote on party and estimated ideal point, the null model in which only the ideal point mattered would be correctly specified. As I discussed in Chapter 2, however, given that probit becomes unreliable at very low levels of error, some safeguards have to be built in to catch perfect and near-perfect roll calls.[13]

The four steps above are repeated until the log-likelihood stops improving. At that point all sets of parameters are reproducing each other. Within each step the maximum of the likelihood function is found for the parameter being estimated, conditioned on all the remaining parameters being held fixed. The algorithm always moves uphill in a city-block-like fashion. At convergence, every parameter is at a maximum conditioned on all the remaining parameters being held fixed and conditioned on the unit hypersphere constraint.[14]

Statistical Issues

Two important statistical issues affect the parameters estimated by DW-NOMINATE and QN: standard errors, and the *incidental parameters* problem that may produce bias in the parameter estimates.

---

[13] As I have shown in Chapter 2 with the cutting plane procedure, the probit coefficients are the components of the normal vector to the plane that divides the choices. As the error goes to zero, these coefficients are identified up to a scalar constant and a slight "wiggle" depending on the number of observations [this problem is known as *complete separation* (Silvapulle, 1981; Albert and Anderson, 1984)]. Although in this instance it is not possible to do inference – there is no error, after all – that also implies that classical inference is technically inappropriate in that before you run the probit, you know you will have to throw away the results if you get perfect classification. Hence the tests *conditional on not getting perfect classification* may not be strictly kosher. I thank Howard Rosenthal for pointing this out to me.

[14] Technically, a slightly stronger statement is true; namely, every parameter is at a maximum conditioned on all the parameters *of the other sets* being held fixed. Each legislator is estimated independently of the remaining legislators, and each roll call is estimated independently of the other roll calls.

In classical maximum likelihood, the maximum of the log-likelihood L is found by taking its first derivatives with respect to all the parameters, setting them equal to zero, and then solving the set of equations for the parameter values. These become the maximum likelihood estimates. For the solution to be a maximum, the matrix of second derivatives must be negative definite. For example, suppose there are 100 legislators and 500 roll calls. QN would require the estimation of 2,300 parameters, so that the vector of parameters, θ, would be a 2,300 by 1 vector. In the BHHH framework, the vector of first derivatives, g_{ij}, for the ith legislator on the jth roll call would be also 2,300 by 1, and the matrix of the sum of the outer products would be

$$\Omega = \sum_{i=1}^{p} \sum_{j=1}^{q} g_{ij} g'_{ij}$$

so that Ω would be a 2,300 by 2,300 matrix. As I noted above, in normal circumstances at convergence, the matrix Ω will closely approximate the *negative* of the matrix of second derivatives (the Hessian matrix). Consequently, at convergence, Ω will be a positive definite matrix, and the variances of the estimated parameters are on the diagonal of the inverse of Ω.

Unfortunately, the presence of constraints and the sheer size of Ω make the classical approach to obtaining standard errors infeasible.

Even if the constraints were not present, the maximum likelihood approaches outlined above have no way of getting around the incidental parameters problem. Simply stated, parameters are estimated for the rows of the data (usually the legislators are the rows) and the columns of the data (usually the roll calls). Every time a roll call is added to the data matrix, $2s$ additional parameters in DW-NOMINATE and $s + 2$ additional parameters in QN must be estimated. If a legislator is added, then s additional parameters in DW-NOMINATE and $s + 1$ (if a legislator-specific variance is estimated) additional parameters in QN must be estimated. That is, as the data grows, so does the number of parameters. Consequently, the standard proof of the consistency of maximum likelihood does not apply (Neyman and Scott, 1948).

Haberman (1977) analyzed the simple version of the item response model developed by Rasch (1961) and was able to show consistency with some restrictive conditions. The simple item response model is mathematically equivalent to the basic spatial model if legislators have quadratic utility functions with additive random error (Ladha, 1991; Londregan, 2000a; Clinton, Jackman, and Rivers, 2004). Haberman (1977) shows that as both the number of legislators and the number of roll calls go to infinity with the restriction that $(\log q)/p$ must go to infinity as well, the simple Rasch model is consistent.

The most important recent work on consistency is by Londregan (2000a). He links the psychometrics testing literature with the spatial theory of legislative voting and derives important statistical results about the parameters of the spatial model. In particular, when the preferential choices are *nominal*, Londregan shows that consistency in its usual statistical sense does not hold. With nominal choices standard maximum likelihood estimators that attempt *simultaneously* to recover legislators' ideal points and roll call parameters inherit the "granularity" of the choice data and so cannot recapture the underlying continuous parameter space.[15] If legislators could report continuous feeling-thermometer scores instead of just Yea or Nay, this source of inconsistency would disappear.

Unfortunately, in the real world of data we are faced with finite sample sizes, so that there is no simple way of ensuring that our estimates of legislator ideal points and roll call parameters are unbiased and no simple way of solving for standard errors. Consequently, there is no substitute for Monte Carlo analysis in establishing the quality of the estimated parameters.

Howard Rosenthal and I performed a large number of simulation studies of our NOMINATE model and found that it performed very well (Poole and Rosenthal, 1991; 1997). Our approach was to create artificial data that met all the assumptions of the model and then test how accurate the method was in reproducing the true legislator ideal points and roll call parameters. We found that when the number of legislators was 50 or more with 100 or more roll calls, the recovery of the true parameters by NOMINATE was very good. We concluded that bias was not a serious problem with reasonable-size roll call matrices.

Obtaining standard errors was a harder problem. We decided to use Efron's (1979) nonparametric bootstrap procedure to obtain standard errors for the legislator ideal points. We sampled roll calls with replacement, holding the number of legislators fixed, and created 50 matrices.[16] We then ran NOMINATE on each of the 50 roll call matrices and computed standard errors for the legislators from the 50 sets of ideal points.

This technique produced nice-looking standard errors, but we were never completely satisfied with it, because it could be used to get the standard errors of only one set of parameters. You had to sample either the rows of the matrix or the columns of the matrix.

In the past few years two approaches have emerged that appear to have successfully solved the standard error problem. The first is based on *Markov chain Monte Carlo* (MCMC) simulation (Metropolis and Ulam, 1949; Hastings, 1970; Geman and Geman, 1984; Gelfand and Smith, 1990; Gelman, 1992) within a Bayesian framework (Gelman et al., 2000; Gill, 2002) and was introduced into political science by Simon Jackman (2000a; 2000b; 2001; Clinton, Jackman,

---

[15]The consistency issue has not been fully sorted out. It might be that the triple-asympotic conditions of Haberman (1977) can be relaxed. See Rivers (2004) for a discussion of identification and consistency issues in multidimensional spatial voting models.

[16]Computing resources were a bit more limited when we did this experiment in 1993 and 1994.

and Rivers, 2004) and Andrew Martin and Kevin Quinn (Schofield et al., 1998; Quinn, Martin, and Whitford, 1999; Martin and Quinn, 2002; Quinn and Martin, 2002; Martin, 2003; Quinn, 2004). I will discuss this innovative approach in the next section. The second is based on the parametric bootstrap (Efron, 1979; Efron and Tibshirani, 1993). Jeff Lewis conceived this approach, and it is discussed in depth by Lewis and Poole (2004). I will outline it after I discuss Bayesian simulation.

The Bayesian Simulation Approach

The basic idea behind Bayesian simulation is to illuminate a probability density function of the parameters – the posterior distribution – through a random tour of the parameter space. At each point of the random tour the value of the parameter is recorded so that when the tour is finished – typically hundreds of thousands or millions of points in the parameter space are visited – the shape of the distribution over the parameter space is known with some accuracy. At the end of the tour the means and standard errors of the parameters can be directly calculated from the tour record.

The random tour is generated using MCMC methods. As Shawn Trier and Simon Jackman (2003, p. 10) note, "the virtue of MCMC methods is that (subject to regularity conditions) they produce random tours that visit locations in the parameter space with frequency proportional to their posterior probability." With respect to estimation of spatial voting models, the advantage of this approach is that it produces estimates of the legislator ideal points and roll call parameters and all of the standard errors as well. In addition, it is possible to estimate and do inference about other quantities of interest, such as the median or any function of the model parameters (Jackman, 2000b). The disadvantage is that the MCMC approach can consume a very large amount of computer time because the bigger the roll call matrix, the larger the number of parameters, and the longer it takes to do a comprehensive random tour of the parameter space.

Technically, the Bayesian simulation approach works with a *posterior* probability distribution. The intuition behind this can be seen by looking at the simple formulas for conditional probability. Let θ and Y be two events; then in classical probability theory,

$$P(\theta \mid Y) = \frac{P(\theta \cap Y)}{P(Y)} \quad \text{and} \quad P(Y \mid \theta) = \frac{P(\theta \cap Y)}{P(\theta)};$$

hence

$$P(\theta \cap Y) = P(\theta \mid Y)P(Y) = P(Y \mid \theta)P(\theta)$$

and

$$P(\theta \mid Y) = \frac{P(Y \mid \theta)P(\theta)}{P(Y)}.$$

In the Bayesian framework, Y is the observed data, the θ are the parameters, $P(\theta \mid Y)$ is the joint distribution of the sample, $P(\theta)$ is the *prior distribution* of the parameters, $P(Y)$ is the marginal distribution of the sample, and $P(\theta \mid Y)$ is the *posterior distribution*. Because $P(Y)$ is a constant, the posterior distribution is proportional to the product of the joint distribution of the sample (which is proportional to the likelihood function) and the prior distribution; that is,

$$P(\theta \mid Y) \propto P(Y \mid \theta)P(\theta). \tag{4.28}$$

In the spirit of Bayes, the researcher specifies the prior distribution of the parameters; that is, $P(\theta)$. Typically the prior distribution is chosen so that when it and the joint distribution of the sample are multiplied, the general form of the posterior distribution is known. For example, if the joint distribution of the sample is normally distributed and the prior distribution is assumed to be a normal distribution, the posterior distribution will be a normal distribution.

If the parameters can be partitioned into k subsets, that is, $\theta_1, \theta_2, \ldots, \theta_k$, then the MCMC random tour through the parameter space is made much more tractable, because it can be "generated by successively sampling from the conditional distributions that together characterize the joint posterior density" (Trier and Jackman, 2003, p. 10). Technically, this is *alternating conditional sampling*, or the *Gibbs sampler* (Geman and Geman, 1984; Gelfand and Smith, 1990).[17] For example, at the hth iteration the MCMC sampling procedure is:

1. Sample $\theta_{1i}^{(h)}$ from $\mathbf{g}_{\theta_1}\left(\theta_{1i} \mid \theta_2^{(h-1)}, \theta_3^{(h-1)}, \ldots, \theta_k^{(h-1)}, \mathbf{Y}\right)$, $i = 1, \ldots, n_1$.

2. Sample $\theta_{2i}^{(h)}$ from $\mathbf{g}_{\theta_2}\left(\theta_{2i} \mid \theta_1^{(h-1)}, \theta_3^{(h-1)}, \ldots, \theta_k^{(h-1)}, \mathbf{Y}\right)$, $i = 1, \ldots, n_2$.

$$\vdots \tag{4.29}$$

k. Sample $\theta_{ki}^{(h)}$ from $\mathbf{g}_{\theta_k}\left(\theta_{ki} \mid \theta_1^{(h-1)}, \theta_2^{(h-1)}, \ldots, \theta_{k-1}^{(h-1)}, \mathbf{Y}\right)$, $i = 1, \ldots, n_k$,

where $\sum_{j=1}^{k} n_j$ is the total number of parameters.

When this framework is applied to roll call data, $\mathbf{Y}$ is the p by q matrix of choices and θ is the vector of legislator ideal points and roll call parameters. With quadratic utility, normally distributed error, and normally distributed prior distributions, the conditional distributions are also normally distributed. This Bayesian QN framework is equivalent to the standard two-parameter item response model widely used in educational testing (see Chapter 2).

Specifically, using equations (4.5) to (4.7), let

$$\alpha_j = \left(\sum_{k=1}^{s} O_{jkn}^2 - \sum_{k=1}^{s} O_{jky}^2\right) = 2\gamma_j \mathbf{Z}_j' \mathbf{N}_j$$

---

[17] See Hitchcock (2003) for a short history of MCMC simulation.

and

$$\beta_j = \begin{bmatrix} -2(O_{j1n} - O_{j1y}) \\ -2(O_{j2n} - O_{j2y}) \\ \vdots \\ -2(O_{jsn} - O_{jsy}) \end{bmatrix} = -2\gamma_j \mathbf{N}_j. \qquad (4.30)$$

This transformation allows the difference between the latent utilities for Yea and Nay to be written in the same form as the item response model; namely,

$$y_{ij}^* = U_{ijy} - U_{ijn} = \alpha_j + \mathbf{X}_i'\beta_j + \varepsilon_{ij} \qquad (4.31)$$

where y_{ij}^* is the difference between the latent utilities, and

$$\varepsilon_{ij} = \varepsilon_{ijn} - \varepsilon_{ijy} \sim N(0,1).$$

If the latent utility differences were observed, then the joint distribution of the sample would be

$$\mathbf{f}(\mathbf{Y}^* \mid \alpha, \beta, \mathbf{X}) = \prod_{i=1}^{p}\prod_{j=1}^{q} \frac{1}{\sqrt{2\pi}} \exp\left(-\frac{1}{2}(y_{ij}^* - \alpha_j - X_i'\beta_j)^2\right) \qquad (4.32)$$

where $\mathbf{Y}^*$ is the p by q matrix of latent utility differences, α is a q by 1 vector of the $2\gamma_j \mathbf{Z}_j' \mathbf{N}_j$ terms, β is a q by s matrix of the $-2\gamma_j \mathbf{N}_j$ terms, and $\mathbf{X}$ is the p by s matrix of legislator ideal points.

Unfortunately, the latent utility differences are not observed, and we do not have any simple expression for $\mathbf{f}(\mathbf{Y} \mid \alpha, \beta, \mathbf{X})$. However, $\mathbf{f}(\mathbf{Y} \mid \alpha, \beta, \mathbf{X})$ is proportional to the likelihood function $\mathbf{L}(\alpha, \beta, \mathbf{X} \mid \mathbf{Y})$ [equation (4.15)], and this fact allows the construction of the conditional distributions for the posterior distribution. Specifically, let

$$y_{ij} = \begin{cases} 1 \text{ (Yea)} & \text{if } y_{ij}^* > 0 \\ 0 \text{ (Nay)} & \text{if } y_{ij}^* \leq 0 \end{cases}$$

so that

$$P(y_{ij}^* > 0) = \Phi(\alpha_j + \mathbf{X}_i'\beta_j)$$
$$P(y_{ij}^* \leq 0) = 1 - \Phi(\alpha_j + \mathbf{X}_i'\beta_j).$$

If the y_{ij} are independent Bernoulli random variables, that is,

$$\mathbf{f}(y_{ij} \mid \alpha_j, \beta_j, \mathbf{X}_i) \sim \text{Bernoulli}(\Phi(\alpha_j + \mathbf{X}_i'\beta_j))$$

then

$$f(\mathbf{Y} \mid \boldsymbol{\alpha}, \boldsymbol{\beta}, \mathbf{X}) \propto \prod_{i=1}^{p} \prod_{j=1}^{q} f(y_{ij} \mid \alpha_j, \beta_j, \mathbf{X}_i) = L(\boldsymbol{\alpha}, \boldsymbol{\beta}, \mathbf{X} \mid \mathbf{Y})$$

$$= \prod_{i=1}^{p} \prod_{j=1}^{q} [\Phi(\alpha_j + \mathbf{X}_i'\boldsymbol{\beta}_j)]^{y_{ij}} [1 - \Phi(\alpha_j + \mathbf{X}_i'\boldsymbol{\beta}_j)]^{(1-y_{ij})}.$$

(4.33)

Note that the reason that the joint distribution of the sample is only *proportional* to the likelihood function is that $L(\boldsymbol{\alpha}, \boldsymbol{\beta}, \mathbf{X} \mid \mathbf{Y})$ in this case is not a proper probability distribution. That is, the multidimensional integral of $L(\boldsymbol{\alpha}, \boldsymbol{\beta}, \mathbf{X} \mid \mathbf{Y})$ is not equal to 1. If the value of that integral were known, then dividing the likelihood function by it would yield the joint distribution of the sample.

Let the prior distribution for the legislator ideal points be

$$\mathbf{X}_i \sim \mathbf{N}(\mathbf{0}, \mathbf{I}_s) = \xi(\mathbf{X}_i)$$

(4.34)

where $\mathbf{0}$ is an s-length vector of zeros and $\mathbf{I}_s$ is an s by s identity matrix. The prior distribution for the roll call outcome parameters is

$$\begin{bmatrix} \alpha_j \\ \beta_j \end{bmatrix} \sim N(\mathbf{b}_0, \mathbf{B}_0) = \xi(\alpha_j, \beta_j)$$

(4.35)

where $\mathbf{b}_0$ is an $(s + 1)$-length vector and $\mathbf{B}_0$ is an $s + 1$ by $s + 1$ variance–covariance matrix. Clinton, Jackman, and Rivers (2004) set $\mathbf{b}_0$ to a vector of zeros and $\mathbf{B}_0$ to $\eta \mathbf{I}_{s+1}$, where η is a large positive constant (typically 25).

With these assumptions, the posterior distribution for the Bayesian QN model is proportional to the product of the joint distribution of the sample and the prior distributions; namely,

$$\xi(\boldsymbol{\alpha}, \boldsymbol{\beta}, \mathbf{X} \mid \mathbf{Y}) \propto f(\mathbf{Y} \mid \boldsymbol{\alpha}, \boldsymbol{\beta}, \mathbf{X})\xi(\mathbf{X})\xi(\boldsymbol{\alpha}, \boldsymbol{\beta}) \propto L(\boldsymbol{\alpha}, \boldsymbol{\beta}, \mathbf{X} \mid \mathbf{Y})\xi(\mathbf{X})\xi(\boldsymbol{\alpha}, \boldsymbol{\beta}).$$

(4.36)

Because the latent utility differences are used in the sampling procedure, it is useful to rewrite the posterior distribution to reflect this:

$$\xi(\boldsymbol{\alpha}, \boldsymbol{\beta}, \mathbf{X} \mid \mathbf{Y}) = \int \xi(\mathbf{Y}^*, \boldsymbol{\alpha}, \boldsymbol{\beta}, \mathbf{X} \mid \mathbf{Y}) \, d\mathbf{Y}^*.$$

Martin and Quinn (2001, p. 12) note that "conditioning on the latent utility differences allows us to recast the item response model for a dichotomous response variable as a factor analysis model for a (latent) continuous response. The integration over $[\mathbf{Y}^*]$ is easily accomplished in the simulation. . . . " In other words, we can pretend that we have all the y_{ij}^*'s from equation (4.32) so that we do not have to use equation (4.33). The sampling is from the conditional distributions of the joint posterior distribution $\xi(\mathbf{Y}^*, \boldsymbol{\alpha}, \boldsymbol{\beta}, \mathbf{X} \mid \mathbf{Y})$ and the draws of the y_{ij}^* can be ignored (Albert and Chib, 1993). What this means is that the Markov chain of the roll call and legislator parameters (under certain regularity conditions) converges to the joint posterior distribution that we are interested in, namely, equation (4.36).[18]

The conditional distributions for $\xi(\mathbf{Y}^*, \alpha, \beta, \mathbf{X} \mid \mathbf{Y})$ that implement equation (4.36) are as follows:

(1) $g_{y_{ij}^*}\left(y_{ij}^* \mid \alpha_j, \beta_j, \mathbf{X}_i, y_{ij}\right) = \begin{cases} \mathbf{N}_{[0,\infty)}(\alpha_j + \mathbf{X}_i'\beta_j, 1) & \text{if } y_{ij} = \text{Yea} \\ \mathbf{N}_{(-\infty,0]}(\alpha_j + \mathbf{X}_i'\beta_j, 1) & \text{if } y_{ij} = \text{Nay} \\ \mathbf{N}_{(-\infty,\infty)}(\alpha_j + \mathbf{X}_i'\beta_j, 1) & \text{if } y_{ij} = \text{Missing} \end{cases}$

where the subscript on the normal distribution indicates the range. For Yea and Nay the normal is truncated as indicated and the missing data is sampled over the entire real line.

(2) $g_{\alpha,\beta}\left(\alpha_j, \beta_j \mid \mathbf{Y}_j^*, \mathbf{X}, \mathbf{Y}_j\right) = \mathbf{N}(\nu_j, \Xi_j)$

where $\mathbf{Y}_j^*$ and $\mathbf{Y}_j$ are the jth columns of $\mathbf{Y}^*$ and $\mathbf{Y}$, respectively, ν_j is an $(s+1)$-length vector of means, and Ξ_j is the $s+1$ by $s+1$ variance–covariance matrix. Specifically,

$$\nu_j = \Xi_j \left[\mathbf{X}^{*'}\mathbf{Y}_j^* + \mathbf{B}_0^{-1}\mathbf{b}_0\right]$$

and

$$\Xi_j = \left[\mathbf{X}^{*'}\mathbf{X}^* + \mathbf{B}_0^{-1}\right]^{-1}$$

where $\mathbf{X}^*$ is the p by $s+1$ matrix of legislator ideal points bordered by ones (that is, $\mathbf{X}^* = [\mathbf{J}_p \mid \mathbf{X}]$), and $\mathbf{J}_p$ is a p-length vector of ones.

(3) $g_X\left(\mathbf{X}_i \mid \alpha, \beta, \mathbf{Y}_i^*, \mathbf{Y}_i\right) = \mathbf{N}(\mathbf{t}_i, \mathbf{T}_i)$

where $\mathbf{Y}_i^*$ and $\mathbf{Y}_i$ are the ith rows of $\mathbf{Y}^*$ and $\mathbf{Y}$, respectively, $\mathbf{t}_i$ is an s-length vector of means, and $\mathbf{T}_i$ is the s by s variance–covariance matrix. Specifically,

$$\mathbf{t}_i = \mathbf{T}_i \left[\beta'(a - \mathbf{Y}_i^*)\right]$$

and

$$\mathbf{T}_i = \left[\beta'\beta + \mathbf{I}_s\right]^{-1}.$$

Note that if a more general prior distribution is used for the legislator ideal points, namely,

$$\mathbf{X}_i \sim N(\mathbf{t}_0, \mathbf{T}_0)$$

---

[18]Conditioning on the latent utilities makes other types of extensions to the model easy to implement. Ordinal (or even multinomial) responses, mixed variables, and so on, can be dealt with efficiently within this framework (Quinn, 2004).

where t_0 is an s-length vector of means and T_0 is an s by s variance–covariance matrix, then the expressions for t_i and T_i are

$$t_i = T_i \left[\beta'(\alpha - Y_i^*) + T_0^{-1} t_0 \right]$$

and

$$T_i = \left[\beta'\beta + T_0 \right]^{-1}.$$

At the hth iteration the MCMC sampling procedure outlined in the equation set (4.29) for these conditional distributions is:

(1) Sample $y_{ij}^{*(h)}$ from $g_{y_{ij}^*} \left(y_{ij}^* \mid \alpha_j^{(h-1)}, \beta_j^{(h-1)}, X_i^{(h-1)}, y_{ij} \right)$,

$i = 1, \ldots, p, j = 1, \ldots, q.$

(2) Sample $\alpha_j^{(h)}, \beta_j^{(h)}$ from $g_{\alpha, \beta} \left(\alpha_j, \beta_j \mid Y_j^{*(h-1)}, X^{(h-1)}, Y_j \right)$,

$j = 1, \ldots, q.$ (4.37)

(3) Sample $X_i^{(h)}$ from $g_X \left(X_i \mid \alpha^{(h-1)}, \beta^{(h-1)}, Y_i^{*(h-1)}, Y_i \right)$,

$i = 1, \ldots, p.$

Sampling from these conditional distributions is straightforward because they are all normal distributions with known means and variances. If the conditional distributions are nonstandard, then a sampling method such as the Metropolis–Hastings algorithm must be used (Metropolis and Ulam, 1949; Hastings, 1970; Gelman et al., 2000, Chapter 11; Gill, 2002, Chapter 9).

Let $\zeta^{(h)}$ denote all the parameters sampled during the hth iteration through the equation set (4.37), that is, $\zeta^{(h)} = \{\alpha^{(h)}, \beta^{(h)}, X^{(h)}\}$. The sequence $\zeta^{(1)}, \zeta^{(2)}, \zeta^{(3)}, \ldots$ is a Markov chain that converges to the posterior distribution $\xi(\alpha, \beta, X \mid Y)$ [equation (4.36)], given certain regularity conditions.[19] (Note that Y^* is not part of the chain.) Typically, tens of thousands of samples are drawn, and inferences – means, medians, and confidence intervals – are based on the final 100,000 or so samples.

This model (with suitable elaborations) has been applied to congressional voting by Clinton, Jackman, and Rivers (2004), to voting in the United Nations by Erik Voeten (2004), to voting in the Continental Congress by Joshua Clinton (2003), to voting in the Supreme Court by Andrew Martin and Kevin Quinn (2002), and to a comparison of voting in the Senate and the Supreme Court by Michael Bailey (2002), to cite just a few papers that have been generated by this approach in the past few years.[20]

---

[19] See Gelman et al. (2000, pp. 325–326) and Gill (2002, pp. 306–311) for a discussion of these conditions. For example, one condition is *irreducibility*. This condition requires that the random walk have a positive probability of jumping from any point to any other point in the distribution.

[20] Software to estimate the IRT model on roll call votes has been developed by Simon Jackman (IDEAL) and by Andrew Martin and Kevin Quinn (MCMCpack). On the website for this book,

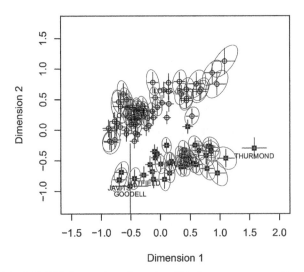

Dimension 1

FIGURE 4.4. *90th U.S. Senate from Bayesian QN. Squares represent Democrats, and circles represent Republicans. The vertical and horizontal lines through each senator's ideal point show the 95 percent confidence intervals for each coordinate of that senator's position. Confidence ellipses are shown for senators whose first-dimension and second-dimension coordinates have a correlation coefficient greater than 0.3 in absolute value.*

Figure 4.4 shows an example of Bayesian QN applied to the 90th U.S. Senate.[21] Squares represent Democrats, and circles represent Republicans. The vertical and horizontal lines through each senator's ideal point show the 95 percent confidence intervals for each coordinate of a given senator's position.[22] For most senators, the posterior correlation between the estimated first- and second-dimension estimates is very low. Normal-theory 95 percent confidence ellipses are shown for senators whose first-dimension and second-dimension coordinates have a correlation coefficient greater than 0.3 in absolute value.

On average the ideal points are precisely estimated. The average standard error on the first dimension is 0.05, and on the second dimension 0.07 (Lewis and Poole, 2004, p. 120). The senator with the largest standard errors around his ideal point is Charles Goodell (R-NY). He was appointed to the Senate in September 1968 to replace Robert F. Kennedy after his assassination that

---

http://k7moa.com/Spatial_Models_of_Parliamentary_Voting.htm, under the Chapter 4 link are links to their websites and examples of the output of both software packages.
[21] The output is from IDEAL (Clinton, Jackman, and Rivers, 2004; Lewis and Poole, 2004, p. 117, Figure 5).
[22] Technically these are ±1.96 times the posterior standard deviations centered at the posterior means.

June. Goodell only voted on 31 scalable roll calls (2.5 percent or more in the minority), so that his standard errors are huge.

The advantage of the Bayesian simulation approach is that it produces parameter estimates and their standard errors in one process. The disadvantage is that it is very computation-intensive. So far, all the applications have used the quadratic utility framework because it is straightforward to write out the conditional distributions in the equation system (4.37). It has not yet been applied to the normal distribution utility model. This is a difficult problem because the conditional distributions do not have a clear-cut form and would themselves have to be simulated.

The simulation approach can only improve over time. Its structure is ideally suited for massively parallel processing, and computers are only going to get faster and cheaper in the coming decades. Howard Rosenthal and I had to use a Cyber 205 vector supercomputer in the 1980s to run D-NOMINATE. Its much more flexible successor, DW-NOMINATE, outlined earlier in this chapter, will run on a personal computer.

The Parametric Bootstrap[23]

In the Bayesian MCMC framework the parameters of interest (the ideal point and roll call parameters) are treated as random variables. Subjective probability distributions are placed over the analyst's uncertainty about the unknown parameters. By Bayes' rule, when the likelihood function is multiplied by these prior distributions, the result is proportional to the posterior distribution of the parameters. The MCMC process approximates draws from the posterior distribution of the parameters. In contrast, the parametric bootstrap takes the classical statistical approach. The parameters are treated as fixed constants to be estimated, and consequently, they are not given probability distributions. Rather, the underlying probability model, with its parameters set equal to the maximum likelihood estimates, is used to generate repeated simulated samples. For each of these repeated samples, the model is refitted, and the empirical distribution of these estimates across the pseudosamples is used to estimate the relevant sampling distributions.

The parametric bootstrap is conceptually simple. In a maximum likelihood framework, the first step is to compute the likelihood function of the sample. The second step is to draw, for example, 1,000 samples from the likelihood density and compute for each sample the maximum likelihood estimates of the parameters of interest. The sample variances computed from these 1,000 values are the estimators of the variances of the parameters (Efron and Tibshirani, 1993, Chapter 6). The parametric bootstrap assumes that the model has been

---

[23] This section draws heavily on the discussion in Lewis and Poole (2004, pp. 109–110).

correctly specified, so that its assumptions are stronger than the nonparametric bootstrap.

When applied to a scaling method such as NOMINATE or QN, the first step is to run the program to convergence and then calculate the probabilities for the observed choices. This produces a legislator by roll call matrix containing the estimated probabilities for the corresponding actual roll call choices of the legislators. Note that the product of these probabilities is the likelihood; that is,

$$L(\hat{\theta} \mid \mathbf{Y}) = \prod_{i=1}^{p} \prod_{j=1}^{q} \prod_{t=1}^{2} \hat{P}_{ij\hat{t}}^{C_{ijt}}$$

where $\hat{\theta}$ is the set of all the estimated ideal point, roll call, and utility function parameters, τ is the index for Yea and Nay, $\hat{P}_{ijc}$ is the estimated probability of voting for choice τ as given by equation (4.10) or (4.13), and $C_{ij\tau} = 1$ if the legislator's actual choice is τ, and 0 otherwise.

To draw a random sample, treat each estimated probability as a weighted coin and flip the coin. Draw a number from a uniform distribution over zero to one – $U(0,1)$. If the estimated probability is greater than or equal to the random draw, the sampled value is the observed choice. If the random draw is greater than the estimated probability, then the sampled value is the opposite of the observed choice; that is, if the observed choice is Yea, then the sampled value is Nay. Note that this is equivalent to drawing a random sample of size one from pq separate Bernoulli distributions with parameters $\hat{P}_{ijc}$. In the context of a Bernoulli distribution the two outcomes are "success" and "failure." Here a "success" is the observed choice and a "failure" is the opposite choice.

The sample roll call matrix is then analyzed by NOMINATE or QN. Repeat this process 1,000 times, and calculate the variances of the legislator ideal points using the 1,000 estimated bootstrap configurations.

Technically, let π be a random draw from $U(0,1)$. The sample rule is as follows: If the observed choice is Yea (Nay), then

$$\text{if } \pi \leq \hat{P}_{ijc}, \text{ then the sample value } \hat{C}_{ij} \text{ is Yea (Nay);} \qquad (4.39)$$
$$\text{if } \pi > \hat{P}_{ijc}, \text{ then the sample value } \hat{C}_{ij} \text{ is Nay (Yea).}$$

This technique allows the underlying uncertainty to propagate through to all the estimated parameters. To see this, note that as $\hat{P}_{ijc} \rightarrow 1$, we have $\hat{C}_{ij} \rightarrow C_{ij}$, that is, sample choices become the observed choices, so that the bootstrapped variances for the parameters of the model go to zero. If the fit of the model is poor, for example, if the $\hat{P}_{ijc}$ are between .5 and .7, then the bootstrapped variances for the parameters will be large.

Let $\hat{\mathbf{X}}$ be the p by s matrix of legislator coordinates estimated by either W-NOMINATE or QN. Let $h = 1, \ldots, m$ be the number of bootstrap trials, and let $\mathbf{X}_h$ be the p by s matrix of legislator coordinates estimated on the hth bootstrap trial. The legislator and roll call coordinates are only identified up to an arbitrary rotation in the s-dimensional space. This arbitrary rotation must be removed to ensure that the bootstrapping process produces accurate estimates of the standard deviations of the parameters. In particular, let

$$\hat{\mathbf{X}} = \mathbf{X}_h \mathbf{V} + \mathbf{E}. \tag{4.40}$$

Here $\mathbf{V}$ is an s by s matrix such that $\mathbf{V}'\mathbf{V} = \mathbf{V}\mathbf{V}' = \mathbf{I}_s$, where $\mathbf{I}_s$ is an s by s identity matrix; and $\mathbf{E}$ is a p by s matrix of errors. In psychometrics, equation (4.40) is known as the *orthogonal Procrustes problem*. Schonemann's (1966) solution is used to remove the arbitrary rotation $\mathbf{V}$. Note that $\mathbf{X}_h$ is being *rigidly rotated*, so that the estimated points are not being altered vis-à-vis one another in any way. Consequently, in the formulas for the mean and standard deviation below I use $\mathbf{X}_h$ to denote the hth bootstrap trial, to reduce notational clutter.

The mean legislator ideal point on the kth dimension is

$$\bar{X}_{ik} = \frac{\sum_{h=1}^{m} X_{hik}}{m} \tag{4.41}$$

where X_{hik} is the estimated coordinate on the hth trial. The corresponding standard deviation is

$$s\{X_{ik}\} = \sqrt{\frac{\sum_{h=1}^{m} (X_{hik} - \hat{X}_{ik})^2}{m-1}} \tag{4.42}$$

where $\hat{X}_{ik}$ is the coordinate estimated by W-NOMINATE or QN.

Jeff Lewis and I (Lewis and Poole, 2004) take a conservative approach and use the estimated coordinate, $\hat{X}_{ik}$, rather than the mean of the bootstrap trials, $\bar{X}_{ik}$, as the "sample mean" in our calculation of the standard deviation. This inflates the standard deviations somewhat, but we feel it is better to err on the safe side and not underreport them.

This technique is superior to the nonparametric bootstrap approach that Howard Rosenthal and I used. The parametric bootstrap allows the uncertainty to be reflected in *all of the choices* and therefore to pass through to the estimates of *all of the parameters*. In addition, it is simple computationally. It consists simply of adding a step at the end of the program to save the probabilities of all the choices and then looping through the scaling program m additional times.

Figure 4.5 shows an example of the parametric bootstrap of QN applied to the 90th U.S. Senate. Squares represent Democrats, and circles represent Republicans. The vertical and horizontal lines through each senator's ideal point show the 95 percent confidence intervals for each coordinate of a given senator's position. For most senators, the correlation between the estimated first- and second-dimension estimates is very low. Normal-theory 95 percent confidence ellipses are shown for senators whose first-dimension and

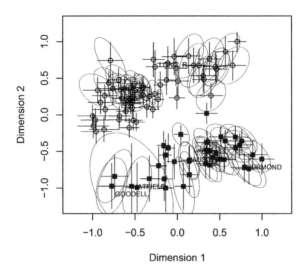

FIGURE 4.5. *90th U.S. Senate from bootstrapped QN. Squares represent Democrats, and circles represent Republicans. The vertical and horizontal lines through each senator's ideal point show the 95 percent confidence intervals for each coordinate of that senator's position. Confidence ellipses are shown for senators whose first-dimension and second-dimension coordinates have a correlation coefficient greater than 0.3 in absolute value.*

second-dimension coordinates have a correlation coefficient greater than 0.3 in absolute value.

The QN ideal points are precisely estimated. The average standard error on the first dimension is 0.05, and on the second dimension 0.08 (Lewis and Poole, 2004, p. 120). The senator with the largest standard errors around his ideal point is Charles Goodell (R-NY). The Pearson correlation between the first-dimension coordinates from QN and those from Bayesian QN (Figure 4.4) is 0.99, and the corresponding second-dimension correlation is 0.97 (Lewis and Poole, 2004, p. 117). The two methods produce essentially the same ideal points.

Conclusion

In this chapter I have outlined the major probabilistic models of legislative voting. Estimation of these models is complicated, and the statistical issues are especially thorny and not fully resolved. Nevertheless, considerable progress has been made in dealing with the two major statistical issues – incidental parameters and standard errors – and it is quite likely that there will be further progress in the near future. The good news is that the major probabilistic methods (Bayesian and non-Bayesian) produce essentially the same spatial maps for large legislatures (Lewis and Poole, 2004). This is important from a scientific standpoint, because it means that the basic theoretical model of choice shared by all the estimation methods produces meaningful results.

The importance that I place on the basic theoretical model of choice (see Chapter 7) is the reason that I am agnostic when it comes to the frequentist versus Bayesian debate.[24] I taught statistics to MBA students for nearly 20 years, and I was invariably asked "How can I *use* this in business?" My answer was always that they should regard these methods as tools. Tools are a means to an end. You must understand how to use the tool and what its limitations are. Sometimes, indeed many times, more than one tool can do the job.

This is how I regard the methods I outlined in this chapter. If roll call voting in a legislature is highly structured, then different methods should produce very similar spatial maps. Now that two methods of obtaining good standard errors are available – MCMC simulation and the parametric bootstrap – both should be used as checks on each other. The aim is to build a science of choice. The methods are a means to this end.

In Chapter 5 I turn to practical issues of estimation of spatial models – how to generate good starting values, how to determine dimensionality, how to interpret the dimensions, and so on, along with some computing tricks I have used over the years that those eager readers who want to "roll their own" might find useful.

---

[24] Jeff Gill (2002) has a comprehensive discussion of the history of this controversy in his excellent textbook on Bayesian methods for social scientists.

CHAPTER 5

Practical Issues in Computing Spatial Models of Parliamentary Voting

Overview

A number of practical issues arise in the real-world estimation of spatial models. This chapter is unavoidably idiosyncratic, because it reflects my experience as a *builder* of computer programs that estimate spatial maps of legislative voting. There is usually more than one way to build a mousetrap, and the practical solutions I offer for problems that arise in estimating spatial models are not necessarily unique nor my exclusive creation. They have one thing going for them, however: They all work. They are the result of 30 years of experimentation in computer code. I have often found that theoretically elegant ways of doing certain tasks – for example, generating starting coordinates when there are missing data – did not work as well as simple "hacks." Consequently, what I discuss below is the chewing gum and baling wire that lie underneath the hood of OC, QN, and NOMINATE.

Unlike the previous chapters, this chapter does not proceed in a nice linear fashion. I have grouped the topics so that similar ones are discussed together. The first section covers standardized measures of fit. I have dealt with this topic tangentially in Chapters 3 and 4 – OC maximizes correct classification, and probabilistic models maximize log-likelihood – but a short discussion is necessary for the remaining topics in the chapter and for the roll call experiments discussed in Chapter 6. The second topic is concerned with how to get reasonable starting values for the legislator ideal points. I have discussed this before in Chapters 2, 3, and 4, but I now turn to the practicalities. For example, how do you deal with the problem of pairs of legislators who do not overlap, so that no agreement score can be computed? This topic naturally flows into the question of how many dimensions you should estimate and what techniques can be used to determine what the dimensions represent. The problem of constraints was discussed a bit in Chapter 4 in terms of what happens to probabilistic models when the error level gets very low; I deal with the issue in more detail in this chapter. I conclude with some advice on designing computer programs to estimate spatial models.

Standardized Measures of Fit

By a *standardized measure of fit* I mean a measure that can be compared across scalings of different legislatures and between different numbers of dimensions for the same legislature. The *percentage of correctly classified choices* is an example of such a measure of fit. This percentage is a useful statistic, but it has some shortcomings. Specifically, it is sensitive to the distribution of margins of the roll calls. For example, suppose the average majority margin in the legislature is 90 percent – that is, on the average roll call 90 percent of the legislators vote Yea (Nay) and 10 percent vote Nay (Yea). Arranging the legislators randomly along a line with all the cutting points at either end of the dimension is guaranteed to achieve a correct classification of 90 percent. But this configuration conveys no information whatsoever about the legislature. Against this standard, a scaling method that estimates a configuration of legislators that correctly classifies 91 percent of the choices is not very impressive.

The *aggregate proportional reduction in error* (APRE) is a statistic that takes into account the distribution of roll call margins. With respect to the example above, a simple *majority voting model* that predicts that every legislator votes with the majority will correctly classify 90 percent of the choices (Weisberg, 1978; Poole and Rosenthal, 1987). Because a *random* spatial map of legislators with the cutting points/lines at the edges of the configuration also correctly classifies 90 percent of the choices, *nonrandom theory-driven* placement can add only 10 percent to the baseline. Hence, finding a configuration that correctly classifies 91 percent really means that the theory-driven configuration is accounting for only 1/10 of the *unexplained* classification. That is, it is reducing the error by only 10 percent.

The aggregate proportional reduction in error is defined as

$$\text{APRE} = \frac{\sum_{j=1}^{q}\{\text{minority vote } - \text{ classification errors}\}_j}{\sum_{j=1}^{q}\{\text{minority vote}\}_j}. \tag{5.1}$$

APRE varies from zero to one. When APRE is equal to zero, the model is explaining nothing. When APRE is equal to one, perfect classification has been achieved. APRE should always be reported along with the simple correct classification percentage for any estimated spatial map.

Note that in an ideal parliamentary two-party system where every member of each party always votes with the party leadership, the APRE will be equal to one, but the spatial map will be meaningless because only two points are required to account for all the ideal points. In this instance a simple *two-party model* (Weisberg, 1978) in which every member is predicted to vote with the majority of her party will achieve perfect classification and an APRE of one. More generally, if the parliament has three or more perfectly cohesive parties, a simple spatial model of three or more points will also perfectly classify the voting behavior, because the parties are behaving, in effect, as individuals. In this case the spatial map will convey more information than the "vote with the majority of her party" model, because of the spatial arrangement of the party points (Weisberg, 1978; 1983; Hammond and Fraser, 1983; Poole and Rosenthal, 1987). As a practical matter, however, even with highly cohesive political parties there are usually enough free or unwhipped votes so that the parties are rarely single points.

With respect to probabilistic spatial models, the standard approach is to find a legislator configuration and roll call parameters that maximize the log-likelihood function. Recall from Chapter 4 that this is

$$L = \sum_{i=1}^{p} \sum_{j=1}^{q} \sum_{t=1}^{2} C_{ijt} \ln P_{ijt}$$

where τ is the index for Yea and Nay, $P_{ij\tau}$ is the probability of voting for choice τ, and $C_{ij\tau} = 1$ if the legislator's actual choice is τ, and 0 otherwise. The magnitude of the log-likelihood will vary with the number of legislators and roll calls. A simple standardized statistic that is comparable between legislatures is the *geometric mean probability*. It is computed by taking the exponential of the average log-likelihood. If there are no missing choices, this formula is simply

$$\text{GMP} = e^{L/pq}. \tag{5.2}$$

The GMP will lie between .5 and 1. If the GMP is near .5, then the model is doing little better than a simple flipping of fair coins. The closer it is to 1, the better the fit of the model. The GMP should always be reported along with the log-likelihood, correct classification, and APRE.

How to Get Reasonable Starting Values for the Legislator Ideal Points

Half the battle in estimating nonlinear models is in the starting values for the parameters. A set of good starting values speeds up the estimation and ensures that you do not end up on a bad local maximum or minimum. In legislative roll call analysis, if you have good starting estimates for either the legislators or the roll calls, you can get the starting estimates for the other set. Unless a Coombs mesh drops into your lap from out of the blue, in my experience the best way to proceed is to generate starting values for the legislator ideal points.

Table 5.1. *Agreement Scores for the First Ten Members of the 90th U.S. Senate*

Johnson	1.000								
Sparkman (D-AL)	0.611	1.000							
Hill (D-AL)	0.510	0.899	1.000						
Gruening (D-AK)	0.524	0.510	0.530	1.000					
Bartlett (D-AK)	0.651	0.650	0.628	0.762	1.000				
Hayden (D-AZ)	0.700	0.850	0.786	0.583	0.704	1.000			
Fannin (R-AZ)	0.371	0.656	0.698	0.435	0.477	0.574	1.000		
Fulbright (D-AR)	0.450	0.703	0.707	0.687	0.694	0.693	0.584	1.000	
McClellan (D-AR)	0.426	0.789	0.809	0.490	0.563	0.686	0.785	0.673	1.000
Kuchel (R-CA)	0.722	0.640	0.568	0.544	0.637	0.635	0.622	0.528	0.570	1.000

The best method I have found to get good starting values for the legislators is to (1) compute the legislator-by-legislator matrix of agreement scores, (2) transform the agreement score matrix into squared distances, (3) double-center the matrix of squared distances, and (4) perform an eigenvalue–eigenvector decomposition of the double-centered matrix. I will discuss each step in turn.

The agreement score between legislator i and legislator m is simply the number of times they voted the same way divided by the total number of times they both voted. This produces a proportion that ranges from zero to one. Technically, let

$$C_{imj} = \begin{cases} 1 & \text{if both vote Yea or both vote Nay on roll call } j \\ 0 & \text{otherwise} \end{cases}$$

and

$$\Delta_{imj} = \begin{cases} 1 & \text{if both vote on roll call } j \\ 0 & \text{otherwise.} \end{cases}$$

Therefore the agreement score is

$$A_{im} = \frac{\sum_{j=1}^{q} C_{imj}}{\sum_{j=1}^{q} \Delta_{imj}}. \tag{5.3}$$

Table 5.1 shows the agreement scores for the first ten members of the 90th U.S. Senate. President Lyndon Johnson is included because *Congressional Quarterly* publishes a list of "presidential support" roll calls indicating whether a Yea or a Nay was a vote in support of the President's position. President Johnson can be treated as a member of the Senate because if he had been able to vote he would have voted Yea or Nay on those roll calls where he had indicated an official White House position.

In the 90th Senate there were 596 roll calls, and *CQ* reported presidential support positions for 327 roll calls. This means that President Johnson did not "vote" on 269 roll calls. Consequently, the denominator of the agreement score formula, $\sum_{j=1}^{q} D_{imj}$, can be at most 327, and the numerator, $\sum_{j=1}^{q} C_{imj}$, by definition, is less than or equal to 327. In fact, it will be less than 327 when the unanimous and near-unanimous votes are discarded. For example, using a cutoff criterion of 2.5 percent or better in the minority – that is, roll calls that are 97–3 to 50–50 in margins – results in 77 roll calls being discarded, leaving a total of 519 in the analysis. Using these roll calls, we see that the agreement score between President Johnson and Senator John Sparkman (D-AL) was .611. They both voted on 257 roll calls. On 64 roll calls they both voted Yea, and on 93 roll calls they both voted Nay; hence the agreement score is $(64 + 93)/257$, or .611.

When members do not overlap, no agreement score can be computed. For example, Charles Goodell (R-NY) was appointed to the Senate on 10 September 1968 to replace Robert F. Kennedy (D-NY) after his assassination that June. There can be no agreement score for Goodell and Kennedy. President Johnson overlapped both senators, voting with Kennedy 196 times for an agreement score of $(75 + 65)/196$, or .714, and voting with Goodell 17 times for an agreement score of $(8 + 7)/17$, or .882.

The agreement scores can be transformed into squared distances by simply applying the transformation

$$d_{im}^2 = (1 - A_{im})^2. \tag{5.4}$$

What should the squared distance be for the missing agreement scores? There is no pat answer. Indeed, there are a plethora of possible solutions. One is to use some existing methods of estimating missing data (King et al., 2001; Gleason and Staelin, 1975). The missing values can be imputed from other members' agreement scores who overlapped the missing pair. President Johnson's agreement scores with Kennedy and Goodell are an example. By looking at the pattern of *all* the other legislators who overlapped *both* members in the missing pair, it is relatively straightforward to make a good guess about the missing value.

Although this method of imputing agreement scores is nice in theory, I found that in practice it was easier simply to put the square of the median distance into the missing entries. For example, the distances range from zero to one. Therefore the median distance is .5, and its square is .25. I simply insert .25 into the squared distance matrix whenever there is a missing value. Although inelegant, this approach is computationally fast, and as long as there are not a lot of missing entries, it really has no effect on the starting values. Note that this is equivalent to assuming that the agreement score is .5. This is the approach I use in OC, QN, and W-NOMINATE.

Let **D** be the p by p matrix of squared distances. **D** is double-centered as follows: from each element subtract the row mean, subtract the column mean, add the matrix mean, and divide by -2. Specifically,

$$d^2_{.m} = \frac{\sum_{i=1}^{p} d^2_{im}}{p} \text{ is the mean of the } m\text{th column of } \mathbf{D}$$

$$d^2_{i.} = \frac{\sum_{m=1}^{p} d^2_{im}}{p} \text{ is the mean of the } i\text{th row of } \mathbf{D}$$

$$d^2_{..} = \frac{\sum_{i=1}^{p} \sum_{m=1}^{p} d^2_{im}}{p^2} \text{ is the matrix mean of } \mathbf{D}.$$

Let $\mathbf{Y}$ be the p by p double centered matrix. The elements of $\mathbf{Y}$ are

$$y_{im} = \frac{d^2_{im} - d^2_{.m} - d^2_{i.} + d^2_{..}}{-2}. \tag{5.5}$$

In the Appendix to Chapter 2 I show that if voting is perfect and in one dimension, then

$$\mathbf{Y} = \mathbf{X}\mathbf{X}'$$

where $\mathbf{X}$ is a p by 1 vector of legislator coordinates such that their rank ordering exactly reproduces the roll call matrix. Even with perfect voting, in more than one dimension it is not necessarily true that $\mathbf{Y}$ is equal to $\mathbf{X}\mathbf{X}'$ (where $\mathbf{X}$ is now the p by s matrix of legislator coordinates), because the *true distances* are not necessarily monotone in the number of cutting lines between pairs of legislators (see Figure 2.10). Furthermore, not every member of a pair will vote on every roll call with a cutting line between them, further compromising the agreement score. Nevertheless, rather than throwing the baby out with the bath water, a sensible way to proceed is to assume that

$$\mathbf{Y} = \mathbf{X}\mathbf{X}' + \mathbf{E}$$

where $\mathbf{E}$ is a p by p matrix of error terms.

This method is again inelegant, but excellent starting values for the legislators can now be gotten from the eigenvalue–eigenvector decomposition of $\mathbf{Y}$; namely,

$$\mathbf{Y} = \mathbf{U}\mathbf{\Lambda}\mathbf{U}'.$$

$\mathbf{U}$ is a p by p matrix of eigenvectors such that $\mathbf{U}'\mathbf{U} = \mathbf{U}\mathbf{U}' = \mathbf{I}_p$, where $\mathbf{I}_p$ is a p by p identity matrix, and $\mathbf{\Lambda}$ is a p by p diagonal matrix containing the eigenvalues in descending order on the diagonal. At least one of these eigenvalues must be zero, because $\mathbf{Y}$ cannot be of rank p, because both the rows and the columns sum to zero.

One method of obtaining starting estimates of the legislator ideal points is

$$\tilde{\mathbf{X}} = \mathbf{U}\mathbf{\Lambda}_s^{1/2} \tag{5.6}$$

where $\mathbf{\Lambda}_s^{1/2}$ contains the square roots of the first s (largest) eigenvalues on the diagonal, and the remaining $p - s$ diagonal terms are set equal to zero. This simple method of scaling was developed by Torgerson (1952).

Equation (5.6) is a *heuristic* formula, but a weak theoretical justification can be made for the Torgerson approach. It requires a digression, but it will make it easier for me to explain the ins and outs of determining dimensionality in the next section, so the side trip is worthwhile. To begin, note that Λ can be written as the sum $\Lambda_s + \Lambda_{p-s}$, where Λ_s is as defined previously, and where Λ_{p-s} contains zeros on the first s diagonal elements and the remaining $p - s$ eigenvalues are in the remaining $p - s$ diagonal entries. Some of the eigenvalues in Λ_{p-s} are going to be *negative*, because $\mathbf{Y}$ is almost certainly not going to be a positive semidefinite matrix.[1] Therefore $\mathbf{Y}$ can be written as

$$\mathbf{Y} = \mathbf{U}[\Lambda_s + \Lambda_{p-s}]\mathbf{U}' = \tilde{\mathbf{X}}\tilde{\mathbf{X}}' + \mathbf{U}\Lambda_{p-s}\mathbf{U}'$$

so that the residual or error matrix is

$$\mathbf{E} = \mathbf{Y} - \tilde{\mathbf{X}}\tilde{\mathbf{X}}' = \mathbf{U}\Lambda_{p-s}\mathbf{U}'. \tag{5.7}$$

Equation (5.6) can be justified through the use of the Eckart–Young (1936) theorem (see Chapter 3 Appendix), but I need to switch to singular value decomposition rather than eigenvalue–eigenvector decomposition. This change will allow me to recast the expression for $\mathbf{E}$ in equation (5.7) in a form that is consistent with the theorem.

Specifically, let the SVD of $\mathbf{Y}$ be

$$\mathbf{Y} = \mathbf{W}\Omega\mathbf{V}'$$

where $\mathbf{W}$ and $\mathbf{V}$ are p by p orthogonal matrices such that $\mathbf{W}'\mathbf{W} = \mathbf{W}\mathbf{W}' = \mathbf{V}'\mathbf{V} = \mathbf{V}\mathbf{V}' = \mathbf{I}_p$, and Ω is a p by p diagonal matrix with the singular values in descending order on the diagonal. The singular values on the diagonal of Ω are the absolute values of the eigenvalues on the diagonal of Λ. Indeed, if the voting space is s-dimensional, then the first s singular values are almost certainly going to be the same as the first s eigenvalues. After the first s eigenvalues, their magnitude drops off sharply.

Table 5.2 shows the eigenvalues and singular values of the double-centered matrix for the 90th U.S. Senate.[2] The first four entries on the diagonals of Λ and Ω are the same, but the fifth value is different, because -0.4875 is the *smallest* eigenvalue but its absolute value is fifth in magnitude. The next smallest eigenvalue is -0.2631, and its absolute value is seventh in magnitude. Consequently, the pth diagonal entry in Λ is the fifth diagonal entry in Ω, and the $p - 1$st entry in Λ is the seventh entry in Ω. Put simply, the order of the

---

[1] Technically, a positive semidefinite matrix $\mathbf{A}$ is a symmetric n by n matrix that can be written as $\mathbf{U}\Lambda\mathbf{U}'$ where all the eigenvalues are greater than or equal to zero; that is, $\lambda_i \geq 0$ for all i.

[2] Only roll calls with at least 2.5 percent in the minority are included in the computations. If all 100 senators are present and voting, roll calls with 97–3 to 50–50 margins are included.

Table 5.2. *Eigenvalues and Singular Values of the*
Double-Centered Agreement Score Matrix for the
90th U.S. Senate

	Eigenvalues	Singular Values
1	4.4382	4.4382
2	1.4493	1.4493
3	0.7678	0.7678
4	0.5063	0.5063
5	0.3198	0.4875
6	0.2269	0.3198
7	0.2015	0.2631
8	0.1711	0.2269
9	0.1572	0.2015
10	0.1529	0.1711

singular values in Ω is *shuffled* vis-à-vis Λ. This shuffling is reflected in the orthogonal matrices W vis-à-vis U. Thus W is exactly the same as U except that the columns of U have been shuffled to form W. The columns of V are also shuffled exactly the same as those of W. There is a further difference between W and V, however; namely, the shuffled columns in V that correspond to the negative eigenvalues have been multiplied by -1. In sum, U, W, and V all have the same p columns, only with some shuffling and multiplications by -1.

Returning to equation (5.7), let $\tilde{Y} = \tilde{X}\tilde{X}'$. Then it is almost certain that

$$\tilde{Y} = U\Lambda_s U' = W\Omega_s V' = W\Omega_s W' = V\Omega_s V'$$

and Y can be written as

$$Y = \tilde{Y} + E = \tilde{Y} + W\Omega_{p-s}V' \tag{5.8}$$

where Ω_{p-s} contains zeros on the first s diagonal elements, and the remaining $p - s$ singular values are in the remaining $p - s$ diagonal entries. Therefore, by construction, according to the Eckart–Young (1936) theorem (see Chapter 3 Appendix), $\tilde{Y}$ is the best least squares approximation of rank s to the matrix Y. Because $\tilde{Y}$ is positive semidefinite, $\tilde{X}$ is unique up to a simple rotation.

The argument above is a weak theoretical justification for the Torgerson approach, because it makes the leap of faith that the first s eigenvalues are not only *positive* but also the largest in absolute value, *and they do not contain any of the error*. Specifically, suppose that the matrix of residuals has the same orthogonal matrices – W and V – as Y. Then, in general,

$$Y = XX' + E = W[\Omega_1 + \Omega_2]V' = W\Omega_1 V' + W\Omega_2 V'$$

where Ω_1 has positive entries on the first s diagonal elements and zeros in the remaining $p - s$ diagonal elements, and Ω_2 has positive entries on all but one diagonal, with one of the elements after the first s entries being zero. This ensures that $\mathbf{Y}$ has rank $p - 1$. Simply put, even if $\mathbf{E}$ has the same orthogonal matrices as $\mathbf{Y}$ – and that is a big "if" – using equation (5.6) for the starts means that it is almost certain that the dimensions are weighted incorrectly. That is, the diagonal elements in Ω_s are almost certainly larger than the diagonal elements in Ω_1.

Given the impossibility of knowing the correct values for the diagonal of Ω_1, I have found that simply using the first s eigenvectors of $\mathbf{Y}$ works very well; specifically, I use the starting values

$$\tilde{\mathbf{X}} = \eta \mathbf{U}_s \qquad (5.9)$$

where $\mathbf{U}_s$ is a p by s matrix consisting of the first s eigenvectors, and η is a positive constant that is an *inflation factor* that scales the starting coordinates so that the legislator who is furthest from the origin lies on the rim of the unit hypersphere. This simple modification of Torgerson's approach works very well. I will refer to these as the *Torgerson coordinates* from now on.

Figure 5.1 shows a plot of the Torgerson coordinates for the 90th U.S. Senate. The S tokens are Southern Democrats,[3] the D tokens are Northern Democrats, and the R tokens are Republicans. The three political parties are quite distinct in the plot. The Southern Democrats are on the conservative side of the first dimension and near the top, or conservative, end of the second dimension. This Senate occurred during the three-political-party period that lasted roughly from 1937 into the 1980s. Voting in Congress was strongly two-dimensional during this period. The second dimension was produced by the split in the Democratic Party between Northerners and Southerners over civil rights. With the passage of the civil rights laws in 1964, 1965, and 1967, this split gradually disappeared, and it was gone by the 1990s (McCarty, Poole, and Rosenthal, 1997; Poole and Rosenthal, 1997; 2001).

The Republicans in the lower left part of the map are senators such as Hatfield (R-OR), Brooke (R-MA), Goodell (R-NY), and Javits (R-NY): liberal Republicans who all but disappeared from the Republican Party by the mid-1990s. The D token down in the midst of the Republicans at roughly $(.4, -.5)$ is Lausche (D-OH). The R up near the Southern Democrats is Young (R-ND). President Johnson (LBJ) is located at roughly $(-.5, -.3)$.

The Torgerson coordinates can be used to obtain starting values for the normal vectors – the $\hat{\mathbf{N}}_j$'s – by running a simple linear regression or a two-group discriminate analysis. These can be used as starts for the cutting plane procedure described in Chapter 3. As a practical matter, however, the cutting plane procedure is insensitive to starting values – it will go into nearly the same solution regardless of the starting values for the $\hat{\mathbf{N}}_j$, especially when the number of legislators is greater than 50.

---

[3] I use the *Congressional Quarterly* definition of the South – the eleven states of the Confederacy plus Kentucky and Oklahoma.

90th U.S. Senate Torgerson Coordinates

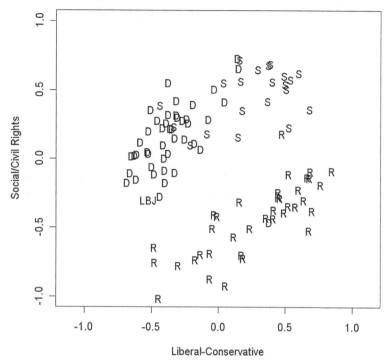

FIGURE 5.1. *90th U.S. Senate Torgerson coordinates. The S tokens are Southern Democrats, the D tokens are Northern Democrats, and the R tokens are Republicans. LBJ is the ideal point for President Lyndon B. Johnson based on the presidential support roll calls from* Congressional Quarterly.

The Torgerson coordinates are excellent starting values for single legislatures, but the method breaks down if multiple legislatures are being evaluated over time. In this instance there will be a large number of legislators with no overlap, so there will be a considerable amount of missing data in the agreement score matrix. This lack tends to make the agreement score approach outlined above unreliable. To get starting coordinates for an application of DW-NOMINATE to multiple legislatures, I apply a scaling method I developed (Poole, 1998) that extracts *common-space scores* (CSS) from multiple sets of legislative coordinates.[4]

---

[4]The scaling method that I discuss in my 1998 *AJPS* article is a general-purpose tool that performs a SVD of a rectangular matrix of real elements with missing entries. In contrast to existing techniques such as factor analysis that work with a correlation or covariance matrix computed from the data matrix, the scaling procedure analyzes the data matrix *directly*. In this chapter I show

The CSS method was developed to be a SVD procedure for matrices with large amounts of missing data. In this application I use it to estimate the latent dimensions underlying the coordinates of a set of legislators over time. The latent dimensions are estimated one at a time. For example, the first latent dimension is extracted from all the first-dimension coordinates over the entire time period, then the second latent dimension is extracted from all the second-dimension coordinates over the entire time period, and so on.

Specifically, let $\mathbf{X}_1, \mathbf{X}_2, \ldots, \mathbf{X}_T$ be the p_t by s matrices of legislator coordinates for the T ($t = 1, \ldots, T$) legislative sessions. These coordinates come from separate scalings of each legislature by NOMINATE or some other scaling method. The CSS method begins by assembling the first dimension of the T coordinate matrices into a single matrix, $\mathbf{X}_0^{(k)}$, where the superscript k indicates the dimension and the subscript 0 indicates that elements are missing from the matrix – not all legislators are in every session of the legislature. To be included in $\mathbf{X}_0^{(k)}$, a legislator must be in at least five sessions of the legislature. $\mathbf{X}_0^{(k)}$ is an n by T matrix, where n is equal to the total number of unique legislators who served in at least five sessions during the T legislative sessions. Let X_{it} be the ith individual's ($i = 1, \ldots, n$) coordinate on dimension k for session t. Let Ψ_{ik} be the ith legislator's position on the kth ($k = 1, \ldots, s$) *basic dimension*. One basic dimension is estimated at a time. The model estimated is

$$\mathbf{X}_0^{(k)} = \left[\boldsymbol{\Psi}_k \mathbf{W}_k' + \mathbf{J}_n \boldsymbol{\mu}_k' \right]_0 + \mathbf{E}_0^{(k)} \tag{5.10}$$

where $\boldsymbol{\Psi}_k$ is the n by 1 vector of coordinates of the individuals on the kth basic dimension, $\mathbf{W}_k$ is a T by 1 vector of weights, $\boldsymbol{\mu}_k$ is a vector of constants of length T, $\mathbf{J}_n$ is an n-length vector of ones, and $\mathbf{E}_0^{(k)}$ is an n by T matrix of error terms. $\mathbf{W}_k$ and $\boldsymbol{\mu}_k$ map the legislators from the basic space onto the individual legislative session dimensions.

I assume that the elements of $\mathbf{E}_0^{(k)}$ are random draws from a symmetric distribution with zero mean.

Without loss of generality, the mean of the coordinates of the legislators on the basic dimensions may be placed at the origin; that is, $\mathbf{J}_n' \boldsymbol{\Psi}_k = 0$. Then, if there were no missing data, we would have $\mathbf{J}_n' [\mathbf{X}^{(k)} - \mathbf{J}_n \boldsymbol{\mu}_k'] = \mathbf{0}'$, where $\mathbf{0}$ is a T-length vector of zeros.

---

only one use of the procedure – creating CSSs. In general, it can be used not only to estimate latent or unobservable dimensions from sets of issue scales, but also to estimate an Eckart–Young lower-rank approximation matrix of a matrix with missing entries. Monte Carlo tests show that the procedure reliably estimates the latent dimensions and reproduces the missing elements of a matrix even at high levels of error and missing data. The programs to compute common-space scores and the other types of matrix decomposition discussed in Poole (1998) are posted at http://k7moa.com/basic.htm.

Equation (5.10) can be written with a product of partitioned matrices:

$$\mathbf{X}_0^{(k)} = [\boldsymbol{\Psi}_k \mid \mathbf{J}_n] \begin{bmatrix} \mathbf{W}_k' \\ \boldsymbol{\mu}_k' \end{bmatrix}_0 + \mathbf{E}_0^{(k)}$$

where $[\boldsymbol{\Psi}_k \mid \mathbf{J}_n]$ is an n by 2 matrix and $[\mathbf{W}_k \mid \boldsymbol{\mu}_k]$ is a T by 2 matrix. If there is no error or missing data, then the rank of $\mathbf{X}^{(k)}$ is *at most* 2. Every column in $\mathbf{X}^{(k)}$ is a multiple of $\boldsymbol{\Psi}_{ik}$ plus a constant. Therefore, subtracting off the column means from $\mathbf{X}^{(k)}$ so that the n entries in each of the T columns sum to zero removes the additive constants, and then it must be the case that the rank of $\mathbf{X}^{(k)} - \mathbf{J}_n \boldsymbol{\mu}_k'$ is one. If there were no missing data in (5.10), it could be estimated quite simply by applying SVD to $\mathbf{X}^{(k)} - \mathbf{J}_n \boldsymbol{\mu}_k'$ where $\boldsymbol{\mu}_k$ is the T-length vector of the column means of $\mathbf{X}^{(k)}$.

The CSS method is an alternating least squares procedure that produces estimates of the basic coordinates and the linear transformations for each dimension; that is, $\hat{\boldsymbol{\Psi}}_1$, $\hat{\mathbf{W}}_1$, and $\hat{\boldsymbol{\mu}}_1$, to $\hat{\boldsymbol{\Psi}}_s$, $\hat{\mathbf{W}}_s$, and $\hat{\boldsymbol{\mu}}_s$. To get estimates for those legislators who served in less than five legislative sessions, I apply the simple linear transformation to their coordinates in each session that they served in, and then compute the mean of these transformed coordinates, namely,

$$\hat{\Psi}_{ik} = \frac{\sum_{t=1}^{T_i} \frac{x_{ikt} - \hat{\mu}_k}{\hat{w}_k}}{T_i} \tag{5.11}$$

where T_i is the number of sessions (<5) that legislator i served in.

The s vectors $\hat{\boldsymbol{\Psi}}_k$ for the legislators serving in five or more sessions are combined with the $\hat{\Psi}_{ik}$'s for the legislators serving fewer than five sessions to form the overall p by s matrix of basic space coordinates, $\hat{\boldsymbol{\Psi}}$. Here p is the number of unique legislators serving in the legislature during the T sessions. Because each dimension is extracted separately from the others, the common-space dimensions are very similar to eigenvectors. At the end of the process I apply an adjustment identical to the Torgerson coordinates shown in equation (5.9) so that the s dimensions lie within the unit hypersphere.

The CSS method should be used only over periods of time where there is good reason to believe that there is no fundamental change in the underlying voting space. For example, it would not be appropriate to apply it to the U.S. Congress during the period from 1840 to 1860, because of the structural change that occurred in congressional voting as the result of the Compromise of 1850. Before the Compromise, the first dimension was based on the role of the government in the economy, and it divided the Whigs from the Democrats. The second dimension divided the two political parties along regional lines – North versus South – and it picked up slavery-related issues. After the Compromise, the party system in the U.S. Congress disintegrated and the first dimension became the slavery dimension (Poole and Rosenthal, 1997).

90th U.S. Senate Common Space Coordinates

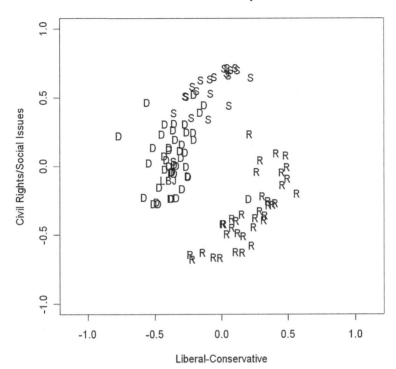

FIGURE 5.2. *90th U.S. Senate common-space coordinates. The S tokens are Southern Democrats, the D tokens are Northern Democrats, and the R tokens are Republicans. LBJ is the ideal point for President Lyndon B. Johnson.*

I developed the CSS method in 1982, and Howard Rosenthal and I used it along with a simple metric scaling method (Poole, 1984, 1990; Poole and Rosenthal, 1997) to get starting coordinates in one and two dimensions for D-NOMINATE.[5] We used common-space coordinates for stable periods and then pieced together all the sets of starting coordinates for Congresses 1 to 100.

For purposes of comparison, Figure 5.2 shows the configuration for the 90th U.S. Senate from common-space coordinates computed using W-NOMINATE scores for the 75th to the 107th Houses and Senates.[6] The configuration is essentially the same as that of the Torgerson coordinates, except that the second dimension is stretched relative to Figure 5.1. The two D tokens that are outliers are Gruening (D-AK) and Morse (D-OR). Both men had very liberal voting records throughout their careers, and the two were the only senators to vote

---

[5]I am a bit slow sometimes in publishing papers. I do not recommend waiting over 15 years to publish your research.

[6]These scores are posted at http://k7moa.com/basic.htm.

against the Tonkin Gulf Resolution on 7 August 1964. Morse's position was determined by his voting as an Independent (83rd and 84th Senates) and as a Democrat (85th to 90th Senates).[7]

How Many Dimensions Should I Estimate?

There is no pat answer to this question. My view is that it is more of a *substantive* question than a *statistical* question. Before turning to the practicalities of deciding on the number of dimensions, I will first discuss two statistical methods for determining dimensionality. The first was developed by Fallaw Sowell, Steve Spear, and me (Poole, Sowell, and Spear, 1992). This method was explicitly designed to address the dimensionality question in spatial voting models. The second method was developed by Cragg and Donald (1997) and is concerned with the more general question of determining the *rank* of a matrix in a broad class of models. I will briefly discuss both methods, beginning with Cragg and Donald.

One of the models that Cragg and Donald consider is estimating the rank of the covariance matrix in the classic factor analysis framework. For the time being I am going to finesse the issue of just what the covariance (correlation) matrix is – that is, how it is computed – and just stick to a mathematical discussion. Namely, let $\mathbf{B}$ be a p by q matrix of data ($q > p$), and let the true p by p covariance matrix for $\mathbf{B}$ be

$$\boldsymbol{\Sigma} = (\mathbf{AF}' + \mathbf{E})(\mathbf{AF}' + \mathbf{E})' = \mathbf{AF}'\mathbf{FA}' + \mathbf{EFA}' + \mathbf{AF}'\mathbf{E}' + \mathbf{EE}' = \mathbf{AA}' + \boldsymbol{\Phi}$$

$$(5.12)$$

where $\mathbf{A}$ is a p by s matrix of rank s, $\mathbf{F}$ is a p by s matrix such that $\mathbf{F}'\mathbf{F} = \mathbf{I}_s$, $\mathbf{E}$ is a p by p matrix of random errors of rank p whose columns are both uncorrelated with the columns of $\mathbf{F}$ and uncorrelated with each other, and $\boldsymbol{\Phi}$ is a p by p diagonal matrix with the variances of the p columns of $\mathbf{E}$ on the diagonal. With these assumptions the rank of $\boldsymbol{\Sigma} - \boldsymbol{\Phi}$ is s.

Let $\hat{\boldsymbol{\Sigma}}$ be the p by p observed covariance matrix. Let ξ be a $p(p+1)/2$-length vector containing the unique elements of $\boldsymbol{\Sigma}$, and let $\hat{\xi}$ be a $p(p+1)/2$-length vector containing the unique elements of $\hat{\boldsymbol{\Sigma}}$. Then as q grows large, $\sqrt{q}(\hat{\xi} - \xi)$ converges to a multivariate normal distribution with zero mean and variance–covariance matrix $\mathbf{V}$; that is,

$$\sqrt{q}(\hat{\xi} - \xi) \to N(\mathbf{0}, \mathbf{V}) \tag{5.13}$$

---

[7]The Tonkin Gulf Resolution was passed 7 August 1964 by a vote of 88–2. The 10 senators who did not vote announced that they would have voted Yea. It passed the House the same day by a vote of 416–0 with 3 announcing Yea and one pair Yea–Nay [Siler (R-KY) was the paired Nay]. It gave President Lyndon Johnson carte blanche to prosecute the Vietnam War. Ernest Gruening lost his party's nomination in 1968 to Mike Gravel, and Wayne Morse lost a close election in 1968 to Robert Packwood. I voted for Morse by absentee ballot from the Republic of Vietnam.

where $\mathbf{V}$ is a $p(p+1)/2$ by $p(p+1)/2$ matrix. From this Cragg and Donald construct a chi-square test:

$$(\hat{\xi} - \xi)'\hat{\mathbf{V}}^{-1}(\hat{\xi} - \xi) \sim \chi_v^2 \qquad (5.14)$$

where the number of degrees of freedom, v, is $(p-s)(p-s+1)/2$, and $\hat{\mathbf{V}}$ is a *fourth moment* matrix constructed from the elements of $\hat{\Sigma}$.

In the roll call framework the matrix $\mathbf{B}$ would be the p by q matrix of roll call choices. Heckman and Snyder (1997) transform the matrix $\mathbf{B}$ of *nominal choices* (just Yea and Nay) into a matrix of *real numbers* by inserting ones for Yeas and zeros for Nays; and by subtracting the column means (the number of Yeas divided by the number of voters) off the resulting matrix, they are able to compute a $\hat{\Sigma}$. They then use a version of equation (5.14) to claim that roll call voting is anywhere from six- to eight-dimensional.

Cragg and Donald's approach has a number of drawbacks. First, the *rank* of the covariance matrix of $\mathbf{B}$ is not quite the correct target. The covariance matrix and the agreement score matrix are very similar and have the same fundamental drawback; namely, the true distances are not necessarily monotone in the number of cutting lines between pairs of legislators. Several hundred roll calls invariably produce a Coombs mesh that fills up the space so that the polytopes are dense almost everywhere except near the rim. The true legislator polytopes could be in a tight ellipsoid in the mesh, but the presence of error could very easily displace legislators in the mesh in such a way that a dimension could look significant when it is not.

Second, with 100 senators $\hat{\mathbf{V}}$ would be a 5,050 by 5,050 matrix. Because of its size, this matrix is almost certain to be singular. The problem is exacerbated by the fact that $\hat{\Sigma}$ is constructed from nominal data and $\hat{\mathbf{V}}$ is constructed from $\hat{\Sigma}$. Empirically, given the way it is constructed, a matrix of this size is almost certain to be singular because of "accidental" linear combinations of rows/columns.

The method developed by Poole, Sowell, and Spear (1992) assumes that the true voting space is high-dimensional and that voting is perfect in the high-dimensional space. Poole, Sowell, and Spear (PSS) assume a uniform distribution of voters within the unit hypersphere, and for every fixed proportion of minority voters, they assume that the alternatives are drawn from a uniform distribution over the hypersphere. This is equivalent to rotating the normal vector randomly around the origin of the space with the cutting plane in a fixed position on the normal vector. PSS then consider the problem of what the *projection* of the roll call onto one dimension would look like. Intuitively, this is like shining a light through a three-dimensional object onto a screen and then trying to figure out what the three-dimensional object looks like from its two-dimensional shadow. The difference is that the hypersphere can have any number of dimensions and the projection is onto a line.

For example, if the true voting space were two-dimensional and the cutting line were perpendicular to the projection dimension, the projection would

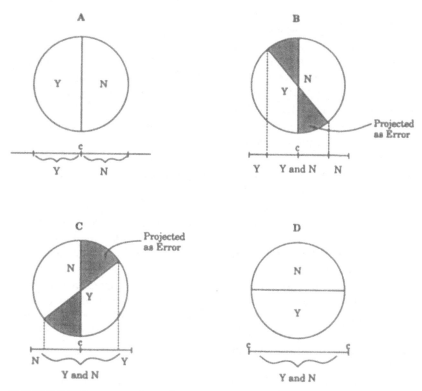

FIGURE 5.3. *Projection of a perfect 50–50 vote in two dimensions onto a line. Voters are uniformly distributed over a circle, and the point c denotes the optimal classification cutting point when the ideal points are projected onto the line below the circle.*

look like a perfect vote in one dimension and would classify perfectly (see Figure 5.3A). If the cutting line were parallel to the projection dimension, the projection would produce a random-looking arrangement of Yeas and Nays along the line and the classification errors would be equal to the minority side of the roll call (see Figure 5.3D). Finally, if the cutting line were not quite perpendicular to the projection dimension, the projection would look like a noisy one-dimensional roll call with Yeas and Nays at the ends and a mix of Yeas with Nays in the middle (see Figure 5.3B and C).

PSS derive the probability distribution of the proportion of classification error, p_c, for all minority margins m and for two or more dimensions. That is,

$$f(p_c \mid m, s). \tag{5.15}$$

Hence, given an empirical distribution of margins – the q m_j's – and classification errors – the q $\hat{p}_{cj}$'s – in one dimension from a scaling procedure, these can then be inserted in equation (5.15), and the likelihood that the observed set of $\hat{p}_{cj}$'s results from a projection of perfect voting in a voting space of s dimensions can be calculated.

PSS evaluated $\hat{p}_{cj}$'s from D-NOMINATE and a simple Guttman scaling of U.S. Houses 1 to 100 and found that the likelihood function (5.15) was a maximum for two dimensions for both methods in all but a handful of Houses – the 32nd House (1851–1852) mentioned above, and several Houses during the Era of Good Feelings (1817–1824).

The method developed by PSS has some obvious drawbacks. The assumptions of high-dimensional *perfect* spatial voting with uniformly distributed legislators and cutting line angles are very strong and clearly not realistic. One justification for them is that the presence of error might make voting *look like* high-dimensional perfect voting, albeit with most of the dimensions above the "true" dimensionality being quite weak. In this case, the PSS method will usually find the correct dimensionality if the number of legislators is 500 or more. Finally, if voting were actually one-dimensional with noise, the PSS method would be of limited use. But the maximum of the likelihood function for this case should be two dimensions.

PSS report an extensive Monte Carlo analysis of their approach that shows that the method is quite accurate for 500 or more legislators with 500 or more roll calls when the true data has four dimensions or less. With real roll call data the method generally indicates a dimensionality consistent with the number of large eigenvalues from the decomposition of the double-centered agreement score matrix.

Given the limitations of the two statistical methods for determining dimensionality, I have found that the most practical approach is to look at the pattern of the eigenvalues of the double-centered agreement score matrix and then simply to estimate the spatial model in one, two, or more dimensions according to whether or not there is an *elbow* in the plot of the eigenvalues. To enhance the comparability of the plots across legislatures, I normalize the eigenvalues by dividing them by the square root of the sum of all the eigenvalues squared; that is,

$$\tilde{\lambda}_i = \frac{\lambda_i}{\sqrt{\sum_{i=1}^{p} \lambda_i^2}}. \tag{5.16}$$

This has the effect of making the largest normalized eigenvalue less than 1.0. It has no impact on the shape of the plot; it is simply a graphical convenience.

I then study the configurations, using letters to represent the members of the political parties (or nations in the case of the United Nations or the European Parliament) or regions of the geographic area that is represented by the legislature. There is no magic to this. As I said in Chapter 1, at this point there is no substitute for the *substantive* knowledge of the researcher. I will illustrate this point with the 90th and 108th U.S. Senates, the first three sessions

Normalized Eigenvalues of Double-Centered Agreement Score Matrix for the 90th Senate

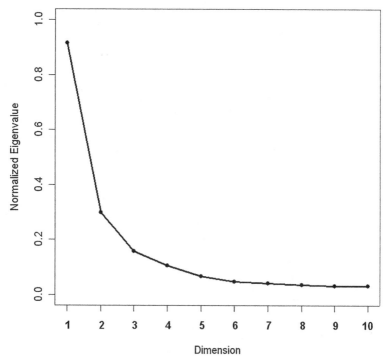

FIGURE 5.4. *Normalized eigenvalues of the double-centered agreement score matrix for the 90th U.S. Senate. The eigenvalues fall off fairly smoothly from the 3rd value through the 10th value. This is a clear indication that the data are most likely to be two-dimensional.*

of the United Nations General Assembly, and the French National Assembly in the Fourth Republic (Rosenthal and Voeten, 2004).

Figure 5.4 shows the normalized eigenvalues for the 90th U.S. Senate. Such plots are known as *scree plots* and have been widely used in psychometrics for decades as indicators for dimensionality (Kruskal and Wish, 1978; Borg and Groenen, 1997).[8] The idea is simply to plot by dimension the measure of fit (R^2, STRESS, eigenvalues, etc.) and see if there is a clear *elbow* in the measure. That is, does the plot fall steeply and then flatten out? In the plot above, the eigenvalues fall off fairly smoothly from the 3rd value through the

---

[8] An R program that computes the double-centered matrix of squared distances computed from the agreement scores and produces a skree plot of the eigenvalues is on the website for this book: http://k7moa.com/spatial_models_of_parliamentary_voting.htm under the link for this chapter.

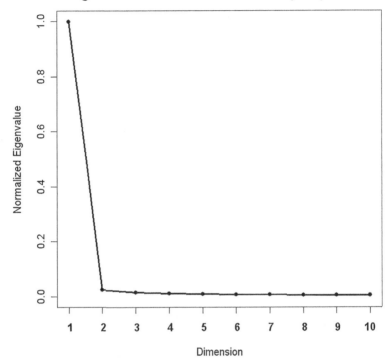

FIGURE 5.5. *Normalized eigenvalues of the double-centered agreement score matrix for the 108th U.S. Senate (2003 only). There is only one large eigenvalue, and the rest are tiny. This is a clear indication that the data are most likely to be one-dimensional.*

10th value. This is a clear indication that the data is most likely to be two-dimensional.

The next step is to make a spatial map in two dimensions like those shown in Figures 5.1 and 5.2 for the 90th U.S. Senate and study the patterns in the spatial arrangements of the legislators. In Figures 5.1 and 5.2, the three-party system (Northern Democrats, Southern Democrats, Republicans) shows up clearly, and the tilt of the "channel" between the Democrats and Republicans shows that there were a substantial number of roll calls that split the two parties internally – for example, the famous conservative coalition of Southern Democrats and Republicans versus the Northern Democrats.

This method of determining dimensionality should never be used mechanically. It is always good practice to estimate spatial maps in higher dimensions and look at the results regardless of the pattern of eigenvalues. For example, Figure 5.5 shows the plot of the normalized eigenvalues of the double-centered agreement score matrix for the first session of the 108th U.S. Senate (2003). Here the elbow is pretty dramatic. There is only one large eigenvalue, and the remaining ones are very tiny. Indeed, a simple one-dimensional scaling using W-NOMINATE correctly classifies 93 percent of the choices (APRE of .822), and a simple rank order using OC correctly classifies 95 percent of the choices (APRE of .861).[9] The voting was clearly almost entirely one-dimensional.

Figure 5.6 shows the final passage vote on a very controversial bill to ban late term ("partial birth") abortions. Even though voting was nearly one-dimensional, the extremely weak second dimension still accounts for some voting on "social" or "lifestyle" issues. The cutting line correctly classifies 89 of 96 senators on this roll call. In general, my advice to researchers is to make plots like Figure 5.6 for several dozen roll calls, to be absolutely certain that your substantive interpretation of the spatial map of the legislators makes sense.[10] In a case like the 108th Senate, where there is an extremely weak second dimension that increases correct classification by 1 percent or less, a researcher can legitimately treat the legislature as one-dimensional. This is a judgment call, and it depends on how important the issues are that have cutting lines with a significant second-dimension component.

The United Nations General Assembly casts roll call votes just like a legislature, but instead of the voters being individuals, they are sovereign nation states. Unlike the modern U.S. Congress, where policy-related abstention is rare (Poole and Rosenthal, 1997), abstention is common in the United Nations General Assembly. In contrast, voting "Present" in the U.S. House of Representatives is very infrequent. Most nonvoting is due to a member simply being absent for some reason, and members are painfully aware of the fact that an opponent in the next election might use their nonparticipation against them. In the United Nations the voters are nation states and are free to abstain as they see fit. Technically, a two-cutting-line model should be applied to United Nations voting because there are three choices. But if the abstention rate is not too high and there are a reasonable number of roll calls, the abstentions can either be treated as missing data or, in the case of the United Nations, be combined with the Nay votes.[11]

---

[9]There were 459 roll calls in 2003, of which 352 had minority margins of 2.5 percent or better. With 100 senators and some missing data, the total number of choices was 33,871. The fits for W-NOMINATE in one dimension were a geometric mean probability of .838, percentage correctly classified 92.8 percent, and an APRE of .822. In two dimensions the fits were .859, 93.8 percent, and .847, respectively. For OC, the correct classification in one dimension was 94.5 percent with an APRE of .864. In two dimensions the fits were 95.6 percent and .891, respectively.

[10]Software to do this for W-NOMINATE, QN, and OC can be found on the website for this book under the link for Chapter 5.

[11]Erik Voeten (2000; 2001; 2004) has an excellent series of papers on voting in the United Nations General Assembly and in the Security Council.

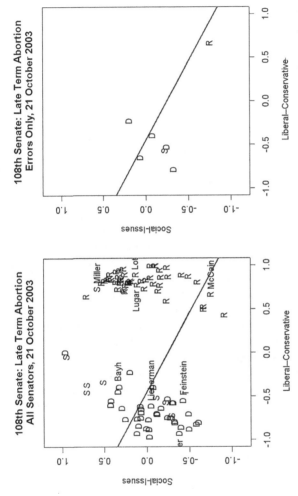

FIGURE 5.6. *Final passage vote on the late term ("partial birth") abortion bill in the 108th U.S. Senate on 21 October 2003. S tokens indicate the ideal points for Southern Democrats, D tokens for Northern Democrats, and R tokens for Republicans. The ideal points of some of the senators are shown in the figure. The errors are concentrated near the cutting line for the roll call.*

**Normalized Eigenvalues of Double-Centered
Agreement Score Matrix for the United Nations**

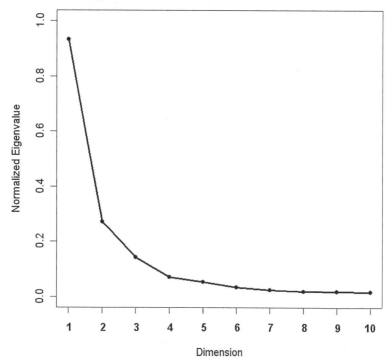

FIGURE 5.7. *Normalized eigenvalues of the double-centered agreement score matrix for the first three sessions of the United Nations (1946–1948). The plot is very similar to that for the 90th U.S. Senate (Figure 5.4). The eigenvalues fall off fairly smoothly from the 3rd value through the 10th value. This is a clear indication that the data are most likely to be two-dimensional.*

For example, during the first three sessions of the United Nations General Assembly (1946–1948), there were 59 nation states and 237 roll calls with a total of 12,707 choices. Of this total only 18.3 percent were abstentions, and I treat them as missing data. Figure 5.7 shows the plot of the normalized eigenvalues of the double-centered agreement score matrix (which had no missing entries) for the first three sessions. The plot is very similar to that for the 90th U.S. Senate (Figure 5.4). The eigenvalues fall off fairly smoothly from the 3rd value through the 10th value. This is a clear indication that the data are most likely to be two-dimensional.

Figure 5.8 shows a two-dimensional plot of the 59 nations in the United Nations during the first three sessions (1946–1948). In one dimension OC correctly classifies 92.6 percent of the 9,527 choices with an APRE of .700.

United Nations: Sessions 1 - 3 (1946-48)

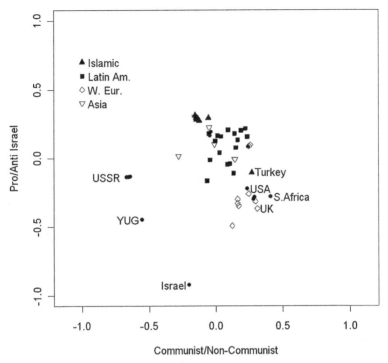

FIGURE 5.8. *Two-dimensional plot of the 59 nations in the United Nations during the first three sessions (1946–1948). The first dimension is communist–noncommunist, and the second dimension is pro–anti-Israel. The USSR has three ideal points, one each for the Russian Federation, Ukraine, and Belarus.*

In two dimensions the correct classification is 95.3 percent with an APRE of .810.[12]

The first dimension in Figure 5.8 is a communist–noncommunist dimension. The USSR is actually *three* points – the Russian Federation, Ukraine, and Belarus. The two adjacent points are Poland and Czechoslovakia, with the remaining communist country, Yugoslavia, a small distance away. On the opposite side of the dimension are the United States and its West European allies and South Africa. The second dimension is essentially a pro–anti-Israel dimension

---

[12]I also scaled the United Nations data with the abstentions treated as Nays. The fit in two dimensions using OC was 92.3 percent with an APRE of .705. The Pearson correlation between the recovered first dimension and the first dimension shown in Figure 5.8 was 0.96, but the correlation for the corresponding second dimensions was only .78. This weaker second-dimension correlation was due to three outliers – Israel, Belgium, and Luxembourg. With these three nations excluded the correlation rose to 0.92 for the 56 remaining countries.

with all the Islamic nations except Turkey clustered at the top of the second dimension and with Israel isolated at the bottom.[13]

Scree plots of the normalized eigenvalues are usually good indicators of the underlying dimensionality, but they do not work well when the agreement score matrix has a substantial number of missing entries. This can happen when a number of sessions of a legislature with a high member turnover are combined into a single roll call matrix for analysis. The reason for this outcome is that the eigenvalues reflect the sum of the squared entries of the matrix.[14] Specifically,

$$\sum_{i=1}^{p} \lambda_i^2 = \sum_{i=1}^{p} \sum_{m=1}^{p} y_{im}^2 \qquad (5.17)$$

where the y_{im} are the entries of the double-centered agreement score matrix given in equation (5.5) above, and the λ_i are the eigenvalues of the matrix. If 0.25 is inserted for all the missing entries in the squared distance matrix computed from the agreement score matrix, this will have the effect of flattening out the distribution of eigenvalues and increasing the apparent rank of **Y**. This flattening happens because the y_{im}^2 corresponding to the missing entries tend to be larger on average than they should be. Mixing in these larger than average entries has the effect of increasing the magnitude of the smaller λ_i's relative to the larger λ_i's. Unless the number of missing entries is well in excess of 50 percent, however, the *eigenvectors* are still fairly reliable as starting values for the legislators.

If the eigenvalues are unreliable indicators of dimensionality, the only thing that can be done is simply to fit the spatial model to the matrix in one and two or more dimensions and look at the fits and the resulting spatial maps. A good example is the work of Rosenthal and Voeten (2004) on voting in the French National Assembly during the Fourth Republic (1946–1958). They analyzed 797 roll calls cast by 1,435 legislators. About 40 percent of the entries in the agreement score matrix are missing data. Rosenthal and Voeten scaled the data in one and two dimensions using OC, and the two-dimensional spatial map is shown in Figure 5.9.

In one dimension OC correctly classifies 93.4 percent of the 423,942 choices with an APRE of .816. In two dimensions the correct classification is 96.5 percent with an APRE of .903! The configuration above is interesting in that

---

[13] My thanks to Erik Voeten for alerting me to this interpretation of the spatial map.

[14] This is a standard result from linear algebra. Let $\mathbf{Y} = \mathbf{U}\boldsymbol{\Lambda}\mathbf{U}'$, and note that because $\mathbf{Y}$ is symmetric, $\mathbf{Y}' = \mathbf{U}\boldsymbol{\Lambda}\mathbf{U}'$. The sum of the squared elements of $\mathbf{Y}$ is

$$\sum_{i=1}^{p} \sum_{m=1}^{p} y_{im}^2 = \text{tr}[\mathbf{Y}'\mathbf{Y}] = \text{tr}[\mathbf{U}\boldsymbol{\Lambda}\mathbf{U}'\mathbf{U}\boldsymbol{\Lambda}\mathbf{U}'] = \text{tr}[\mathbf{U}\boldsymbol{\Lambda}^2\mathbf{U}'] = \text{tr}[\mathbf{U}'\mathbf{U}\boldsymbol{\Lambda}^2]$$

$$= \text{tr}[\boldsymbol{\Lambda}^2] = \sum_{i=1}^{p} \Lambda_i^2$$

where tr[] is the trace of the matrix, that is, the sum of the diagonal elements, and the order of multiplication of the matrices under a trace operator can be cyclically changed as long as the rules of matrix multiplication are followed.

French National Assembly 1946-1958
(Rosenthal and Voeten, 2004)

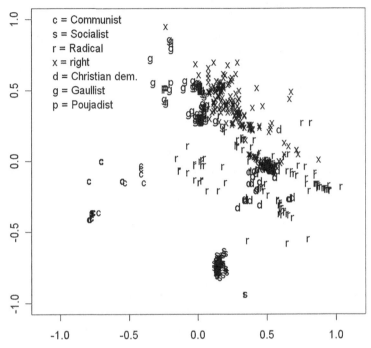

FIGURE 5.9. *French National Assembly, 1946–1958. The mathematical dimensions are not necessarily the same as the substantive dimensions. Rosenthal and Voeten (2004) show that the two substantive dimensions of the spatial map run at 45-degree angles through the space. From southwest to northeast the dimension is left versus right, and from southeast to northwest the dimension is pro-regime to anti-regime.*

Rosenthal and Voeten show that the two *substantive dimensions* of the spatial map run at 45-degree angles through the space. From southwest to northeast the dimension is left versus right, and from southeast to northwest the dimension is pro-regime to anti-regime. This pattern illustrates the fact that *substantive* dimensions do not necessarily coincide with *mathematical* dimensions.

Although I have emphasized the importance of the researcher's substantive knowledge in the interpretation of spatial maps, even a well-informed researcher may not be able to predict what the dimensions will be in advance, nor will the obvious interpretation leap out of the spatial map at first glance, as shown by the clever work of Rosenthal and Voeten. A tried and true technique for interpreting the structure of spatial maps is to use the estimated dimensions as independent variables in a simple linear regression where the dependent variable is some characteristic of the legislators (or nations, objects, etc.) (Kruskal and Wish,

106th (1999-2000) U.S. House W-NOMINATE Coordinates

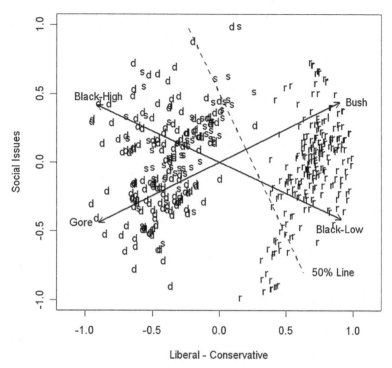

FIGURE 5.10. *Interpreting the dimensions of the 106th (1999–2000) U.S. House. The line connecting Gore and Bush is produced by regressing the 2000 election vote percentage for Bush by congressional district minus the corresponding percentage for Gore on the two W-NOMINATE dimensions. The line connecting Black–High and Black–Low is produced by regressing the percentage African-American of the congressional district on the two W-NOMINATE dimensions.*

1978; Borg and Groenen, 1997). Two examples of this method are shown for the 106th U.S. House in Figure 5.10.

The line connecting Gore and Bush in Figure 5.10 is produced by regressing the 2000 election vote percentage for Bush by congressional district minus the corresponding percentage for Gore on the two W-NOMINATE dimensions. Specifically, the simple OLS is[15]

$$\text{Bush\%} - \text{Gore\%} = -8.864 + 36.581 \times \text{WNOM\_1} + 17.710 \times \text{WNOM\_2}.$$
$$(0.870) \quad (1.452) \quad\quad\quad\quad (2.399)$$

The simple R^2 for this regression was 0.626 with 432 observations.

---

[15] The standard errors are shown in parentheses below the coefficient estimates.

In Chapter 2 I showed with respect to probit and logit that the coefficients of the independent variables in the equation (that is, the coefficients other than the intercept term) can be treated as elements of a normal vector. This normal vector and its reflection yield a *projection line* through the space of the independent variables much like the one discussed in Chapter 3. In this case the normal vector is

$$\left[\begin{array}{c} \frac{36.581}{(36.581)^2 + (17.710)^2} \\ \frac{17.710}{(36.581)^2 + (17.710)^2} \end{array} \right] = \left[\begin{array}{c} .900 \\ .436 \end{array} \right].$$

This vector and its reflection form the line from Gore to Bush in Figure 5.10. In terms of the regression equation, what this means is that as we move along the line from Gore to Bush the predicted value of the difference in the percentages goes from highest possible negative to highest possible positive. The dotted line perpendicular to the line connecting Gore and Bush shows where the prediction is zero (the "50 percent line" in a two-person race). That is, every congressional district on the Bush side of the line should have voted for Bush over Gore, and every congressional district on the Gore side of the line should have voted for Gore.

Regressing the percentage African-American of the congressional district on the two W-NOMINATE dimensions produces the second line, connecting Black–High and Black–Low, in Figure 5.10. Specifically, the simple OLS is

(% African-American) $= 13.440 - 10.466 \times \text{WNOM\_1} + 4.744 \times \text{WNOM\_2}.$
        (0.725)   (1.951)   (1.238)

The simple R^2 for this regression was 0.143 with 435 observations. The normal vector from the regression coefficients is $\left[\begin{array}{c} -0.911 \\ 0.413 \end{array} \right]$. It and its reflection form the percent African-American line in Figure 5.10.

The slopes and positions of both lines in Figure 5.10 make sense. The realignment of the South into the Republican Party and the virtual disappearance of moderate Republicans have left very few Democratic districts with conservative-leaning electorates and very few Republican districts with liberal-leaning electorates. The lower fitting percentage African-American line also makes sense, because it neatly divides the two political parties. Democrats tend to get a higher percentage of African-American voters than do Republicans. Nevertheless, many Republicans have sizable percentages of African-Americans in their congressional districts (e.g., in Southern states), and many Democrats have very low percentages of African-Americans in their districts (e.g., in Oregon and Washington), and this depresses the R^2.

Although these regressions do not reveal much beyond what well-informed observers of American politics already know, they illustrate the utility of the simple regression analysis approach to uncovering the structure in spatial maps. Simple probit or logit or ordered probit also can be used in exactly the same way to study structure if the dependent variable is categorical. As I demonstrated in Chapter 2, the coefficients can be converted into a normal vector and displayed in the same fashion as the lines in Figure 5.10.

The Problem of Constraints

Because roll call data are nominal – that is, just Yea and Nay – they have no natural metric. Consequently, any scaling of roll call data that produces a spatial map must determine the underlying metric of the dimensions. The basic spatial model I have used throughout this book simply assumes that legislators are represented by points and roll calls are represented by cutting points or lines in a Euclidean space, and that legislators vote for the outcome closest to them in the space. Clearly, once the ideal points and cutting points or lines have been estimated, any rigid rotation or uniform expansion of the space will produce the same correct classification and, in a probabilistic model, the same log-likelihood if the utility function is adjusted accordingly (e.g., the β parameter in the NOMINATE model).

I have always designed my scaling programs to estimate legislator ideal points within a hypersphere of radius one. In one dimension this simply trans-lates into an interval from -1 to $+1$, in two dimensions a circle with radius one, and in three dimensions a sphere with radius one. This is, of course, an arbitrary decision, but I think it makes intuitive sense in that the underlying geometry that I discussed in Chapter 2 is centered on the normal vectors for the roll calls. Having these vectors be of unit length makes the geometry particularly elegant and easy to illustrate, so I think the radius one assumption is the best one to make.

Within OC the radius one constraint does not pose any problems. During the legislator procedure it is a simple matter to confine the polytope search to the interior of the unit hypersphere. As I discussed in Chapter 4, with proba-bilistic spatial voting models, the unit hypersphere constraint means that the log-likelihood of a legislator's ideal point is not necessarily at a maximum. This typically happens when some legislators are so ideologically consistent that they fit the spatial model "too well." Simply put, they make too few voting errors: either they vote for the conservative outcome on nearly ev-ery roll call or they vote for the liberal outcome on nearly every roll call. Consequently, a *sag* in the ideal point configuration can occur, in that a legisla-tor appears at the edge of the space with the other legislators recovered to the interior. Figure 5.11 shows an example of the sag problem for the 107th U.S. Senate.

In the 107th Senate, Paul Wellstone (D-MN) voted almost perfectly liberal. Before his death in October 2002, Wellstone had voted on 444 nonunanimous roll calls and made only 18 voting "errors." Consequently, his fit to the spatial

107th Senate (2001-2002): Illustration of Sag Problem

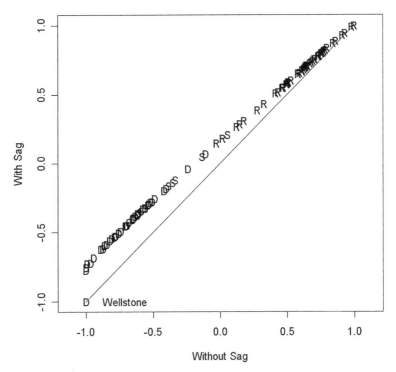

FIGURE 5.11. *An example of the sag problem, using the 107th (2001–2002) U.S. Senate. Paul Wellstone (D-MN) voted almost perfectly liberal, so that his ideal point is pushed away from those of the remaining senators.*

model is nearly perfect. In a probabilistic spatial voting model, the tendency is to push a perfect liberal or conservative away from the other legislators. Such a legislator is on the correct side of all the cutting points or planes, so pushing her out increases all the distances of the perfect legislator from the cutting points or planes. In the NOMINATE framework, as I illustrated with Figure 4.3, the probabilities eventually begin to decrease at some point, but this will not be true of the quadratic utility function.

In the original one-dimensional NOMINATE, the legislator configuration was normalized by placing the furthest left legislator at −1 and the furthest right legislator at +1. If the furthest right or left legislator was more than 0.1 units away from the next nearest legislator, then her coordinate is constrained in that it is not estimated during the next iteration. This has the practical effect of setting the legislator's coordinate to −1 or +1, because it is very unlikely that another legislator will "pass over" the extreme legislator. Consequently, at the

Table 5.3. *The Supreme Court and the Sag Problem*

Justice	W-NOMINATE	QN	OC	OC(1)	OC(2)
Stevens	−1.000	−1.000	1	−0.794	−0.491
Breyer	−0.454	−0.644	2	−0.576	0.906
Ginsburg	−0.302	−0.498	3	−0.357	−0.357
Souter	−0.175	−0.237	4	−0.270	−0.078
Kennedy	0.273	0.210	5	0.160	−0.287
O'Connor	0.319	0.381	6	0.194	0.790
Rehnquist	0.558	0.675	7	0.416	0.022
Scalia	0.782	0.895	8	0.554	−0.309
Thomas	1.000	1.000	9	0.593	−0.211

end of the next iteration the original extreme legislator and the next nearest legislator are both assigned coordinates of −1 or +1. Figure 5.11 shows a W-NOMINATE one-dimensional scaling of the 107th Senate with and without this sag constraint.

Without the constraint, the gap between Wellstone and the next most liberal senator, Barbara Boxer (D-CA), is about .2 units. The coordinates of the two scalings have the same rank ordering, but it seems to me that placing Wellstone .2 units to the left of Barbara Boxer simply lacks face validity. From what I know of American politics, Paul Wellstone was one of the most liberal senators in the past 50 years, but is he that much more liberal than Barbara Boxer − 1/10 of the span of the dimension? I do not think so.[16]

There is no easy fix for this problem. Ultimately, it is a judgment call. When we first encountered the sag problem in our early work with NOMINATE in 1983, we decided to impose the .1 unit constraint on substantive grounds. In our D-NOMINATE and DW-NOMINATE work, we did not have to impose this constraint, because a legislator's ideal point was estimated using her *entire* roll call record.

The sag problem can be especially serious if probabilistic methods are used on small voting bodies, such as the U.S. Supreme Court. For example, Table 5.3 shows the recovered one-dimensional ideal points of the current court if we use W-NOMINATE with no sag constraint, QN (which has no sag constraints), OC one-dimensional rank ordering, and OC two-dimensional coordinates.[17]

---

[16] For a further analysis of Wellstone's liberalism relative to the other members of the Senate, see http://k7moa.com/Paul_Wellstone_RIP.htm.

[17] The data consisted of 293 nonunanimous Supreme Court votes by the current court with a total of 2,624 choices. The fits for W-NOMINATE were a GMP of .819, 90.0 percent correctly classified, and an APRE of .644. The fits for QN were a GMP of .828, 89.0 percent correctly classified, and an APRE of .607. The one-dimensional rank ordering from OC correctly classified 93.1 percent of the choices with an APRE of .755. In two dimensions OC correctly classified 97.0 percent with an APRE of .893.

All three methods produce the same rank ordering of the nine Justices. Both W-NOMINATE and QN, however, show a considerable gap between Stevens and Breyer. What is driving this result is that Stevens almost always votes for the liberal alternative in every decision. The two probabilistic models compensate for this by pushing Stevens well away from Breyer. In the OC rank ordering, Stevens makes only 10 voting "errors" out of 291 choices. When we produce a two-dimensional configuration using OC, the coordinates on the first dimension have the same ordering as all the other techniques, but the relative locations make much more sense (at least to me). The second dimension separates Breyer and O'Connor from the other Justices and increases the correct classification from 93.1 percent (.755 APRE) to 97.0 percent (.893 APRE).

As I discussed in Chapter 4, NOMINATE and QN should not be used on small data sets, because of consistency issues. I use them here for illustrative purposes only. Martin and Quinn (2002) avoid the problems inherent in using probabilistic models on small data sets by analyzing all Supreme Court decisions from 1953 to 1999 using a highly innovative MCMC method that allows the Justices to alter their ideal points through time.

Constraints also must come into play with roll calls, although the problem is quite different. With legislators, problems arise only for those individuals who vote too perfectly near the edges of the space – that is, it is a *low-error problem*. With roll calls it is a *high-error problem*. If a roll call has very low error – that is, if the cutting point or plane nearly perfectly classifies the legislators – then, as I discussed in Chapter 4, in NOMINATE the distance between the two outcomes cannot be identified. Similarly, in QN the distance parameter tends to get very large. In both cases this is a very easy problem to catch and has no effect on the cutting line, which is sharply identified. The distance parameter is simply constrained not to grow beyond a reasonable value, and this fact is flagged in the computer output.

Constraints really come into play when a roll call is lopsided and is also noisy. As I noted in Chapter 4, in this instance a probabilistic model will do best when it predicts unanimity. It will try to push the cutting line to the edge of the legislator configuration. In this case, I restrict the cutting line to be tangent to the unit hypersphere. Again, the result is that the log-likelihood of the roll call parameters is not necessarily at a maximum.

Constraints pose an especially difficult problem for probabilistic models as the level of the error in the data decreases. After all, probability assumes the presence of random error. As the error in a voting data set declines, probabilistic models will of necessity become unstable. Rosenthal and Voeten (2004) find that the roll call voting in the French National Assembly during the Fourth Republic is so highly structured that OC correctly classifies more than 96 percent of the choices in two dimensions and that W-NOMINATE produces spatial maps with large numbers of legislators at the edges of the space – sag writ large. This is why OC is an important check on all probabilistic methods. Because it is built directly on the geometry, OC is not subject to the vagaries of the error. When the error level is a bit higher, as it is, for example, for the 90th U.S. Senate, then the spatial maps of all the probabilistic methods are essentially the same (Lewis and Poole, 2004).

Computing Made Easy – Some Simple Tricks to Make Estimation Tractable

If I had written this chapter 30 years ago, this section would have been at the beginning and much longer. With the revolution in computing, the standard "hacks" that all programmers had to learn to get around memory and disk problems are now for the most part irrelevant. Consequently, I will discuss only two tricks that I still think are useful regardless of the increase of computer speed.

The first is *table lookup*. I have always used table lookup for normal probabilities and their associated natural logs and first derivatives. Most computer languages have built-in function calls to either the distribution function of the standard normal, $\Phi(x)$, or the error function. The two are related by the equation $\Phi(x) = [erf(x) + 1]/2$, where erf(x) is the error function. These function calls are to subroutines that simply use an infinite series of some form to approximate $\Phi(x)$. For example,

$$erf(x) = \frac{2}{\sqrt{\pi}} \sum_{k=0}^{\infty} (-1)^k \left(\frac{x^{2k+1}}{(2k+1)k!} \right). \tag{5.18}$$

When the function is called, the normal probability is calculated to any degree of accuracy by running a "do" loop or a "for" loop using an equation like (5.18).

Table lookup is a simple idea that dramatically reduces the number of computations necessary to compute log-likelihoods. At the beginning of the program, a table is created that holds the values of the standard normal distribution, the distribution function of the normal, the natural log of the distribution function, and a critical portion of the first and second derivatives of the log-likelihood, namely, the inverse of the *Mills ratio*, the ratio of the function to the distribution function. Then, during the program, instead of using the built-in function call for the distribution function quite literally millions of times during a typical computer run, simply look the value up in the table instead.

For example, to create a table of values for the normal distribution with four-digit accuracy over the range of -5.0 to $+5.0$ requires that the table have 100,001 rows. The first row will correspond to -5.0, the second to -4.9999, the third to -4.9998, and so on, with row 50,001 corresponding to 0.0000 and row 100,001 corresponding to 5.0000. The first column simply contains the standard normal distribution value in increments of 0.0001 from -5.0

to 5.0, namely, $\phi(-5.0)$, $\phi(-4.9999)$, $\phi(-4.9998)$, ..., $\phi(4.9999)$, $\phi(5.0)$. The second column contains the corresponding distribution function values from $\Phi(-5.0)$ to $\Phi(5.0)$. The third column contains the natural logs of the third column, and the fourth column contains the inverse of the Mills ratios, $\phi(-5.0)/\Phi(-5.0)$, $\phi(-4.9999)/\Phi(-4.9999)$, etc. The fourth column is needed to compute first and second derivatives.

To do a table lookup, simply take the argument, multiply it by 10,000 (the reciprocal of the accuracy 0.0001), round off to the nearest integer, and add the result to 50,001; that gives the correct row of the table. Note that to get higher levels of accuracy it is a simple matter to scale up the size of the lookup table.

The other trick I have always used is to store the roll call data matrix two ways in the computer memory: in its original form, where the rows are legislators and the columns are roll calls, and transposed, where the rows are roll calls and the columns are legislators. Depending on the programming language, matrices are stored in computer memory as one long vector with the columns or the rows stacked on top of each other. For example, in FORTRAN matrices are stored in contiguous computer memory with the columns stacked. Consequently, doing mathematical operations down a column was faster than doing mathematical operations across rows, because row elements of a matrix were not contiguous. Having the matrix stored both column- and row-stacked means that mathematical operations can always be designed to work with contiguous elements of memory, and that increases the speed of the program. Both D-NOMINATE and DW-NOMINATE are designed this way because of the very large matrices that they analyze.

Even these two useful tricks may become increasingly irrelevant as processor speed increases – especially if the CPU becomes significantly faster than retrieving information from memory. I suspect, however, that computer engineers will redesign memory systems to keep up with the ever-faster CPUs. Regardless of what happens, it's a much better world than the card readers and card sorters of 30 years ago.

Conclusion

In this chapter I have covered a variety of purely practical issues that arise in the estimation of spatial models. As I pointed out in the introduction, this chapter is the most idiosyncratic, because it reflects my experience with building computer programs that implement the methods I outlined in Chapters 2, 3, and 4. My published work is the tip of a computer code iceberg that I have built up over 30 years. The purpose of this chapter is simply to give some practical advice based on all that work – the many elegant but dead-end programs, and the many inelegant but practical programs that I have written to implement spatial models of voting.

In Chapter 6 I will show a variety of natural experiments that can be performed with roll call matrices. For example, simple ways to combine roll call data matrices to test whether or not legislators alter their ideal points when they change political parties, when they are in their last term (the so-called "shirking" phenomenon), when they move from one chamber of a legislature to another chamber, when their geographic districts are redrawn, and so on. Chapter 6 is the applied chapter of this book, and it builds on Chapters 2 through 5.

CHAPTER 6

Conducting Natural Experiments with Roll Calls

Overview

A variety of natural experiments can be performed using roll call matrices. Some consist mainly of combining roll call matrices over time or introducing additional rows into the matrices to allow legislators to be treated as multiple individuals. Additional experiments are possible if the legislature is bicameral (that is, it has two chambers). For a bicameral legislature, the roll call matrices from the two chambers can be combined *via the columns* if enough roll calls with identical content were cast in the two chambers. Likewise, *over time*, if some legislators served in both chambers, then on the assumption that the legislator has the same ideal point in both chambers, we can combine the roll call matrices using these legislators.

Although I will concentrate my analysis below on bicameral legislatures, the same methods can be used for multiple legislatures provided that there are enough legislators who served in all combinations of the legislatures. An example would be a federal system where legislators serve at one time in a regional or state legislature and later in the national legislature. Provided there is enough overlap, the roll call matrices can be combined and analyzed.

We would use additional rows for a legislator who switches political parties. The question is: When a legislator switches from one political party to another, does her roll call voting behavior change? In order to test for the change, the simplest approach is to treat the legislator as *two individuals* – one before the switch and one after. This is equivalent to adding a row to the matrix. The new row contains only the roll calls the legislator voted on after the switch, and the original row is changed to contain only the roll calls the legislator voted on before the switch. A spatial map is produced for this matrix, and the distance between the before and after ideal points of the party switcher can be computed. This distance is the basis for deciding whether or not the legislator's party switch had a *meaningful* change in her roll call voting behavior.

162

Here is where the hard part comes in. How do we decide what constitutes a meaningful change? Meaningful compared to what? My answer is that every legislator must be subjected to the same experiment, so that the party switcher's change can be compared with everyone else's change. I will discuss this method in detail in the next section.

This method (treating party-switching legislators as multiple individuals to test whether or not their voting behavior changed) can be extended to studying whether or not legislators alter their ideal points when they are in their last term (the so-called *shirking* phenomenon), when their geographic districts are redrawn, when they are within a year of running for reelection, and when they are in a lame-duck session after they have been voted out of office. I show several examples of this multiple-individuals experimental setup in the next section.

In order to study changes in the structure of legislative voting behavior over time, the roll call matrices of consecutive sessions of a legislature must be combined, treating each unique legislator who served in one or more sessions as an individual. The DW-NOMINATE scaling method discussed in Chapter 4 is designed to analyze roll call data organized in this form. I discuss several examples of large-scale experiments using DW-NOMINATE in the third section below. These experiments are concerned with party switching (Nokken and Poole, 2004), last-period effects (Goodman, 2004), and agenda effects. Unfortunately, because the matrices for these experiments are very large, it is not possible (at this time) to compute standard errors for the legislator ideal points. Nevertheless, much can be learned by comparing the ideal points of groups of legislators with one another over time.

Finally, if the legislature is bicameral, we can combine the roll call matrices of both chambers over time, using the legislators who served in both chambers. The spatial maps produced by analyzing these combined sets of roll call matrices have the great advantage of jointly displaying members of both chambers, allowing the chambers to be compared over time. But great care must be taken in analyzing roll call data organized in this framework. I discuss the ins and outs of cross-chamber scaling methods in the last section of this chapter.

Multiple-Individuals Experiments

Testing the Effect of a Party Switch

Does a legislator who switches from one political party to another change her voting behavior? Substantively, if the legislative parties are highly disciplined so that all the members of each party all vote alike, then if a legislator changed political parties (assuming that the new party would even accept someone from the opposition), her voting behavior would obviously change. But suppose that there is no party discipline whatsoever. That is, no member is ever put under pressure by her party to vote a particular way. Then her behavior may or may not change. For example, suppose voting is one-dimensional (liberal–conservative) and every legislator votes perfectly. Suppose further that there are only two political parties and that they overlap at the center of the dimension, so that there are moderates in both parties. What does party affiliation mean in this simple left–right perfect-voting world? Not much! Would party switching ever occur in this environment? Probably not.

It is the in-between case that we are likely to face, that is, the case where political parties appear to be composed of ideologically like-minded legislators *and* there is reason to believe that political party affiliation is important either in the geographic constituency or within the legislature. This is clearly the case for the U.S. Congress.

A substantial literature on party switching in the U.S. Congress has developed during the past ten years, partly in response to Keith Krehbiel's famous "Where's the party?" challenge (Krehbiel, 1993). That is, to what extent do political parties affect how members vote on roll calls over and above their personal preferences (Krehbiel, 1993; Snyder and Groseclose, 2000; McCarty, Poole, and Rosenthal, 2001; Cox and Poole, 2002a; 2002b)? If party pressure on members to vote the party line is an important factor, then when a legislator changes her political party affiliation there should be a nontrivial change in the switcher's roll call voting behavior. Nokken (2000), McCarty, Poole, and Rosenthal (2001), Oppenheimer (2000), and Nokken and Poole (2004) have documented such changes using a variety of approaches.

A simple method of testing for the effect of a change in party affiliation is to combine the roll call matrices of the legislature before and after a legislator's switch into a single matrix with the party switcher treated as two legislators – one before and one after the switch. To illustrate this technique I will use U.S. Senator Ben Nighthorse Campbell from the state of Colorado.

Senator Campbell switched from the Democratic to the Republican Party in March 1995 during the 104th Senate. In the 104th Senate he cast 98 roll calls as a Democrat and 919 as a Republican. I combined the 103rd, 104th, and 105th (1993–1998) Senates into one matrix with Campbell's voting record broken into two rows – one row for his voting as a Democrat from the beginning of the 103rd (724 roll calls) until his change after the 98th roll call of the 104th, and one containing roll calls 99 through 919 of the 104th and the 612 roll calls of the 105th Senate. In the combined matrix there are 2,255 roll calls and 132 unique senators (counting Campbell as two senators).[1]

The experiment is performed in one dimension, because by the 103rd U.S. Congress roll call voting was nearly one-dimensional (McCarty, Poole, and

---

[1] All of the data sets and programs discussed in this chapter are posted on the website for this book, http://k7moa.com/Spatial_Models_of_Parliamentary_Voting.htm, under the Chapter 6 link.

Rosenthal, 1997; Poole and Rosenthal, 2001).[2] The experiment consists of three steps. First, estimate a spatial map from the matrix and obtain the two points for Campbell. The distance between these two points is a measure of the effect of the party switch. Second, perform the same experiment for every other senator who served in all three Senates (71 senators besides Campbell), and compute the distance for each senator. These 71 distances can be compared with Campbell's distance to see whether or not his distance is out of the ordinary. Note that technically the 72 roll call matrices being analyzed are all different, so that the spatial maps are not strictly comparable. Nevertheless, all 72 matrices have the same number of nonmissing entries, and they differ only in the fact that each has a different senator divided into two records. Consequently, I believe it is safe to compare the 72 distances with each other, because the differences between the configurations will be trivial.

The third step of the experiment is to compute measures of uncertainty for the distances. Because I use W-NOMINATE to estimate the spatial maps, I use the parametric bootstrap to obtain the standard errors. Namely, for each of the 72 matrices I performed 101 trials to obtain 101 sets of coordinates. For each set of coordinates I computed the distance between the pair of points for the senator in question and then computed the standard deviation of these 101 distances using the *true* distance as the "sample mean" rather than the mean of the bootstrap trials. This procedure has the effect of inflating the standard deviation somewhat, but it is better to err on the safe side and not underreport the standard deviation (Lewis and Poole, 2004, p. 8). The results are shown in Figure 6.1.

Figure 6.1 shows the 72 shift distances for the Campbell party-switch experiment. Senator Campbell is a clear outlier. Three other senators are shown for comparison. The vertical lines through the points show the 95 percent confidence limits for the distances. The overall mean shift distance is 0.081 with a standard deviation of 0.095. Excluding Campbell, the mean for the 71 remaining senators is 0.072 with a standard deviation of 0.055. Campbell's shift distance is 0.733, or almost 10 times the average shift distance of the remaining

---

[2] For the combined matrix of the 103rd to the 105th Senates, using W-NOMINATE, the correct classification in one dimension was 87.5 percent, with an APRE of .637 and a geometric mean probability of .742. In two dimensions, the fits were 88.3 percent, .662, and .765, respectively. Applying W-NOMINATE to the 103rd Senate in one dimension produced a correct classification of 87.1 percent, an APRE of .606, and a GMP of .742. In two dimensions, the fits for the 103rd were 88.4 percent, .646, and .764, respectively. Applying W-NOMINATE to the 104th Senate in one dimension produced a correct classification of 87.9 percent, an APRE of .666, and a GMP of .752. In two dimensions the fits were 88.5 percent, .685, and .769, respectively. Finally, applying W-NOMINATE to the 105th Senate in one dimension produced a correct classification of 87.9 percent, an APRE of .642, and a GMP of .751. In two dimensions the corresponding fits were 88.6 percent, .662, and .771, respectively.

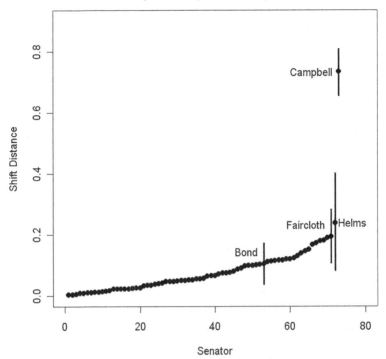

FIGURE 6.1. *Campbell party-switch experiment using the combined 103rd to 105th U.S. Senate roll call voting matrices. The vertical axis is the magnitude of the distance shifted, and the horizontal axis sorts the shifts from low to high. The vertical lines around selected senators show the 95 percent confidence limits for the shift distances.*

71 senators. In any meaningful statistical sense, Campbell's party switch is clearly significant.

This experimental framework consists of three steps only if scaling methods such as W-NOMINATE or QN are used. If Bayesian simulation is used, both the ideal points and the standard errors are estimated in one step. In either case the basic logic of the framework is the same: Every legislator's change must be compared with everyone else's change.

This simple experimental framework is easily extended to other questions. Below I show three more examples using W-NOMINATE: a test of whether or not U.S. senators alter their voting behavior in the last two years of their term before running for reelection; a test of whether or not legislators alter their ideal points when they are in their last term (shirking); and a test of whether or not legislators alter their behavior when their geographic districts are redrawn.

Testing for Shifts in Position Before an Election

U.S. senators have the luxury of serving six-year terms. Consequently, if voters do not have long memories, a senator is free to vote pretty much the way she pleases the first four years and pay close attention to her voting pattern only in the two years before her run for reelection. This is the basis for the conjecture that U.S. senators modify their voting behavior in the last two years of their terms.[3]

I am greatly simplifying a complex subject for the sake of making the experiment simpler. In the real world most senators really do believe what they say. That is, they are either Democrats or Republicans (except for James Jeffords), and they tend to vote in predictable ways on basic issues that divide the two political parties, such as labor regulation, minimum wages, taxes, and so on. Consequently, even if senators shift position before an election, the shifts are likely to be small.

To illustrate the test I use the same set of roll calls that were the basis of the Campbell party-switch experiment shown in Figure 6.1. The difference here is that at the second step I break the roll call record for each senator at the 105th Senate. That is, the 71 senators (Campbell and Shelby are excluded because they switched political parties) who served in all three Senates were each treated as two legislators – one for the 103rd and 104th Senates, and one for the 105th – to obtain a shift distance.[4] As I noted previously, technically the 71 roll call matrices being analyzed are all different, so the spatial maps are not strictly comparable. But all 71 matrices have the same number of nonmissing entries, and they differ only in the fact that each has a different senator divided into two records. Finally, in the third step I used the parametric bootstrap (Lewis and Poole, 2004) to obtain 95 percent confidence limits for selected senators. The results are shown in Figure 6.2.

There are six clear outlying senators, three of whom ran for reelection in 1998: D'Amato (R-NY), McCain (R-AZ), and Specter (R-PA). The senator with the largest shift is "Pothole Al" D'Amato of New York. Senator D'Amato shifted 0.278 units to the left (0.434 to 0.155) during the 105th Senate. In the 1998 election D'Amato was defeated by Charles Schumer, 55 to 44 percent. McCain shifted to the left (0.708 to 0.506) and won reelection with 69 percent of the vote. Specter shifted from the right of center to the left of center (0.061 to –0.099) and won reelection with 61 percent of the vote. The other large shifts are by Moynihan (D-NY), who shifted right (–0.748 to –0.540) and retired in 2000; Bumpers (D-AR), who shifted left (–0.701 to –0.886) and did not run for reelection in 1998; and Harkin (D-IA), who shifted left (–0.756 to –0.921)

---

[3] For tests of the conjecture, see Amacher and Boyes (1978), Poole (1981), Elling (1982), Thomas (1985), Wright and Berkman (1986), Abramowitz and Segal (1992), Bernhard and Sala (2004), and Goodman (2004).

[4] Three senators whose terms ended with the 105th Senate are excluded. Campbell and Shelby switched political parties – Campbell (CO) switched during the 104th, and Shelby (AL) switched between the 103rd and 104th. Robert Packwood (R-OR) resigned his seat in late 1995.

103rd–105th Senates: Shift-at-105th Experiment

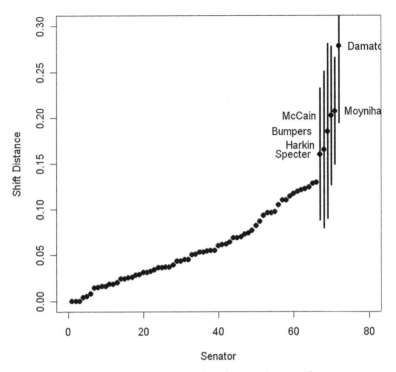

FIGURE 6.2. *Testing for an ideal point shift before an election. The experiment uses the combined 103rd to 105th U.S. Senate roll call voting matrices. The vertical axis is the magnitude of the distance shifted, and the horizontal axis sorts the shifts from low to high. The vertical lines around selected senators show the 95 percent confidence limits for the shift distances.*

after being reelected in 1996. The vertical lines through the points show the 95 percent confidence limits for the distances.

The overall mean shift distance is 0.068 with a standard deviation of 0.055. Excluding D'Amato, the mean for the 70 remaining senators is 0.065 with a standard deviation of 0.049. For the 26 senators who ran for reelection in 1998, the mean shift distance was 0.080 with a standard deviation of 0.063. Excluding D'Amato, the numbers are 0.072 and 0.049, respectively. D'Amato's shift distance of 0.278 is about four times the overall mean, and his shift toward the center makes sense. Pothole Al's shift is clearly significant, but the results for the remaining senators are not clear-cut. For example, two other senators, Moseley-Braun (D-IL) and Faircloth (R-NC), were also defeated for reelection in 1998. Moseley-Braun shifted right (−0.734 to −0.617), and Faircloth shifted left (1.000 to 0.907). Neither shift distance is much above the mean, and it would be hard to argue that Faircloth's shift is substantively significant.

In addition to the 26 senators who served in all three Senates and ran for reelection in 1998, 4 senators did not run for reelection and retired at the end of the 105th – Bumpers (D-AR), Coats (R-IN), Ford (D-KY), and Glenn (D-OH). Their shifts were 0.185, 0.016, 0.039, and 0.096, respectively. These four were in their last Senate and were free of any electoral accountability. Consequently, they were free to shirk and vote their "personal preferences" as opposed to their state's preferences.[5] Except for Bumpers, who became more liberal (–0.701 to –0.886), there is little evidence of any last-period effect that is dramatically different from the average shifts of other groups of senators.

Testing for Last-Period and Redistricting Effects

We can test for last-period effects better by using the U.S. House of Representatives, because of its larger membership and more frequent elections. To illustrate this test, I combined the 96th, 97th, and 98th (1979–1984) Houses into one matrix. In the combined matrix there are 2,984 roll calls and 612 unique representatives. With this matrix I can show a test for last-period effects as well as a test for the effect of changing the boundaries of a geographic district (redistricting).

During this period U.S. congressional voting was weakly two-dimensional. The primary dimension was liberal–conservative and separated the two political parties, and the second dimension mainly served to separate Northern from Southern Democrats (Poole and Rosenthal, 1997). I will conduct the experiments using only the first dimension, because the second dimension is weak and the two types of changes that I consider should take place along the first dimension and not the second.[6]

---

[5] There is a substantial literature on shirking. Poole and Romer (1993) found little evidence for shirking in the U.S. House during the 1947–1983 period. They used exit codes developed by Loomis (1995) and performed their tests using transformed D-NOMINATE scores. Lott and Bronars (1993) used interest group ratings of members of the U.S. House and also found little last period movement. In contrast, Stratmann (2000) and Rothenberg and Sanders (2000) find evidence of shirking in the U.S. House of Representatives. Poole and Rosenthal (1997) find that shirking mainly consists of lower rates of voting in the U.S. House.

[6] For the combined matrix of the 96th to the 98th Houses, using W-NOMINATE, the correct classification in one dimension was 84.6 percent, with an APRE of .475 and a geometric mean probability of .705. In two dimensions, the fits were 85.9 percent, .519, and .723, respectively. Applying W-NOMINATE to the 96th House in one dimension produced a correct classification of 84.3 percent, an APRE of .473, and a GMP of .700. In two dimensions, the fits for the 96th were 85.9 percent, .526, and .724, respectively. Applying W-NOMINATE to the 97th House in one dimension produced a correct classification of 84.6 percent, an APRE of .453, and a GMP of .700. In two dimensions the fits were 86.2 percent, .509, and .725, respectively. Finally, applying W-NOMINATE to the 98th House in one dimension produced a correct classification of 85.5 percent, an APRE of .509, and a GMP of .721. In two dimensions the corresponding fits were 87.0 percent, .561, and .743, respectively.

96th–98th Houses: Shift-at-98th Experiment

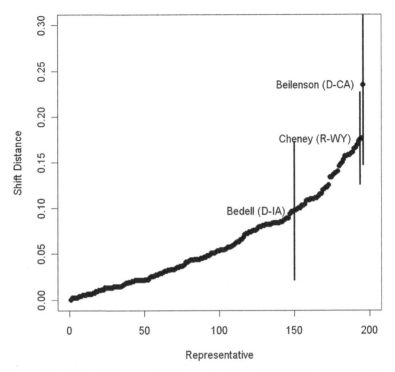

FIGURE 6.3. *Testing for last-period effects using the combined 96th to 98th U.S. House roll call voting matrices. The vertical axis is the magnitude of the distance shifted, and the horizontal axis sorts the shifts from low to high. The vertical lines around selected representatives show the 95 percent confidence limits for the shift distances.*

To implement the test I broke the roll call record for each representative at the 98th House. That is, the 198 representatives who served in all three Houses were each treated as two legislators – one for the 96th and 97th Houses, and one for the 98th – to obtain a shift distance. To reiterate the warnings given above, the roll call matrices are all different, so the spatial maps are not strictly comparable. Nevertheless, they all have the same number of nonmissing entries, and they differ only in the fact that each has a different representative divided into two records. Finally, because I use W-NOMINATE, I use the parametric bootstrap to obtain 95 percent confidence limits for selected representatives. (If Bayesian simulation is used, both the ideal points and the standard errors are estimated in one step.) The results are shown in Figure 6.3.

There is only one clear outlier – Representative Anthony Beilenson (D-CA). Beilenson shifted 0.235 units to the right (–0.896 to –0.661) from the 97th to the 98th House. The overall mean shift distance was 0.063 with a standard deviation of 0.048. Twenty representatives left the House at the end of the 98th Congress. Their mean shift distance was 0.056 with a standard deviation of 0.049. The 178 members who continued to the 99th House had a mean shift distance of 0.064 and a standard deviation of .048. There was essentially no difference between the two groups.

In the 1982 elections at the end of the 97th Congress, 192 of the 198 representatives who served in all three Houses were reelected from geographic districts whose boundaries had changed. Since the Supreme Court rulings in the 1960s, states are required to draw district boundaries very precisely so that the populations are nearly equal within states. These court rulings resulted in more frequent redistricting and had a great impact upon U.S. politics (Cox and Katz, 2002).[7]

The mean shift distance for the 192 representatives who were redistricted was 0.064 with a standard deviation of 0.048. For the six representatives who were not redistricted, the mean was 0.049 and the standard deviation was 0.064. Unfortunately, because the number of representatives who were not redistricted is so small, it is difficult to say much about the redistricting issue. But comparing the shift distances of the 192 representatives who were redistricted with their shift distances between the 96th and the combined 97th and 98th can at least give us an idea whether redistricting has some systematic impact.

To perform the comparison test I broke the roll call record for each representative at the 97th House. That is, the 192 representatives who served in all three Houses and were redistricted are each treated as two legislators – one for the 96th House, and one for the 97th and 98th Houses. The results are shown in Figure 6.4.

The shift distances in Figure 6.4 are very similar to those shown in Figure 6.3. The mean shift distance for the 192 redistricted representatives is 0.065, and the standard deviation is 0.050. This is indistinguishable from the shift distances from the 96th and 97th to the 98th House. Although there almost certainly were members of the House who shifted position in response to a new geographic district, in the aggregate there is no significant effect.

To reiterate a point I made earlier, the basic experimental framework used above consists of three steps only if scaling methods such as W-NOMINATE

---

[7]Cox and Katz (2002), in their impressive book *Elbridge Gerry's Salamander: The Electoral Consequences of the Reapportionment Revolution,* look at the impact of *Baker v. Carr* by political party. They consider the effect of the partisan composition of the federal courts that were involved in the redistricting decisions and find that the political party affiliation of the judges was a significant determinate of how a judge ruled. Cox and Katz set up a simple model of the redistricting process that takes into account the role of the federal courts and the change in the structure of incentives by *all* the actors brought about by *Baker v. Carr.* They show that their model can account for the "mystery of the vanishing marginals" as well as the steep rise in the incumbency advantage in congressional elections.

96th - 98th Houses: Shift-at-97th Experiment

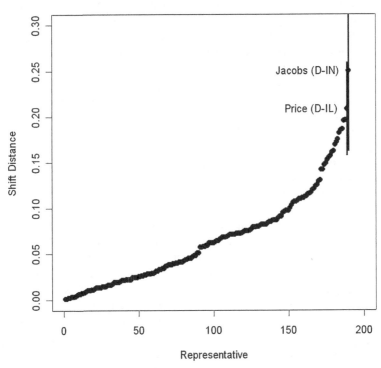

FIGURE 6.4. *Testing for redistricting effects using the combined 96th to 98th U.S. House roll call voting matrices. The vertical axis is the magnitude of the distance shifted, and the horizontal axis sorts the shifts from low to high. The vertical lines around selected representatives show the 95 percent confidence limits for the shift distances.*

or QN are used. If Bayesian simulation is used, both the ideal points and the standard errors are estimated in one step. In either case the change in position of each legislator is compared with the changes for all other legislators.

Large-Scale Experiments Using DW-NOMINATE

Two sets of large-scale experiments, described here, can be done with DW-NOMINATE. The first set deals with shift distances, and the second with agendas – that is, scaling subsets of the roll calls to see whether the legislator ideal points are affected by *adding* or *subtracting* sets of votes.

In principle, we could do the shift distance experiments described above using any number of legislative sessions. Technically, the correct baseline for the shift distances over time would be to use *all* the legislative sessions and break *every legislator* between *every adjacent pair* of sessions. For large legislatures over a long period of time this is not yet computationally feasible. A reasonable approximation to this ideal setup is to use the modified DW-NOMINATE method developed by Nokken and Poole (2004) to compute shift distances.

Experiments with Shift Distances

The experiments described in the previous section were all small-scale, that is, confined to three adjacent U.S. Congresses. Although these matrices were quite large by conventional standards – 612 by 2,984 for the U.S. House example – either the parametric bootstrap or Bayesian simulation can be used to compute confidence limits for the various shift distances. Now I will outline several large-scale experiments using DW-NOMINATE applied to all U.S. Houses from 1789 to 2002 (the 1st to 107th Congresses). By scaling up the size of the experiments we can compute shift distances over long periods of time so that more comprehensive experiments can be conducted. The downside is that with experiments this large it is not yet possible to use the parametric bootstrap or Bayesian MCMC methods to obtain measures of uncertainty for the shift distances. In the not too distant future, methods to obtain standard errors will be computationally possible, however, so I will show how such experiments can be conducted.

To obtain shift distances between adjacent legislative sessions I use the modified version of DW-NOMINATE developed by Nokken and Poole (2004). To briefly recap the discussion of DW-NOMINATE in Chapter 4, let T denote the number of Congresses (indexed by $t = 1, \ldots, T$); s denote the number of policy dimensions ($k = 1, \ldots, s$), p_t denote the number of legislators in Congress t ($i = 1, \ldots, p_t$); q_t denote the number of roll call votes in Congress t ($j = 1, \ldots, q_t$); and T_i denote the number of Congresses in which legislator i served ($t = 1, \ldots, T_i$). Legislator i's coordinate on dimension k at time t is given by equation (4.17); for the *linear model* the coordinate is

$$X_{ikt} = \chi_{ik0} + \chi_{ik1} T_{t1} \qquad (6.1)$$

where T_{t1} is a Legendre polynomial [equation (4.18)]:

$$T_{tl} = -1 + (t - 1)\frac{2}{T_i - 1}, \qquad t = 1, \ldots, T_i. \qquad (6.2)$$

To employ the Nokken–Poole method I use DW-NOMINATE to estimate the two-dimensional linear model for the 1st to 107th U.S. Houses. Then, holding the roll call outcomes from the two-dimensional linear model fixed, I estimate an ideal point for every legislator in every Congress. This allows me to compute a shift distance for every legislator between Congresses, *controlling for the linear time trend*. That is, loosely speaking, the shift distances are the "residuals" from fitting a two-dimensional linear model to roll call data over time.

Following the notation in Chapter 4, let X_{ikt}; O_{jkyt} and O_{jknt}; and β and w_2 through w_s be the estimated legislator ideal point coordinates; roll call outcome point coordinates; and utility function parameters from running DW-NOMINATE to convergence. Let $\tilde{X}_{ikt}$ be the ith legislator's coordinate on the kth dimension in the tth Congress estimated from the converged roll call outcomes, O_{jkyt} and O_{jknt}, and the utility function parameters β and w_2 through w_s for Congress t from DW-NOMINATE [$\tilde{X}_{ikt}$ should not be confused with X_{ikt} from equation (6.1) previously].

Given this framework, the squared distance of legislator i to the Yea outcome on the kth dimension for roll call j at time t is

$$\tilde{d}^2_{ijkyt} = (\tilde{X}_{ikt} - O_{jkyt})^2. \tag{6.3}$$

The probability that legislator i votes Yea on the jth roll call at time t is

$$\tilde{P}_{ijyt} = \Phi\left[\beta\left\{\exp\left(-\frac{1}{2}\sum_{k=1}^{s} w_k \tilde{d}^2_{ijkyt}\right) - \exp\left(-\frac{1}{2}\sum_{k=1}^{s} w_k \tilde{d}^2_{ijknt}\right)\right\}\right] \tag{6.4}$$

and the natural log of the likelihood function is

$$L = \sum_{t=1}^{T}\sum_{i=1}^{p_t}\sum_{j=1}^{q_t}\sum_{\tau=1}^{2} C_{ij\tau t} \ln \tilde{P}_{ij\tau t} \tag{6.5}$$

where τ is the index for Yea and Nay, $\tilde{P}_{ij\tau t}$ is the probability of voting for choice τ as given by equation (6.4), and $C_{ij\tau t} = 1$ if the legislator's actual choice is τ, and 0 otherwise. Equations (6.4) and (6.5) are the same as equations (4.23) and (4.24), respectively, with the only unknowns being the time-specific legislator ideal point coordinates, the $\tilde{X}_{ikt}$. Everything else is from the converged DW-NOMINATE estimation.

Given the $\tilde{X}_{ikt}$, the shift distances controlling for the linear trend are easily computed; namely,

$$d_{itt-1} = \left|\sqrt{\sum_{k=1}^{s} w_k^2(\tilde{X}_{ikt} - \tilde{X}_{ikt-1})^2} - \sqrt{\sum_{k=1}^{s} w_k^2(X_{ikt} - X_{ikt-1})^2}\right| \tag{6.6}$$

where $\sqrt{\sum_{k=1}^{s} w_k^2(X_{ikt} - X_{ikt-1})^2}$ is the distance between legislator i's ideal points at times t and time $t - 1$ from DW-NOMINATE. This distance is usually very small (Poole and Rosenthal, 1997), so that the distance between the respective time-specific legislator ideal points largely determines d_{itt-1}.

Following Nokken and Poole (2004), to check this approach I computed measures of fit for DW-NOMINATE, the time-specific legislator ideal point model (fixed cutting lines with legislators estimated for each Congress), and NOMINATE applied to each Congress separately (cutting lines and legislators estimated for each Congress). If the time-specific legislator ideal point model

U.S. House: Mean of Shift Distances
Two-Dimensional DW-NOMINATE (1789-2002)

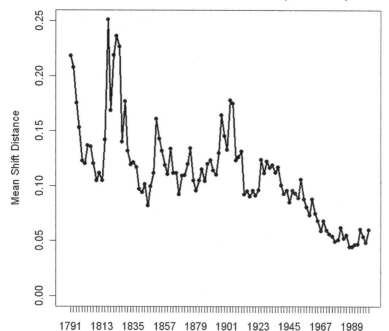

FIGURE 6.5. *Average shift distances for all the adjacent pairs of U.S. Houses, 1789–*
2002. The shift distances are computed from DW-NOMINATE two-dimensional dynamic
coordinates. The mean shift distance tends to track the fit of the two-dimensional dynamic
model.

accounts for most of the increase in fit from DW-NOMINATE to scaling each
Congress separately, the assumption of fixed cutting lines is reasonable.

For the 1st to 107th U.S. Houses, the two-dimensional dynamic DW-
NOMINATE scaling correctly classified 86.5 percent of member votes with
an aggregate proportional reduction in error (APRE) of 0.592 and a geometric
mean probability of 0.740. For the time-specific legislator ideal point model
the correct classification was 86.9 percent, with an APRE of 0.606 and a GMP
of 0.747. For each Congress separately the figures are 87.0 percent, an APRE
of 0.607, and a GMP of 0.748. In sum, the time-specific legislator ideal point
model fits almost as well as estimating each Congress separately. This means
that most of the change of fit from DW-NOMINATE to the separate Congress
scalings is being captured by the time-specific ideal points model. That is, most
of the difference in fit is due to shifting ideal points, not to shifting cutting lines.

Figure 6.5 shows the mean of the shift distances – the d_{itt-1} – for all
the adjacent pairs of U.S. Houses 1–2, 2–3, ..., 106–107. The mean shift distance is essentially a measure of fit for the two-dimensional dynamic spatial

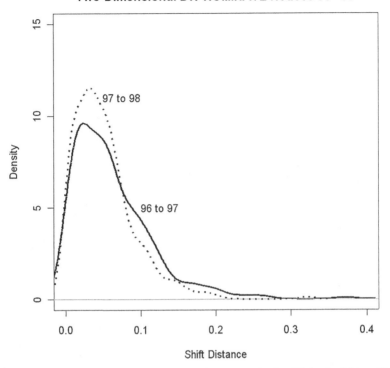

FIGURE 6.6. *Distribution of shift distances from DW-NOMINATE for the 96th to 98th U.S. Houses. There is essentially no difference between the two distributions, even though representatives serving in the 98th House were redistricted.*

model: The larger the mean shift distance, the lower the fit. Consequently, the basic pattern is consistent with the findings of Poole and Rosenthal (1997). The mean shift distance is large in the first few Houses and then drops dramatically when the Federalist–Jeffersonian Republican party system emerges. The mean shift distances are high during the Era of Good Feelings (1815–1824) and in the early 1850s when the two-party system was weakest. During the twentieth century the mean shift distance fell steadily.

The standard deviations are roughly on a par with the means. In the early part of the nineteenth century they vary from below 0.10 to about 0.20 during the Era of Good Feelings. After the early 1850s they are all below 0.12, and they fall below 0.10 for the entire twentieth century. In the past 30 years they have all been below 0.055.

Figure 6.6 shows the distribution of shift distances for the 96th to 98th U.S. Houses that were examined in the previous section. The number of

Table 6.1. *An Analysis of Shift Distances of the Exits of U.S. House Members,*
1947–1984

Shiftdist	Coef.	Std. Err.	t	$P > |t|$	[95% Conf. Interval]	
appoint	.0103272	.0086743	1.19	0.234	−.0066774	.0273318
died	.0168357	.0057399	2.93	0.003	.0055835	.028088
hirun	.0024771	.0040324	0.61	0.539	−.0054278	.010382
lost	.0062945	.0030628	2.06	0.040	.0002903	.0122987
retire	−.0006396	.0033617	−0.19	0.849	−.0072298	.0059506
missvote	.0475206	.0081348	5.84	0.000	.0315735	.0634676
redistrict	.0032472	.0023797	1.36	0.172	−.0014179	.0079123
vsharetm1	−.0003384	.0000432	−7.84	0.000	−.000423	−.0002537

Number of obs. = 6280
$F(25, 6254) = 28.65$
Prob. $> F = 0.0000$
$R^2 = 0.1028$
Adj. $R^2 = 0.0992$
Root MSE = 0.0551

representatives serving in both the 96th and 97th Houses was 354, with a mean shift distance of 0.058 and a standard deviation of 0.049. The number in both the 97th and 98th Houses was 351, with a mean shift distance of 0.051 and a standard deviation of 0.041. Of these 351 members serving in the 97th and 98th Houses, 343 were redistricted and 8 were not (these numbers differ from those in the previous section because of members who did not serve in the 96th House). The corresponding mean shift distances were 0.051 and 0.074 with standard deviations of 0.040 and 0.064, respectively. Again, at least with respect to the redistricting of the 98th U.S. House, there is little evidence that members *in the aggregate* shifted position in response to a new geographic district.

These shift distances can be used for a variety of experiments. I will illustrate this by replicating the analysis done by Poole and Romer (1993) and Poole and Rosenthal (1997) of the types of exit from the 80th through the 99th U.S. Houses. The dependent variable in the analyses is a measure of how different one-dimensional W-NOMINATE coordinates were from one-dimensional D-NOMINATE coordinates. In this analysis the dependent variable is 6,280 shift distances for House pairs 80–81, 81–82, . . . , 97–98. The independent variables are indicators for the type of exit [appointed to a judgeship or executive position (appoint); died in office (died); ran for higher office (hirun); lost bid for reelection in either the primary or general election (lost); and retired (retire)], the proportion of missing votes in the final House (missvote), an indicator for redistricting (redistrict), the percentage of the two-party vote in the last election (vsharetm1), and fixed-effect indicators for the 18 House pairs. The results are shown in Table 6.1.

The results are essentially the same as discussed in Poole and Rosenthal (1997). The fixed-effect coefficients (not shown) are all statistically significant, and the redistricting and retirement indicators are not statistically significant. The exit indicators "died" and "lost" reach statistical significance in this analysis, in contrast to Poole and Romer (1993) and Poole and Rosenthal (1997), but they were close to being statistically significant in those previous analyses using a different but similar dependent variable. The basic finding remains the same: "shirking is not an ideological matter; it is simply voting less. Shirking, interpreted as indulging one's own preferences, rather than representing the district's preferences, is, at best, a second-order phenomenon" (Poole and Rosenthal, 1997, p. 75).

The analysis of shift distances can be pushed only so far. *I am not arguing that there are no redistricting or last-period effects*. Pothole Al D'Amato clearly moved to the left to try to win reelection in 1998. Some members of Congress clearly become "statesmen" when they know that they are going to retire and no longer have to face the folks back home. Tests for shifts in position by *groups of legislators* cannot use aggregate variation and expect to be very successful. Simply put, as the previous figures show, this variation is very likely going to be near or within the noise level – that is, what is left over after you have controlled for the systematic ideological content of voting using the spatial model.

In order to detect shifts in position due to redistricting and other similar effects, it is necessary *to sign the shifts*, that is, actually work with the *direction of movement* from legislative session to legislative session. For example, if a legislator's geographic district is redrawn so that it is more liberal, the direction of the shift of the legislator's ideal point should be toward more liberal members of the legislature. Properly detecting these kinds of effects is very difficult, because the first step must be to estimate the spatial component of choice properly so that the shifts are meaningful. Interest-group ratings are not usually appropriate for these tasks, because of the flaws that I discussed in Chapter 2; namely, they are inherently one-dimensional, and the researcher must assume that the interest group is exterior to the legislators being rated. The use of an appropriately specified and estimated spatial model of choice is the necessary first step of any investigation into position shifts in roll call voting over time.

Experiments with Adding and Subtracting Sets of Roll Calls

A spatial map does not necessarily have to be constructed from *all* the roll call votes cast by a legislature. Making spatial maps using subsets of roll calls is relatively easy. Depending on what subset of roll calls is selected, the spatial map of the legislators may change from that produced by scaling all the roll calls. The important question is: Why do it? Before turning to this question, I show in Figures 6.7 and 6.8 an example of the effect of a subset of roll calls on a spatial map.

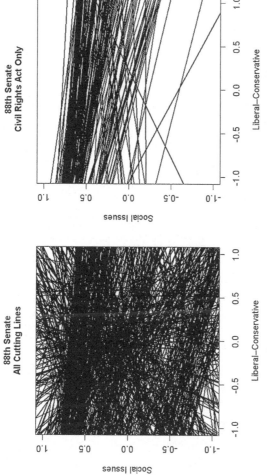

FIGURE 6.7. *Cutting lines from DW-NOMINATE for the 88th U.S. Senate. The cutting lines for the 1964 Civil Rights Act are almost all at the same angle through the two-dimensional space, because the roll calls almost always split some number of Southern Democrats from a coalition of the Northern Democrats plus most of the Republicans.*

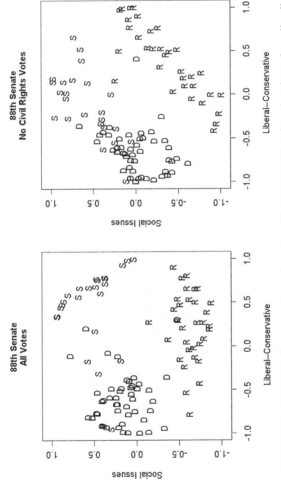

FIGURE 6.8. 88th U.S. Senate configurations from W-NOMINATE with and without the roll calls on the 1964 Civil Rights Act. The configuration on the right for the non–Civil Rights Act roll calls is rotated about 45 degrees counterclockwise, and the Southern Democrats are somewhat more dispersed. However, allowing for the rotation, the two configurations are very similar.

Figure 6.7 shows the cutting lines for the 505 scalable roll calls cast in the 88th U.S. Senate from DW-NOMINATE, along with just the 134 roll calls cast on the landmark 1964 Civil Rights Act.[8] The difference is obvious to the eye. The Civil Rights Act roll calls almost always split some number of Southern Democrats from a coalition of the Northern Democrats plus most of the Republicans (see Figure 1.2) so that the angles of the cutting lines through the two-dimensional space are almost all the same. Indeed, a simple one-dimensional OC scaling of these 134 roll calls produces a rank ordering of the senators that correctly classifies 95.3 percent of the 12,960 total choices with an APRE of 0.846.

This simple example shows that if a large number of roll calls are cast on a single well-defined issue, the voting on that set of roll calls can easily form a one-dimensional track through the two-dimensional space. This can affect the spatial map of the legislators, as we see in Figure 6.8.

Figure 6.8 shows the spatial maps produced by applying W-NOMINATE to the 505 scalable roll calls cast in the 88th Senate and to the 371 scalable non-Civil Rights Act roll calls.[9] The configuration from the non-Civil Rights Act votes is rotated about 45 degrees counterclockwise, and the Southern Democrats are a bit more dispersed. Allowing for the rotation, the Pearson correlation between the corresponding first dimensions is 0.985 and the correlation between the corresponding second dimensions is 0.883. These correlations are almost exactly the same for the Democrats only and for the Republicans only.

The configurations in Figure 6.8 make sense because Civil Rights-related issues were *secondary*. That is, most roll calls before the 88th Senate and after it were concerned with the standard bread-and-butter issues that divided the two political parties. Consequently, when a large number of roll calls have cutting lines that are primarily along the second dimension, it is very likely that their inclusion or exclusion will affect the second dimension of the spatial map. Consequently, analyzing the 88th Senate in isolation can be quite misleading.

Analyzing legislative sessions over longer periods of time is less sensitive to these kinds of agenda effects. I show this with two examples using DW-NOMINATE applied to the 1st through 107th U.S. Houses.

For my first example I analyze those U.S. Houses, *constraining every House to have the same distribution of roll call majority margins*. The average distribution of majority margins for all 107 Houses was used for each House, and

[8] The second dimension is shown unweighted so that the structure is easier to see.

[9] For all the roll calls in two dimensions, the percentage correctly classified was 87.5 percent with an APRE of 0.601 and a geometric mean probability of 0.750. For the non-Civil Rights roll calls the percentage correctly classified was 85.5 percent with an APRE of 0.542 and a geometric mean probability of 0.717. Including the Civil Rights Act roll calls improves the fit of the spatial model.

Table 6.2. *Distribution of Majority Margins,*
1st to 107th U.S. Houses

Majority Margin (%)	Number	Proportion
50–55	92	0.23
56–60	80	0.20
61–65	60	0.15
66–70	44	0.11
71–75	32	0.08
76–80	24	0.06
81–85	20	0.05
86–90	16	0.04
91–95	20	0.05
96–97.5	12	0.13

the number of roll calls for each House was set equal to 400. This common distribution of majority margins is shown in Table 6.2.

To construct the artificial margins data for each House I sampled each majority margin category *with replacement* to get the required number of roll calls. For example, if for some House there were 75 roll calls with majority margins in the range 66–70 percent, then 44 roll calls from those 75 were drawn with replacement. If there were no roll calls in the range, no roll calls could be included. Hence there are a few Houses with fewer than 400 roll calls. For example, the 58th House had no roll calls with margins 71–75, 81–85, 86–90, or 91–95. It was the most extreme case. The 2nd, 3rd, 4th, 15th, 17th, 19th, 22nd, 23rd, and 78th Houses each had one missing margin, and the 18th had two missing margins. In sum, 96 of the 107 Houses had no missing margins, and 105 of 107 Houses had either no missing margins or only one.

The two-dimensional linear model was used to analyze the artificial margins data, so that the results are comparable to the two-dimensional linear model applied to the actual roll call matrices. The results are shown in Table 6.3.

Table 6.3. *Correlations Between Margins Scaling and Regular*
DW-NOMINATE Scaling of the 1st to 107th U.S. Houses

	Number of Legislators	1st Dim.	2nd Dim.
	All	All	All
Houses 1–107	34,817	.983[a]	.975
	All	All	All
	Dem. Rep.	Dem. Rep.	Dem. Rep.
Houses 80–107	12,330	.990	.985
	7,014 5,299	.979 .960	.981 .976

[a]All entries are Pearson correlations.

The legislator ideal points recovered from the margins experiment are almost identical to those estimated from the actual roll call matrices.[10] Table 6.3 shows the Pearson correlations between various subsets of legislators on the first and second dimensions. The correlations are computed between ideal points over Congresses. There were 10,322 unique representatives and 34,817 estimated ideal points. The upper half of Table 6.3 shows the correlations for all 34,817 estimated ideal points, and the lower half shows just the post-World War Two legislators overall and broken down by political party. The correlations are uniformly high.

Figure 6.9 shows the spatial map for the 88th U.S. House (1963–1964) from the actual votes and the margins experiment votes. There are only slight differences between the two configurations. The Pearson correlations for all legislators between the two configurations are 0.991 for the first dimension and 0.987 for the second dimension. The corresponding correlations for the Democrats only are 0.986 and 0.973, respectively. The corresponding correlations for the Republicans only are 0.959 and 0.978, respectively.

For my second example I analyze the 1st through 107th U.S. Houses *excluding the Southern states.*[11] The *second* dimension of the spatial maps for the U.S. Congress roughly from 1823 to 1850 and roughly from 1937 to 1990 separated members of Congress along North–South lines. The *first* dimension was primarily a North–South dimension from roughly 1815 to 1822 and 1852 to 1861. Given, however, that there is always some dispersion of the Northern state members of Congress over both dimensions, excluding the Southern states should be a good test of the stability of the spatial maps. The two-dimensional linear model was used to analyze the no-South data, so that the results are comparable to the two-dimensional linear model applied to the actual roll call matrices. The results are shown in Table 6.4.

The legislator ideal points recovered from the no-South experiment are almost identical to those estimated from the actual roll call matrices.[12] Table 6.4 shows the Pearson correlations between various subsets of legislators on the first and second dimensions. The correlations are computed between ideal points over Congresses. There were 7,585 unique non-South representatives and 24,465 estimated ideal points. The upper half of Table 6.4 shows the correlations for all 24,465 estimated ideal points, and the lower half shows just the post-World War Two non-South legislators overall and broken down by political party. The correlations are again uniformly high.

[10] In the margins experiment, the correct classification was 85.53 percent with an APRE of 0.581 and a geometric mean probability of 0.729. The total number of choices was 10,841,319. For the DW-NOMINATE scaling of the actual roll calls the total number of choices was 11,141,903. The percentage correctly classified was 86.47 percent with an APRE of 0.592 and a geometric mean probability of 0.740.

[11] Recall that the Southern states are the 11 states of the Confederacy plus Kentucky and Oklahoma.

[12] In the no-South experiment the correct classification was 86.68 percent with an APRE of 0.572 and a geometric mean probability of 0.744. The total number of choices was 7,814,794.

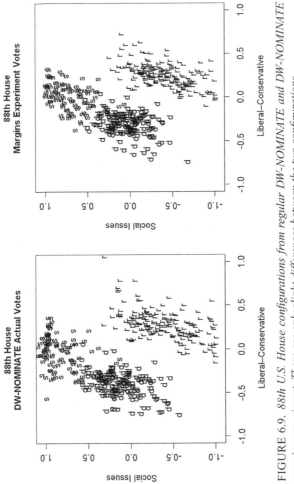

FIGURE 6.9. *88th U.S. House configurations from regular DW-NOMINATE and DW-NOMINATE margins experiment. There are only slight differences between the two configurations.*

184

Table 6.4. *Correlations Between No-South Scaling and Regular*
DW-NOMINATE Scaling of the 1st to 107th U.S. Houses

	Number of Legislators	1st Dim.	2nd Dim.
Houses 1–107	All 24,465	All .993[a]	All .967
Houses 80–107	All Dem.[b] Rep. 8,795 4,454 4,327	All Dem. Rep. .994 .967 .967	All Dem. Rep. .964 .954 .958

[a] All entries are Pearson correlations.
[b] Northern Democrats and Northern Republicans only.

Figure 6.10 shows the spatial map for the 88th U.S. House (1963–1964) from the actual votes (Southern legislators not shown) and the spatial map estimated without the Southern representatives. There are only slight differences between the two configurations. The Pearson correlations for all non-Southern legislators between the two configurations are 0.994 for the first dimension and 0.973 for the second dimension. The corresponding correlations for the (Northern) Democrats only are 0.975 and 0.943, respectively. The corresponding correlations for the (Northern) Republicans only are 0.966 and 0.969, respectively.

The examples above show that the selection of what roll calls to scale can definitely affect the structure of a spatial map. This is particularly true if a single legislative session is analyzed, but will be less true if legislative sessions are analyzed over longer periods of time. The reason is simple. Over time, short-run agenda effects will be smoothed out because the primary issues dividing the political parties (or nations) represented in the parliament will tend to be voted on in every legislative session.

Returning to the question I raised at the beginning of this subsection, why should we scale *subsets* of roll calls at all? I think this is useful for two purposes. The first is to uncover the microstructure of the spatial map. The 88th Senate roll calls on the 1964 Civil Rights Act are a good example of this type of research. The Civil Rights Act roll calls form a one-dimensional track through the two-dimensional space, and this result makes a great deal of sense from the legislative history of the Act. Second, I think it is a useful tool to uncover what is going on when *structural change* is occurring, either in the electorate that is selecting the legislature or in the legislature itself. For example, the Compromise of 1850 in the U.S. tried to settle the outstanding issues regarding Southern slavery. The result was the disintegration of the Whig party and an electoral realignment that produced the Republican Party. The structure of Congressional voting changed dramatically beginning in 1853. Slavery-related roll calls before 1850 fell along the second dimension, whereas slavery-related roll calls after 1852 fell along the first dimension (Poole and Rosenthal, 1997).

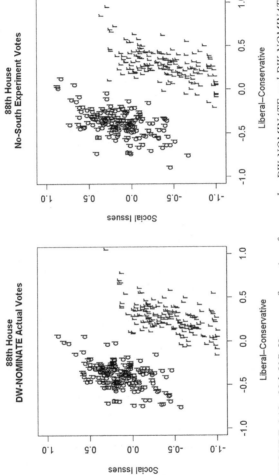

FIGURE 6.10. *88th U.S. House configurations from regular DW-NOMINATE and DW-NOMINATE no-South experiment. There are only slight differences between the two configurations.*

Estimating a Common Spatial Map for
Two Different Legislatures

The problem of estimating a common spatial map for two different legislatures, or a legislature and an executive or judicial body, is very hard to solve. Placing different governmental institutions in a common spatial map is important, however, because a large body of spatial theory predicts how legislative, executive, and judicial institutions should interact (e.g., McCarty and Poole, 1995; Krehbiel, 1998; Brady and Volden, 1998; McCarty and Razaghian, 1999; Shipan and Moraski, 1999; McCarty, 1997, 2000; Bailey and Chang, 2001; Bailey, 2002; and the citations therein).

The simplest example of this problem is a bicameral legislature – that is, a legislature that has two distinct voting bodies, like the British Parliament, the U.S. Congress, and 49 of the 50 U.S. state legislatures. The roll call matrices from the two chambers of a bicameral legislature can be combined via the columns if enough roll calls are cast in the two chambers with identical content, or via the rows if some legislators serve in both chambers. If both chambers voted on exactly the same motions, the roll call matrix would be functionally equivalent to one from a legislature formed from the combined membership of the two chambers, and the problem would be trivial. In fact, however, in the U.S. Congress it is very difficult to match up identical roll calls. Such roll calls are usually on conference reports, and many of these are passed by very lopsided margins in both the House and the Senate.

A workable solution is to combine some common roll calls with some common legislators. In the U.S. context one can use interest groups that issue ratings of members of Congress. Typically an interest group like Americans for Democratic Action (ADA) selects 20 to 50 roll calls that its leaders regard as important, and they publish a "report card" showing the percentage of those roll calls that each member of the House or the Senate voted with their preferred position. In other words, interest groups that issue ratings of members of Congress "vote" on a subset of roll calls in *both* chambers. To make the idea work, you must assume that the interest groups have the same ideal points in both chambers.

Howard Rosenthal and I performed such an experiment using the 96th (1979–1980) U.S. Congress (Poole and Rosenthal, 1997, chapter 8). We found 8 roll calls with identical content, and used 27 interest groups[13] and President

---

[13] The interest groups are: American Civil Liberties Union (ACLU), American Conservative Union (ACU), Americans for Constitutional Action (ACA), Americans for Democratic Action (ADA), American Farm Bureau Federation (AFBF), American Federation of State, County and Municipal Employees (AFSCME), American Federation of Teachers (AFT), American Security Council (ASC), Bread for the World (BFW), Building and Construction Trades Department AFL-CIO (BCTD), Chamber of Commerce of the United States (CCUS), Child Welfare League of America (CWLA), Christian Voice (CV), Coalition for a New Foreign and Military Policy (CFNFMP),

Carter to glue the chambers together. President Carter can be treated as voting in both chambers because *Congressional Quarterly* reports the President's position on many roll calls. (These roll calls are used by *CQ* to construct its Presidential-Support Score for every member.) We used W-NOMINATE to analyze the combined matrix of senators, representatives, 27 interest groups, and President Carter. Figure 6.11 shows the estimated spatial map.

Figure 6.11 is the same as Figure 8.6 in Poole and Rosenthal (1997) except that I show the interest groups and President Carter separately from the members of Congress. These results are analyzed in detail in Poole and Rosenthal (1997, Chapter 8), and I will not repeat that analysis here except to say that all the checks we did on the results show that combining two chambers using interest groups *and* some common roll calls is a reasonable approach.

Although Rosenthal and I found that this method of combining two chambers works well, a few words of caution are in order. Great care must be taken in analyzing roll call data organized in this framework. Because interest groups typically pick only 20 to 50 roll calls, this by itself cannot provide enough glue to combine the two chambers. Recall from Chapter 2 that with small numbers of roll calls a sizable number of open polytopes may be present. In the case of an interest group "voting" only 20 times in each chamber, the overall meshes for the separate chambers can be slid around a lot vis-à-vis one another because of all the big polytopes in the separate submeshes for the chosen roll calls. Consequently, to make this approach work it is essential to have some roll calls that are common to both chambers. This has the effect of gluing the meshes together. The more common roll calls there are, the better the results. The difficulty is that this is a very labor-intensive approach.

Another approach to estimating a common spatial map for two chambers of the same legislature (or two different legislatures) together is to analyze multiple legislative sessions. *Over time*, if some legislators served in both chambers, then on the assumption that the legislator has the same ideal point in both chambers, we can combine the roll call matrices using these legislators, and a spatial map can be estimated.

I have developed two methods for doing this. The first is an extension of a scaling method I developed (Poole, 1998) that extracts common-space scores (CSSs) from multiple sets of legislative coordinates. In Chapter 5 I discussed this method in some detail and showed how it can be used to obtain good starting coordinates for DW-NOMINATE or other procedures that analyze a large number of legislative sessions over time. Here I will show a simple

---

Committee on Political Education AFL-CIO (COPE), Congress Watch (CW), Consumer Federation of America (CFA), Friends' Committee on National Legislation (FCNL), League of Conservation Voters (LCV), League of Women Voters (LWV), National Alliance of Senior Citizens (NASC), National Council of Senior Citizens (NCSC), National Farmers Organization (NFO), National Farmers Union (NFU), National Federation of Independent Business (NFIB), United Auto Workers (UAW), and United Mine Workers (UMW).

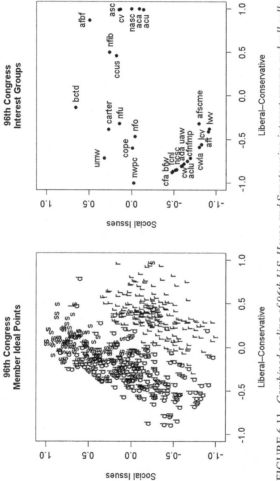

FIGURE 6.11. *Combined scaling of 96th U.S. House and Senate using interest groups and roll calls common to both chambers.*

189

extension of the CSS method that extracts common-space coordinates for two chambers simultaneously so that they are in the same space.

The second method is an extension of OC to multiple legislative sessions and two chambers.

As I noted in Chapter 5, the CSS method was developed to be a singular-value decomposition procedure for matrices with large amounts of missing data. In this application I use it to estimate the latent dimensions underlying the coordinates of a set of legislators over time. The latent dimensions are estimated one at a time. The first latent dimension is extracted from all the first-dimension coordinates over the entire time period. Then the second latent dimension is extracted from all the second-dimension coordinates over the entire time period, and so on.

The model estimated is

$$X_0^{(k)} = [\Psi_k W_k' + J_n \mu_k']_0 + E_0^{(k)} \tag{6.8}$$

where Ψ_k is the n by 1 vector of coordinates of the individuals on the kth basic dimension, W_k is a T by 1 vector of weights, μ_k is a vector of constants of length T, J_n is an n-length vector of ones, and $E_0^{(k)}$ is an n by T matrix of error terms. W_k and μ_k map the legislators from the basic space onto the individual legislative session dimensions. I assume that the elements of $E_0^{(k)}$ are random draws from a symmetric distribution with zero mean.

The CSS method is an alternating least squares procedure that produces estimates of the basic coordinates and the linear transformations for each dimension; that is, from $\hat{\Psi}_1$, $\hat{W}_1$, and $\hat{\mu}_1$ to $\hat{\Psi}_s$, $\hat{W}_s$, and $\hat{\mu}_s$. To get estimates for those legislators who served in less than five legislative sessions, I apply the simple linear transformation to their coordinates in each session that they served and then compute the mean of these transformed coordinates; namely,

$$\hat{\psi}_{ik} = \frac{\sum_{t=1}^{T_i} \frac{X_{ikt} - \hat{\mu}_k}{\hat{w}_k}}{T_i} \tag{6.9}$$

where T_i is the number of sessions (<5) that legislator i served in. Equation (6.8) is the same as equation (5.10), and equation (6.9) is the same as equation (5.11).

The CSS method is easily extended to the case of two legislatures. To see how, let n_U be the number of legislators who served in the first (upper) chamber only, let n_L be the number of legislators who served in the second (lower) chamber only, let n_B be the number of legislators who served in both chambers, and let Ψ_{Uk}, Ψ_{Lk}, Ψ_{Bk} be the corresponding vectors of underlying coordinates on the kth basic dimension of lengths n_U, n_L, and n_B, respectively.

This produces the equations

$$X_{U0}^{(k)} = \begin{bmatrix} \Psi_{Uk} \\ \Psi_{Bk} \end{bmatrix} W_U' + J_{U+B} \mu_U' + E_{U0}^{(k)}$$

$$X_{L0}^{(k)} = \begin{bmatrix} \Psi_{Lk} \\ \Psi_{Bk} \end{bmatrix} W_L' + J_{L+B} \mu_L' + E_{L0}^{(k)}$$

(6.10)

where $X_{U0}^{(k)}$ and $X_{L0}^{(k)}$ are the $n_U + n_B$ by T and $n_L + n_B$ by T matrices of estimated ideal points for the kth dimension in each of the T time periods for the two chambers, respectively.

The procedure to estimate equations (6.10) is the same as that discussed in Chapter 5, only now some bookkeeping is necessary when the legislator coordinates are estimated. Given $\hat{W}_U$, $\hat{\mu}_U$, $\hat{W}_L$, and $\hat{\mu}_L$, the coordinate for a legislator who served only in the upper chamber can be estimated by using $\hat{W}_U$ and $\hat{\mu}_U$ via simple ordinary least squares (Poole, 1998). Similarly, if a legislator served only in the lower chamber, then $\hat{W}_L$ and $\hat{\mu}_L$ are used to estimate the legislator coordinate via simple ordinary least squares. If a legislator served in both chambers, a W matrix can be formed from $\hat{W}_U$ and $\hat{W}_L$ by using the rows corresponding to the chamber served in, and a μ vector can be formed from $\hat{\mu}_U$ and $\hat{\mu}_L$ by using the entries corresponding to the chamber served in. Given estimates of the legislator coordinates, $\hat{\Psi}_{Uk}$, $\hat{\Psi}_{Lk}$, and $\hat{\Psi}_{Bk}$, respectively, it is a simple matter to estimate W_{Uk} and μ_{Uk} and W_{Lk} and μ_{Lk} with simple ordinary least squares (Poole, 1998). This alternating least squares process can be repeated as many times as desired. Monte Carlo work reported in Poole (1998) shows the algorithm to be very stable, and it accurately reproduces the "true" coordinates even with high levels of missing data and error.

I will illustrate the CSS method by analyzing U.S. House and Senate two-dimensional W-NOMINATE scores for the 75th to 107th Congresses (1937–2002). It is possible to analyze the House and Senate W-NOMINATE scores together because 162 legislators served in both chambers for at least five Congresses during this period. I make the assumption that legislators maintain a fixed position in the underlying basic space when they move from the House to the Senate or vice versa. In this application, the overall X_0 has 33 columns – one for each Congress – and a row for each person serving in at least five Congresses from 1937 to 2002. A total of 1,570 legislators served in at least five Congresses during this period – 1,219 in the House only, 189 in the Senate only, and 162 in both chambers.[14] Equation (6.10) is used to estimate the basic dimensions, and equation (6.9) is used to estimate the basic coordinates for those legislators

---

[14] The matrices $X_0^{(1)}$ through $X_0^{(s)}$ have 1,570 rows and 33 columns. The total number of entries in each matrix is $1,570 \times 33 = 51,810$, of which 37,855 are missing data and 13,955, or 26.9 percent, are W-NOMINATE coordinates. The fit of the first basic dimension was a Pearson R^2 of 0.957, and the fit of the second basic dimension was 0.888.

serving in fewer than five total Congresses. Figure 6.12 shows the chamber and party first-dimension (liberal–conservative) common-space coordinate means for the 75th to 107th Congresses.

The ability to study the changes in chamber and political party means and medians over time illustrates the advantage of being able to place two different legislatures in a common spatial map. Despite their different electoral rules, geographic constituencies, and internal procedures, the U.S. House and Senate have essentially the same overall patterns over time. There is a slight tendency for the means of the political parties in the House to be more extreme than in the Senate, simply because there is slightly more ideological variance within parties in the House. House geographic districts tend to be subsets of Senate geographic districts (entire U.S. states). Even so, this is a minor effect. The trend to partisan polarization is also evident in both chambers (Poole and Rosenthal, 1984b; 1991; 1997; 2001; McCarty, Poole, and Rosenthal, 1997). This trend has been evident since the early to mid-1970s and shows no sign of slowing down.

The CSS method extracts basic dimensions from the separately estimated spatial maps for legislatures over time. In contrast to the interest group experiment discussed above, the separately estimated spatial maps are based on all the roll call votes, so that the basic coordinates for a legislator who served in both chambers are indirectly based on all the roll call votes the legislator cast in both chambers, albeit in different Congresses. This raises the obvious question: Why not analyze the roll call matrices directly? The answer is that it is doable, but there are problems with the approach. I first show some results from using OC to analyze the U.S. House and Senate, and then discuss the limitations of the general approach.

Recall from Chapter 3 that OC is based directly on the underlying geometry of roll call voting, and the only assumptions made to implement it are that the choice space is Euclidean and that legislators making choices behave as if they had symmetric, single-peaked preferences. Other than these assumptions, no assumptions are made about the functional form of individuals' preferences and no assumptions are made about the distributional form of individuals' errors in making choices. In one dimension, OC produces a rank order that maximizes the number of correctly classified roll call voting decisions. In two dimensions, it produces ideal points and cutting planes for the roll call votes that maximize the number of correctly classified choices.

I applied OC to all the U.S. Houses and Senates for the 1st to 107th Congresses (1789–2002). All roll calls with at least 2.5 percent in the minority (40,292 roll calls in the House and 42,149 roll calls in the Senate) were included in the scaling. I did the scaling on both chambers simultaneously, using the 615 members who served in both the House and Senate as glue to define a common metric. The overall fit of the scaling was 87.34 percent in two dimensions – 12,171,199 of 13,935,976 total choices were correctly classified, for an APRE

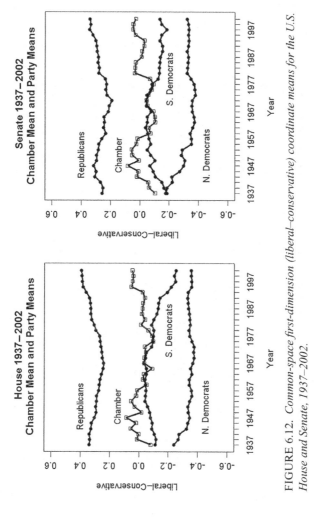

FIGURE 6.12. *Common-space first-dimension (liberal–conservative) coordinate means for the U.S. House and Senate, 1937–2002.*

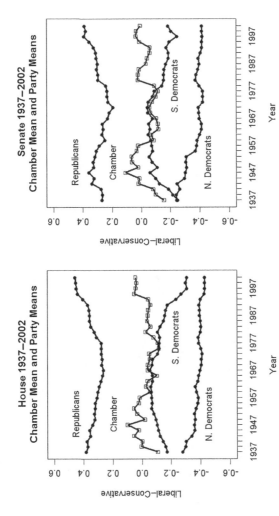

FIGURE 6.13. *Optimal classification first-dimension (liberal–conservative) coordinate means for the U.S. House and Senate, 1937–2002. The patterns are very similar to the corresponding common-space means shown in Figure 6.12.*

of .619. There were 10,299 unique members of the House, 1,808 unique members of the Senate, and 615 legislators who served in both chambers. Hence there were $10,299 + 1,808 - 615 = 11,492$ unique legislators who served in Congress in American history. Known major political party switchers (e.g., Strom Thurmond of South Carolina) are in the data twice. Figure 6.13 shows the chamber and political party means on the first dimension for the 75th to 107th Congresses (1937 to 2002).

Figure 6.13 is almost identical to Figure 6.12, even though the OC scaling is for all 107 Congresses rather than just for the last 33 Congresses. The Pearson correlations between the corresponding means in the two figures are all above 0.95 except for the Northern Democrats. For the House the correlation is 0.863, and for the Senate it is 0.917.[15] The fact that these two very different methods yield essentially the same result over time is important validation for both approaches and means that, at least over reasonably short time frames, estimating a spatial map for more than one legislature is possible and the results are meaningful.

The fly in the ointment is the assumption that legislators who serve in both legislatures have fixed ideal points. This is clearly a very strong assumption and, in the case of the U.S. House and Senate, a questionable one because of the different geographic constituencies. Most members of the House represent portions of states, whereas senators represent whole states. Conventional wisdom tells us that when members of the House want to win election to the upper body they must moderate their views because of the broader statewide constituency. A predictable spatial change should occur, but building that into OC or DW-NOMINATE is a formidable problem. If every member who served in both chambers were allowed to "move" when she made the change, then *there would be no glue*. It would be the functional equivalent of scaling the two chambers separately.

I have no doubt that this problem will be solved in the not too distant future. In the meantime, the CSS method appears to give reasonable results over time spans where the structure of the voting space is stable.

Conclusion

In this chapter I have discussed a variety of natural experiments that we can perform using roll call matrices. These experiments consist of combining roll call matrices over time or introducing additional rows into the matrices to allow legislators to be treated as multiple individuals.

---

[15]The correlations for the U.S. House are: chamber, 0.994; Republicans, 0.991; Northern Democrats, 0.863; Southern Democrats, 0.995. The correlations for the U.S. Senate are: chamber, 0.983; Republicans, 0.989; Northern Democrats, 0.917; Southern Democrats, 0.990.

In the first part of the chapter I outlined a general method of testing for changes in the voting behavior of legislators by treating them as multiple individuals. The idea is to compare the change of a specific legislator – e.g., a legislator who switches political parties – with the change of every other legislator who serves during the same period of time. The method is applied to a combined roll call matrix that consists of all roll calls cast during several legislative sessions before and after the change in question. In this combined matrix, the legislator who is the focus of the experiment is treated as two individuals. The method has three steps: (1) estimate a spatial map from the matrix, obtain the two points for the legislator who is the object of the experiment, and calculate the *shift distance* between the two estimated ideal points; (2) perform the same experiment for every other legislator with the same period of service as the targeted legislator – that is, treat them as multiple individuals, and compute the corresponding shift distances; and (3) compute measures of uncertainty for the shift distances, using either the parametric bootstrap (Lewis and Poole, 2004) or Bayesian MCMC methods. The shift distance for the legislator who is the focus of the experiment can then be compared with all the other shift distances to see whether or not the legislator is an outlier.

In the second half of the chapter I showed how to estimate a spatial map for multiple legislatures. For a bicameral legislature the roll call matrices from the two chambers can be combined via the *columns* if enough roll calls with identical content were cast in the two chambers. Likewise, *over time*, if some legislators served in both chambers, then on the assumption that the legislator has the same ideal point in both chambers, we can combine the roll call matrices using those legislators.

CHAPTER 7

Conclusion

Overview

I conclude with short discussions of two topics. The first is the scientific status of the state of knowledge about geometric representations of human choice and judgment. I believe that research in this area, encompassing work in psychology, political science, economics, and other disciplines, is a classic example of scientific progress.

In the final section I discuss what I believe to be the important unsolved problems in the study of geometric models of legislative choice: specifying the sources of constraint, and determining precisely how the level of error interacts with the underlying geometry. I believe that these problems can be solved, and I hope the readers of this book take them as a challenge and push the field even further.

The Scientific Status of Geometric Models of Choice and Judgment

"[Textbooks] address themselves to an already articulated body of problems, data, and theory, most often to the particular set of paradigms to which the scientific community is committed at the time they are written" (Kuhn, 1962/1996, p. 136). This book, together with textbooks written for psychometricians interested in multidimensional scaling techniques (Borg and Groenen, 1997; Cox and Cox, 2001), researchers in item response theory (Andrich, 1988; Fischer and Molenaar, 1995; Embretson and Reise, 2000), and students of social choice (Sen, 1970; Austen-Smith and Banks, 2000; 2004) fits Kuhn's definition.

I believe this to be so because of the relationship between the work on multidimensional scaling methods in psychology and the development of the spatial theory of choice in political science and economics. Both have reached

197

essentially the same conclusion – low-dimensional spatial maps accurately summarize similarities and preference judgments. But the two fields use different paradigms to reach this end point. The spatial model is based upon rational choice theory, while the psychological approach is based upon cognitive process theory.

Rational choice is a general theory of human behavior that assumes individuals attempt to make the most efficient decisions possible in an environment of scarce resources. Rational choice theory can be seen as an extension of what philosophers call *folk psychology*. "Core" folk psychology consists of an ordinary belief–desire psychology and a maximization hypothesis. Actions are taken in light of beliefs to bring about desired states of affairs (Ferejohn and Satz, 2000; Cox, 2004). The spatial theory of parliamentary voting outlined in Chapter 1 rests not only upon the basic theory of rational choice but also upon a specific application of a theory of ideology based upon the work of Hinich and Ordeshook (Cahoon, Hinich, and Ordeshook, 1976; Ordeshook, 1976; Hinich and Pollard, 1981) and Converse (1964).

Cognitive process models attempt to represent similarities and choice behavior as a function of how the mind processes external information and translates it into action. These models are typically based on theories of cognition that describe how knowledge is accessed, represented, and manipulated in our minds. "Objects that are perceived or remembered receive some internal representation. Various cognitive processes are then assumed to act upon that representation. The particular processes that operate are task dependent – they will vary depending on whether subjects are asked to discriminate among objects, identify, categorize or recognize them, supply similarity ratings, make preference judgments, and so forth. Thus, to understand performance in tasks involving similarity data requires not only the specification of an underlying similarity representation, but also the cognitive processes that act on that representation" (Nosofsky, 1992, p. 25).

Within psychology, surveys and experiments over the past 50 years of how people make similarities and preferential choice judgments show that very simple geometric models appear to structure responses to these tasks (Shepard, 1987). When individuals make a judgment of how similar two stimuli are, they appear to base the judgment upon how close the two stimuli are in an abstract psychological space (Nosofsky, 1984; 1992; Shepard, 1987; Gluck, 1991). The dimensions of these psychological spaces correspond to the attributes of the stimuli. A strong regularity is that these psychological spaces are low-dimensional – very rarely above two dimensions – and that the stimulus judgments are either additive (that is, a city-block metric is being used) or simple Euclidean (Garner, 1974; Shepard 1987; 1991; Nosofsky, 1992).[1]

---

[1] Tversky (1977) argues that traditional MDS methods cannot account for well-documented asymmetries in similarity judgments (e.g., the famous Morse code data set, Rothkopf, 1957).

Another strong regularity is that the reported similarities are an exponential function of the distance in the abstract psychological space. That is, if d is the distance between two stimuli, then the reported similarity tends to be e^{-kd}, where k $(k > 0)$ is a scaling constant (Shepard, 1987; Nosofsky, 1992; Cheng, 2000).[2] In the Shepard–Ennis–Nosofsky model of stimulus comparison the individual compares two stored *exemplars* (models; patterns; typical cases) in psychological space and reports the distance between them. "The similarity between two exemplars is computed according to a rule that assumes similarity decays exponentially with increasing distance in...psychological space" (Gluck, 1991, p. 50). Ennis (1988a) shows that if these exemplars are treated as multivariate normal distributions in psychological space so as to allow for "irreducible noise in the perceptual/memory system" (Shepard, 1986, p. 60), then the expected value of the reported distance has a Gaussian distribution. That is, if there is some perceptual error, the expected value of the response function tends to be Gaussian, of the form $e^{-k\delta}$, where $\delta = d^2$ (Shepard, 1987; 1988b; Nofosky, 1988; 1992; Ennis, 1988a; 1988b; Ennis, Palen, and Mullen, 1988).[3,4]

He proposes a set-theoretic model of similarity based upon feature matching. Part of the difficulty is that similarity judgments between multiple pairs may be mixing dimensions and thereby producing asymmetries and violations of the distance axioms (Borg and Groenen, 1997, p. 299; Nosofsky, 1992). However, the asymmetries can be modeled adequately within the MDS framework in many circumstances (Borg and Groenen, 1997, pp. 402–407; Nosofsky, 1991).

[2] Shepard (1987) proposes a universal law of generalization for psychological science: "Because any object or situation experienced by an individual is unlikely to recur in exactly the same form and content, psychology's first general law should, I suggest, be a law of generalization" (p. 1317). Shepard's universal law of generalization is concerned both with *confusable* stimuli (similarity judgments) and *discriminable* stimuli (which *cannot* be confused). An example of the latter is an animal's search for food. An animal finds food in a container at a specific location (called S+ in the literature). The animal then returns somewhat later, and the container is in a noticeably different location (the animal can *discriminate* the two locations). "Will the animal still 'bet' on finding food in the container?" (Cheng, 2000, p. 403) That is, how much effort will the animal put into searching the area (the *consequential region*) near where it found the food originally? This *effort* is governed by an exponential law and has been confirmed by a variety of studies (Shepard, 1987). It is the conditional probability "that an encountered location is in the consequential region, given that S+ is in the consequential region" (Cheng, 2000, p. 403). This makes evolutionary sense. The search effort should be concentrated in the area closest to the original food source and decline sharply with increasing distance (broadly defined). Shepard (1987) shows that the exponential form can be derived from a very wide class of assumptions about the consequential region.

[3] Shepard's exponential law is very robust and does not strictly depend upon a comparison of points in an internal psychological space. Chater (1999) argues that it can be applied to distances computed using algorithmic information theory. Namely, the distance between two stimuli is defined as the sum of the lengths of the shortest computer program that maps one into the other. Gluck (1991) argues that it holds for adaptive network models.

[4] An R program illustrating the Shepard–Ennis–Nosofsky model is on the website for this book at: http://k7moa.com/Spatial_Models_of_Parliamentary_Voting.htm under the link for this chapter.

The evidence compiled in psychology on how individuals make similarity judgments produces results that are very similar to the spatial model of parliamentary voting. This is not surprising, because the economists' notion of preference can be *reduced* to the psychologists' notion of similarity. Let Ms. Smith prefer **A** to **B** when (1) Ms. Smith has an ideal standard, X_{Smith}, against which she judges stimuli of type **A**, **B**; and (2) Ms. Smith judges the similarity between X_{Smith} and **A** to be greater than the similaity between X_{Smith} and **B**.[5] In this regard, spatial models of parliamentary roll call voting are a subspecies of the similarity model.

Specifically, the random utility model with a normal distribution utility function and random error is essentially the same as the Shepard–Ennis–Nosofsky model of stimulus comparison. Namely, in a choice situation, the individual is comparing her ideal point with the Yea alternative *and* comparing it with the Nay alternative. In each comparison the individual's utility plays the role of a similarity judgment. By definition, the expected value of this utility when plotted against the distance between the ideal point and the outcome location is Gaussian. In the Shepard–Ennis–Nosofsky model, when the expected value of the reported similarity is graphed against the true distance between two stimuli, the response function is Gaussian. Even with a quadratic deterministic utility function there will be a reasonably close correspondence between the two models.

This remarkable convergence of disciplines provides powerful support for the spatial theory of parliamentary choice detailed in this book. The computer programs that produce the spatial maps only assume that the choice space is Euclidean and that the legislators' utility functions are symmetric. They are simply measuring instruments. The low dimensionality that they reveal in most applications is explained by the rational-choice-based two-space theory of Hinich and Ordeshook (Cahoon, Hinich, and Ordeshook, 1976; Ordeshook, 1976; Hinich and Pollard, 1981). The key assumption of the two-space theory is that individuals' issue positions are highly correlated – what Converse (1964) called *constraint*. Constraint may or may not be present, and the conditions that produce it are not fully understood. I discuss constraint in the next section.

Both cognitive process theory and rational choice theory are limited in what they can explain. The empirical evidence at hand simply does not determine *logically* which theory is correct. Laudan (1984; 1996), in his criticism of Kuhn's account of paradigm change, argues that it is *underdetermination* not *incommensurability* that is the key. Intuitively, underdetermination means that we are dealing with a situation where we have more parameters to estimate than we have data.[6] "Thus, we ought to abandon paradigms primarily when

---

[5] I thank Gary Cox for suggesting this formulation to me.

[6] Laudan makes the telling criticism of Kuhn that in the history of science, paradigm debate is brought to closure fairly quickly. Empirical knowledge builds up to the point that there comes

better ones come along – where I would define 'better' not simply in terms of empirical but also in terms of theoretical values" (Cox, 2004, p. 14). The power of the rational choice approach is its simplicity. "Theories are conventionally valued not just for their ability to generate predictions that survive empirical testing but also for their parsimony, rigor, and generality" (Cox, 1999, p. 13). The spatial model of parliamentary voting used in this book passes this test.

The spatial maps produced by the computer programs discussed in previous chapters have, for the first time, enabled scholars to test a multitude of hypotheses, including the existence of responsible party government in the United States (Cox and McCubbins, 1993; 2004), whether or not there was a "corrupt bargain" in the 1824 Presidential election in the U.S. House (Jenkins and Sala, 1998), the existence of sophisticated voting in the U.S. Congress (Jenkins and Munger, 2003; Clinton and Meirowitz, 2003; 2004), the structure of voting in the U.N. General Assembly over time (Voeten, 2000), candidate positioning in U.S. House elections (Ansolabehere, Snyder, and Stewart, 2001), whether or not U.S. Congressional committees are preference outliers (Londregan and Snyder, 1994), the effect of the Presidential veto on the U.S. Congress (McCarty and Poole, 1995), minority representation in the U.S. Congress (Lublin, 1997), political action committee donations to members of the U.S. Congress (McCarty and Rothenberg, 1996), the U.S. congressional appropriations process (Kiewiet and McCubbins, 1991), constituency interests and legislative behavior in the nineteenth century British Parliament (Schonhardt-Bailey, 2003), financial institutions in the U.S. (Romano, 1997), predicting decisions of the U.S. Supreme Court (Martin and Quinn, 2002; Ruger et al., 2004), coalition formation in Latin American legislatures (Morgenstern, 2004), and how ideology affects decision making in the Chilean legislature (Londregan, 2000b), along with a host of other examples.

It seems to me that if science is the observation, identification, description, experimental investigation, and theoretical explanation of natural phenomena, then the study of geometric models of human choice and judgment – encompassing work in psychology, political science, economics, and other disciplines – is a textbook case of scientific progress.[7]

---

a time when rational disagreement becomes unsustainable. In the short run there is disagreement about paradigms. In the long run it is not true that "anything goes" – that is, that there is no rational justification for one paradigm over the other and hence no scientific "progress" (as suggested, e.g., by Feyerabend, 1975). For example, if it is true that "anything goes" why don't the losers of the paradigm debate start their own journals (e.g., *The Journal of Cartesian Physics, The Journal of Newtonian Mechanics*, or *The Journal of Phlogiston Theory*)?

[7]Some readers may be wondering about the "dog that didn't bark" – namely, why I have not addressed Green and Shapiro's (1994) critique of rational choice theory. First of all, Green and Shapiro do not address spatial models of parliamentary voting in their book. Their chapter on spatial models is concerned only with electoral competition. Their chapter on legislative behavior only mentions roll calls in the context of Riker's examples of voting cycles (Riker, 1982/1988; see

Unsolved Problems

In this section I discuss what I believe to be the important unsolved problems in the study of geometric models of legislative choice. My talents lie in the *engineering* side of the discipline, not in the *theory* side. My contribution has been the construction of measuring instruments (Poole, 1999). Consequently, my discussion of "important" problems will be primarily focused upon unsolved engineering issues. However, I will begin by discussing what I believe to be the most important theoretical issue – the sources of constraint – because it has so many engineering implications.

Specifying the Sources of Constraint

The two-space theory of Hinich and Ordeshook rests upon the assumption that individuals' issue positions are correlated, or *constrained* (Converse, 1964). Constraint means that certain issue positions are bundled together, and the knowledge of one or two issue positions makes the remaining positions very predictable. What is unclear is how these issue bundles are held together and why they persist over time. For example, it is clear that this bundling does not have to be a function of a logically consistent philosophy. This in turn raises the questions: (1) if there is no coherent political philosophy underlying the bundling, how does the system persist; and (2) how do new issues get drawn into the current bundle? The answers to these two questions are obviously closely interrelated, because if we know how the system persists, we should know how new issues get drawn in. In addition, the answers to these questions also must take into account the role that intensity of belief – *passion* – plays in providing the glue that holds issue bundles together.

Mathematically, to recap the discussion in Chapter 1, suppose there are s basic dimensions, p voters, and n issue dimensions, where $s < n$. Let $\mathbf{X}$ be the p by s matrix of ideal points of the p voters on the s basic dimensions, and let $\mathbf{Y}$ be the p by n matrix of voters' ideal points on the n issue dimensions. The presence of constraint means that the voters' positions on the basic dimensions, $\mathbf{X}$, generate all the issue positions, $\mathbf{Y}$; that is,

$$\mathbf{XW} = \mathbf{Y} \tag{7.1}$$

Poole and Rosenthal, 1997, Chapter 7, for an analysis of the examples). Second, in fairness to Green and Shapiro, most of the literature that is the basis of this book appeared after they wrote their book. Rosenthal and I did have two papers in *AJPS* (Poole and Rosenthal, 1985; 1991) on the subject, but Green and Shapiro do not discuss them. Finally, I believe that their arguments have been adequately addressed, and I need not do so here. In particular, see Cox (1999; 2004), Diermeeier (1996), Ferejohn and Satz (1996), Fiorina (1996), Ordeshook (1996), Schofield (1996), and Shepsle (1996).

where the *s* by *n* matrix **W** maps the basic dimensions onto the issue dimensions. The matrix **X** is the spatial map produced by the computer programs from the roll call votes. The mapping matrix **W**, the source of constraint, is not observed.

W incorporates a very strong assumption, namely, that the mapping is the same for every legislator. Although this is a very restrictive assumption, it is not as severe as it appears. Intuitively, if we are given **X**, then the *j*th column of **W**, the *s* by 1 vector $\mathbf{w}_j$, can be treated as a normal vector, so that $\mathbf{Xw}_j = \mathbf{y}_j$, where the *p* by 1 vector $\mathbf{y}_j$ defines a projection line through the spatial map just like those discussed in Chapter 3. Because the projection line can go through the space in any direction, this does tend to ameliorate the mapping constraint. However, it is quite possible that there could be different $\mathbf{w}_j$'s for different groups of legislators.

From an engineering standpoint, it might be possible to make some headway on the problem of different projections for different groups of legislators. For example, I conjecture that the problem of *party pressure* on roll call votes (Snyder and Groseclose, 2000; McCarty, Poole, and Rosenthal, 2001; Cox and Poole, 2002a; 2002b; Clinton, Jackman, and Rivers, 2004) is related to differing $\mathbf{w}_j$'s. This would be akin to allowing two projection lines or something similar to the two-cutting-point model of Poole and Rosenthal (1997, pp. 155–157; McCarty, Poole, and Rosenthal, 2001).

An important aspect of constraint is that it does not have to be strictly logical *in a deductive sense*. That is, a coherent philosophy is *not* a necessary condition for constraint to exist. "What is important is that the elites familiar with the total shapes of these belief systems have *experienced* them as logically constrained clusters of ideas, within which one part necessarily follows from another" (Converse, 1964, pp. 210–211; emphasis in original). An example of this is current U.S. politics. One party – the Republicans – favors tight regulation of private personal behavior (abortion, homosexual rights, assisted suicide, etc.) and loose regulation of the economy; while the opposite party – the Democrats – favors little if any regulation of private personal behavior and much greater regulation of economic behavior (cf. Hinich and Munger, 1994, p. 100; Poole, 2003). There is no logically consistent philosophy that underlies these issues. To make matters even more incoherent, the issue of gun control does not fit comfortably into the category of an economic issue or a social issue. Viewed as a social issue, gun control has the two parties on the "wrong" sides – the Republicans oppose further regulation; the Democrats want *more* regulation.[8]

---

[8]Constraint and passion are well illustrated by several letters to the public editor of the *New York Times* published on 1 August 2004. Daniel Okrent, the public editor, had written a column on 25 July 2004 titled "Is the New York Times a Liberal Newspaper," to which he answered "Of course it is." One letter writer responded: "Is it liberal to be concerned by huge budget deficits? Is it liberal to think that the Constitution is not to be trifled with? Is it liberal to be against the erasing of lines separating church and state? Is it liberal to worry that special interest money is harming

The fact that almost all of these issues in recent roll call voting in the U.S. Congress can be accounted for by a single voting dimension that is commonly labeled liberal–conservative underlines the questions that I raised above: "How do such disparate policy positions get bound together?" and "How could such an incoherent system persist?" and "Why is the 'belief gravity' so strong that it draws new issues into the current alignment?"

Part of the answer to these questions is that political elites are *passionate* about their beliefs. James Madison in *Federalist 10* points out that "as long as the connection subsists between his reason and his self-love, his opinions and his passions will have a reciprocal influence on each other; and the former will be objects to which the latter will attach themselves" (Wills, 1982, p. 43). For political elites, constraint and intensity of belief (passion) appear to be two sides of the same coin.

Another part of the answer to these questions is that political elites, in contrast with the mass public, possess high levels of information about issues. This should make political elites more ideologically consistent than the mass public, and it is quite likely that this has an influence on how issues are packaged (Converse, 1964; Hinich and Munger, 1997, Chapter 9).

How all the above can be reconciled I do not know. Clearly, political parties and legislative institutions are the most important sources of constraint for legislators.[9] For example, in a study of U.S. state legislatures, Wright and Schaffner (2002) find that political parties that are effective in electing their members to a legislature appear to strongly affect the expression of constraint in roll call voting. In addition, new issues are almost certainly being mapped onto the basic dimensions rather than the other way around. Specifically, $y_{new}w'_{new} = X$, where y_{new} is the p by 1 vector of positions on the new issue and the s by 1 vector w_{new} maps y_{new} onto the basic dimensions (Poole and Rosenthal, 1997, Chapter 5).

A thorough cross-national study of roll call behavior over time is badly needed to start the process of sorting out the role of political parties, information, and legislative institutions in determining constraint. I believe that this can be achieved within the rational choice framework. To paraphrase

---

our democracy? Is it liberal to think that government must be transparent because it is supposed to represent its citizens?" Another letter writer responded: "Your examination of where The Times fits – left or right – seems to accept the right's contention that there should be equality between the two. But where the left looks for empirical evidence to support its views, the right already has the theological received wisdom that brooks no contradiction. Why give the right's views the same weight as the left's? Why present religiously based arguments as equally valid?" The latter letter writer was responding to the public editor's criticism of the coverage of the gay marriage issue by the *Times*.

[9]This is especially true of political parties that arise from mass movements. For an insightful discussion of this fact see Eric Hoffer's (1951) masterpiece *The True Believer*. Hoffer analyzes the nature of mass movements – both religious and political.

Hinich and Munger (1994, p. 236), I believe that constraint is *not irrational.* "[Ideology] is not a residual or random component of conscious human decision making. So long as social science does not take ideology into account, it cannot make claims either to descriptive accuracy or to theoretical closure."

Unsolved Engineering Problems

The most important unsolved engineering problem is determining precisely how the level of error *interacts* with the underlying geometry of parliamentary roll call voting. Without knowing this relationship, we cannot be certain about the interval scale information that is being recovered by the various scaling programs. In fact, the interaction of error and geometry is not a single problem but a family of problems – hence the plural in this section title. In addition, the problem becomes qualitatively different as we move from a one-dimensional to a multidimensional world.

Hence, in the remainder of this section I will discuss the relationship between error and geometry for the one-dimensional case before turning to the multidimensional case. In these discussions I will mention other unsolved problems of lesser importance that are closely related to the basic problem of the interaction of the error and the geometry.

With respect to one dimension, the puzzle of how error interacts with the underlying geometry can be summarized in two closely related questions: (1) how high does the error level have to be so that interval scale information is recovered; and (2) under what circumstances will the true rank ordering be recovered?

With regard to the first question, as I demonstrated in the Appendix of Chapter 2, some of the interval-level information may be an illusion. Namely, if voting is perfect, an interval-level set of points is always recovered using the eigenvalue–eigenvector decomposition of the double-centered agreement score matrix. However, *this is an artifact of the distribution of cutting points.* The intervals between adjacent legislators are simple functions of the number of cutting points between them. In addition, as I discussed in Chapter 3, when the error level is very low, it only affects *adjacent* legislators, so that the presence of error is very difficult to detect. The effect will be to perhaps slightly scramble the "true" ordering, but we might never know, because with very low error voting may appear to be perfect.

Clearly, to recover accurate interval-level information a *necessary* condition is that the error level must be high enough so that the rows and columns of the roll call matrix cannot be swapped (transposed) so as to produce a perfect voting matrix (e.g., Figures 3.1, 3.4, and 3.5), and it also must negate the artificial effect of the distribution of cutting points. (Note that this question is related to the *sag problem* that I discussed in Chapter 5. The sag problem can be especially serious when small voting bodies such as the U.S. Supreme Court are being analyzed [see Table 5.3].)

The answer to the first question I believe crucially depends upon the answer to the second question – a proof of the *Quinn conjecture*[10]:

If the voting space is one-dimensional and the noise process is symmetric, then as the number of roll calls goes to infinity, the true rank ordering of the legislators will be recovered.

More technically, suppose the error ε is drawn from some continuous symmetric probability distribution with mean 0 and finite variance σ^2 having support on the real line; then the Quinn conjecture is: If $s = 1$ and $\varepsilon \sim f(0, \sigma^2)$ with $-\infty < \varepsilon < \infty$ and $\sigma^2 < \infty$, then as $q \to \infty$,

$$P(X_1 < X_2 < X_3 < \cdots < X_{p-2} < X_{p-1} < X_p | V) \to 1$$

where V is the p by q matrix of observed votes and the legislator indices have been permuted so that they correspond to the true ordering of the ideal points.

One approach to proving this would be to work directly with the agreement scores and see if it is possible to state conditions such that all the triangle inequalities are equalities. Recall from Chapter 2 that with perfect voting the distance between any pair of legislators was a simple function of the number of roll call cutting points between them. For any triple of points $X_a < X_b < X_c$, the distances are

$$d_{ab} = \frac{\sum_{i=a}^{b-1} k_i}{q} \quad \text{and} \quad d_{bc} = \frac{\sum_{i=b}^{c-1} k_i}{q} \quad \text{and} \quad d_{ac} = \frac{\sum_{i=a}^{c-1} k_i}{q}$$

where k_i is the number of cutting points between legislators i and $i + 1$. Hence, if voting is perfect,

$$d_{ac} = d_{ab} + d_{bc}.$$

With error, some of the cutting points that are between a pair of legislators would appear to not be between, and some of the cutting points that are not between would appear to be between. Hence, the trick to proving the Quinn conjecture using the agreement scores is to show that those two cases balance out, so that $d_{ac} = d_{ab} + d_{bc}$ holds. An important stumbling block to getting the cases to balance out is that many of the patterns for the legislators near the ends of the dimension are likely to be unanimous when error is present.

If the Quinn conjecture is true (and I think that it is), then this suggests a possible avenue for answering the interval scale question. Turning the Quinn conjecture on its head, suppose we know the true ordering of the legislators. Taking account of polarity, this means that there are $2(p - 1)$ possible *perfect*

---

[10]This conjecture is due to Kevin Quinn. He outlined it to me over a fine dinner on a very, very cold night in Cambridge, MA, in January 2004.

roll call voting patterns consistent with the ordering (ignoring the possibility of ties in the legislator ordering). Now let the number of roll calls go to infinity as in the conjecture, and consider two adjacent legislators somewhere in the interior of the ordering. Suppose for simplicity that Yea is always the left outcome and Nay is always the right outcome. Consider the four possible patterns for the adjacent pair on every roll call with a cutting point between them: YN, NY, YY, NN. Only the YN pattern is correct; the rest are errors. However, it only makes sense that the closer the two legislators actually are on the dimension, the more frequent the error patterns YY and NN will be relative to the error pattern NY. This is clearly the source of the interval scale information.

Note that I am greatly simplifying things in that each one of the two legislators is in turn adjacent to another legislator and the error patterns from those pairs will partly negate the YY and NN pattern of the specific pair. For example, suppose the pair of legislators votes YY but the legislator adjacent to but to the left of the pair votes Nay; that is, NYY. If no other legislators make errors, then this pattern looks like

$$\ldots YYYYYNYYNNNN.\ldots$$

From the point of view of optimal classification, the cutting point should be placed to the *right* of the specific pair. However, this pattern is offset by

$$\ldots YYYYYYYYYNNN\ldots$$

where the legislator adjacent to but to the right of the pair votes Yea when she should have voted Nay.

Hence, interval-level information in one dimension must be a result of the frequency of the YY and NN error patterns relative to the NY pattern coupled with the degree of offsetting of nearby error patterns. This would account for why the various scaling procedures produce very similar one-dimensional interval scales (Lewis and Poole, 2004; Clinton, Jackman, and Rivers, 2004).[11]

In two or more dimensions, while interval scale information is more easily obtained simply due to the geometry, the problem of determining the interaction of error and geometry becomes more difficult. As I discussed in Chapter 2, with 100 or so roll calls the polytopes for most legislators are so small that recovering interval scale information is straightforward. However, the lack of a solution to the *perfect*-voting problem makes determining the interaction of error and geometry much more difficult than for the one-dimensional case.

---

[11] Note that in one dimension the roll call voting problem is *symmetric*. That is, the roll call voting matrix can be transposed and the roll calls treated as "legislators." Hence, the Quinn conjecture can be restated to apply to the cutting points by simply transposing the matrix and interchanging the roles of p and q.

Nevertheless, some headway could be made if the properties of Coombs mesh uniqueness were better understood. Every method of scaling produces a Coombs mesh, and for each mesh the p legislator ideal points lie within p polytopes and each polytope corresponds to a q-length vector of choices. Comparing the sets of polytopes produced by the various scaling procedures would give us insight into how the assumptions about the error process and the form of the utility function deform one mesh with respect to another. While these meshes must correspond to a *reasonable* extent because W-NOMINATE, OC, QN, and Bayesian QN produce similar legislator configurations in more than one dimension (Poole and Rosenthal, 1997; Poole, 2000a; 2001; Lewis and Poole, 2004), we do not know whether the differences are negligible or not.

By "reasonable" I mean the following. Given the Coombs meshes from two scaling procedures, can the polytope pattern for a specific legislator in one mesh be found in the second mesh? Note that this could be possible without the two polytope patterns being exactly the same. If the polytope pattern for a specific legislator does not exist in the second mesh, is it possible to transform the second mesh by moving its cutting lines around slightly in order to create the missing polytope pattern *while preserving the estimated legislator polytopes*? For example, suppose there is a Coombs mesh such that two or more scaling solutions are contained within it. That is, the polytope patterns for the p legislators from each solution exist in the mesh. Consider a specific legislator. It is possible to calculate the probabilities corresponding to placing the legislator in every polytope in the mesh (a maximum of $\sum_{k=0}^{s}\binom{q}{k}$ polytopes if it is a *complete* Coombs mesh). Suppose the scaling procedures have done this, so that the legislator is in the maximum probability polytope for each procedure. Consequently, if the legislator's polytope location differs across scaling procedures, then this difference is not due to the underlying geometry, but to the probability distributions that are laid over the top of the mesh.

In sum, solving the engineering problem of mapping Coombs meshes into each other would show how differing assumptions about the error process deform the meshes and would lead to a much better understanding of why the various scaling procedures produce very similar spatial maps.[12]

---

[12]The problem of the interaction of the error process with the underlying geometry would be even more severe with more than two choices. In this book I have confined my analysis to the simple spatial model of only two outcomes per roll call. The geometry of more than two choices is a fairly simple extension of the geometric framework developed in Chapter 2, but the engineering problems are formidable. For example, in a three-choice framework there would be two cutting planes. Should these cutting planes be parallel, with a common normal vector, as in ordered probit or logit, or should there be multiple normal vectors, as in multinomial probit or logit? I believe that this can be done in either case; but that would take yet another book.

Conclusion

I conclude with a point I made in Chapter 1. Anyone can construct a spatial map using the computer programs I discussed in this book. But the maps are worthless unless the user understands both the spatial theory that the computer program embodies and the politics of the legislature that produced the roll calls. Never forget that this book can only supply the former – not the latter. Both are equally important.

References

Abramowitz, Alan I. and Jeffrey A. Segal. 1992. *Senate Elections*. Ann Arbor, MI: University of Michigan Press.

Albert, A. and J. A. Anderson. 1984. "On the Existence of Maximum Likelihood Estimates in Logistic Regression Models." *Biometrika*, 71:1–10.

Albert, James H. and Siddhartha Chib. 1993. "Bayesian Analysis of Binary and Polychotomous Response Data." *Journal of the American Statistical Association*, 88:669–679.

Aldrich, John H. and Michael D. McGinnis. 1989. "A Model of Party Constraints on Optimal Candidate Positions." *Mathematical and Computer Modeling*, 12:437–450.

Amacher, Ryan C. and William J. Boyes. 1978. "Cycles in Senatorial Voting Behavior: Implications for the Optimal Frequency of Elections." *Public Choice*, 33(3): 5–13.

Andrich, David. 1988. *Rasch Models for Measurement*. Newbury Park, CA: Sage.

Andrich, David. 1995. "Hyperbolic Cosine Latent Trait Models for Unfolding Direct Responses and Pairwise Preferences." *Applied Psychological Measurement*, 19:269–290.

Ansolabehere, Stephen, James M. Snyder, Jr., and Charles Stewart, III., 2001. "Candidate Positioning in U.S. House Elections." *American Journal of Political Science*, 45:136–159.

Austen-Smith, David. 1987. "Interest Groups, Campaign Contributions, and Probabilistic Voting." *Public Choice*, 54:123–139.

Austen-Smith, David and Jeffrey S. Banks. 2000. *Positive Political Theory I: Collective Preference*. Ann Arbor, MI: University of Michigan Press.

Austen-Smith, David and Jeffrey S. Banks. 2004. *Positive Political Theory II: Strategy and Structure*. Ann Arbor, MI: University of Michigan Press.

Bailey, Michael. 2002. "Comparing Presidents, Senators, and Justices, 1946–2002." Working Paper, Georgetown University.

Bailey, Michael and Kelly Chang. 2001. "Comparing Presidents, Senators, and Justices: Inter-institutional Preference Estimation." *Journal of Law, Economics and Organization*, 17:477–506.

Bennett, Joseph F. and William L. Hays. 1960. "Multidimensional Unfolding: Determining the Dimensionality of Ranked Preference Data." *Psychometrika*, 25:27–43.

Berndt, E. K., Bronwyn H. Hall, Robert E. Hall, and Jerry Hausman. 1974. "Estimation and Inference in Nonlinear Structural Models." *Annals of Economic and Social Measurement*, 3/4:653–666.

Bernhard, William and Brian R. Sala. 2004. "The Dynamics of Senate Voting: "Ideological Shirking" and the 17th Amendment." Paper Presented at the Annual Meetings of the Southern Political Science Association, New Orleans, LA.

Bernhardt, M. Daniel and Daniel E. Ingberman. 1985. "Candidate Reputations and the 'Incumbency Effect'." *Journal of Public Economics*, 27:47–67.

Best, Alvin M., Forrest W. Young, and Robert G. Hall. 1979. "On the Precision of a Euclidean Structure." *Psychometrika*, 44:395–408.

Black, Duncan. 1948. "On the Rationale of Group Decision Making." *Journal of Political Economy*, 56:23–34.

Black, Duncan. 1958. *The Theory of Committees and Elections*. Cambridge, England: Cambridge University Press.

Blokland-Vogelesang, Rian van. 1991. *Unfolding and Group Consensus Ranking for Individual Preferences*. Leiden: DWSO Press.

Borg, Ingwer and Patrick Groenen. 1997. *Modern Multidimensional Scaling: Theory and Applications*. New York: Springer.

Brady, Henry. 1990. "Traits Versus Issues: Factor Versus Ideal-Point Analysis of Candidate Thermometer Ratings." *Political Analysis*, 2:97–129.

Brady, David W. and Craig Volden. 1998. *Revolving Gridlock Politics and Policy from Carter to Clinton*. Boulder, CO: Westview Press.

Cahoon, Lawrence S. 1975. *Locating a Set of Points Using Range Information Only*. Ph.D. Dissertation, Department of Statistics, Carnegie-Mellon University.

Cahoon, Lawrence S., Melvin J. Hinich, and Peter C. Ordeshook. 1976. "A Multidimensional Statistical Procedure for Spatial Analysis." Manuscript, Carnegie-Mellon University.

Cahoon, Lawrence S., Melvin J. Hinich, and Peter C. Ordeshook. 1978. "A Statistical Multidimensional Scaling Method Based on the Spatial Theory of Voting." In *Graphical Representation of Multivariate Data*, edited by P. C. Wang. New York: Academic Press.

Calvert, Randall. 1985. "Robustness of the Multidimensional Voting Model: Candidates' Motivations, Uncertainty, and Convergence." *American Journal of Political Science*, 29:69–95.

Campbell, Angus, Philip E. Converse, Warren E. Miller, and Donald E. Stokes. 1960. *The American Voter*. New York: Wiley.

Carmines, Edward G. and James A. Stimson. 1989. *Issue Evolution: Race and the Transformation of American Politics*. Princeton, NJ: Princeton University Press.

Carroll, J. Douglas. 1972. "Individual Differences and Multidimensional Scaling." In *Multidimensional Scaling: Theory and Applications in the Behavioral Sciences*, edited by A. Kimball Romney, Roger N. Shepard, and Sara Beth Nerlove. New York: Seminar Press.

Carroll, J. Douglas. 1980. "Models and Methods for Multidimensional Analysis of Preferential Choice (or Other Dominance) Data." In *Similarity and Choice*, edited by E. D. Lantermann and H. Feger. Bern, Switzerland: Huber.

Carroll, J. Douglas and Jih-Jie Chang. 1970. "Analysis of Individual Differences in Multidimensional Scaling via an *N*-Way Generalization of 'Eckart–Young' decomposition." *Psychometrika*, 35:283–320.

Chang, Jih-Jie and J. Douglas Carroll. 1969. "How to Use MDPREF, a Computer Program for Multidimensional Analysis of Preference Data." Multidimensional Scaling Program Package of Bell Laboratories, Bell Laboratories, Murray Hill, NJ.

Chater, Nick. 1999. "The Search for Simplicity: A Fundamental Cognitive Principle?" *Quarterly Journal of Experimental Psychology*, 52A:273–302.

Cheng, Ken. 2000. "Shepard's Universal Law Supported by Honeybees in Spatial Generalization." *Psychological Science*, 5:403–408.

Clinton, Joshua D. 2003. "Same Principals, Same Agents, Different Institutions: Roll Call Voting in the Continental Congress, Congresses of Confederation and the U.S. Senate, 1774–1786." Working Paper, Princeton University.

Clinton, Joshua D. and Adam H. Meirowitz. 2003. "Integrating Voting Theory and Roll-Call Analysis: A Framework." *Political Analysis*, 11:381–396.

Clinton, Joshua D. and Adam H. Meirowitz. 2004. "Testing Accounts of Legislative Strategic Voting: The Compromise of 1790." *American Journal of Political Science*, 48:675–689.

Clinton, Joshua D., Simon D. Jackman, and Douglas Rivers. 2004. "The Statistical Analysis of Roll Call Data: A Unified Approach." *American Political Science Review*, 98:355–370.

Converse, Philip E. 1964. "The Nature of Belief Systems in Mass Publics." In *Ideology and Discontent,* edited by David E. Apter. New York: Free Press.

Coombs, Clyde. 1950. "Psychological Scaling Without a Unit of Measurement." *Psychological Review*, 57:148–158.

Coombs, Clyde. 1964. *A Theory of Data.* New York: Wiley.

Courant, Richard and David Hilbert. 1937. *Methods of Mathematical Physics: Volume I.* Berlin: Julius Springer.

Cox, Gary W. 1999. "The Empirical Content of Rational Choice Theory: A Reply to Green and Shapiro." *Journal of Theoretical Politics*, 11:147–169.

Cox, Gary W. 2004. "Lies, Damned Lies and Rational Choice Analysis." In *Problems and Methods in the Study of Politics*, edited by Ian Shapiro, Rogers M. Smith, and Tarek E. Masoud. Cambridge: Cambridge University Press.

Cox, Gary W. and Jonathan N. Katz. 2002. *Elbridge Gerry's Salamander: The Electoral Consequences of the Reapportionment Revolution.* New York: Cambridge University Press.

Cox, Gary W. and Mathew D. McCubbins. 1993. *Legislative Leviathan.* Berkeley, CA: University of California Press.

Cox, Gary W. and Mathew D. McCubbins. 2004. "Setting the Agenda: Responsible Party Government in the US House of Representatives." Manuscript, University of California, San Diego.

Cox, Gary W. and Keith T. Poole. 2002a. "On Measuring Partisanship in Roll Call Voting: The U.S. House of Representatives, 1877–1999." *American Journal of Political Science*, 46:477–489.

Cox, Gary W. and Keith T. Poole. 2002b. "Measuring Group Differences in Roll Call Voting." Manuscript, University of Houston.

Cox, Trevor F. and Michael A. A. Cox. 2001. *Multidimensional Scaling*. New York: Chapman and Hall/CRC.

Cragg, John G. and Stephen G. Donald. 1997. "Inferring the Rank of a Matrix." *Journal of Econometrics*, 76:223–250.

D'Andrade, Roy G., Naomi R. Quinn, Sara Beth Nerlove, and A. Kimball Romney. 1972. "Categories of Disease in American-English and Mexican-Spanish." In *Multidimensional Scaling: Theory and Applications in the Behavioral Sciences*, edited by A. Kimball Romney, Roger N. Shepard, and Sara Beth Nerlove. New York: Seminar Press.

Davis, Otto A. and Melvin J. Hinich. 1966. "A Mathematical Model of Policy Formation in a Democratic Society." In *Mathematical Applications in Political Science, II*, edited by J. L. Bernd. Dallas: SMU Press, pp. 175–208.

Davis, Otto A. and Melvin J. Hinich. 1967. "Some Results Related to a Mathematical Model of Policy Formation in a Democratic Society." In *Mathematical Applications in Political Science III*, edited by J. Bernd. Charlottesville, VA: University of Virginia Press, pp. 14–38.

Davis, Otto A., Melvin J. Hinich, and Peter C. Ordeshook. 1970. "An Expository Development of a Mathematical Model of the Electoral Process." *American Political Science Review*, 64:426–448.

DeSarbo, Wayne S. and Jaewun Cho 1989. "A Stochastic Multidimensional Scaling Vector Threshold Model for the Spatial Representation of 'Pick Any/N' Data." *Psychometrika*, 54:105–129.

DeSarbo, Wayne S. and Donna L. Hoffman. 1987. "Constructing MDS Joint Spaces from Binary Choice Data: A Multidimensional Unfolding Threshold Model for Marketing Research." *Journal of Marketing Research*, 24:40–54.

Dhrymes, Phoebus J. 1978. *Introductory Econometrics*. New York: Springer-Verlag.

Diermeier, Daniel. 1996. "Rational Choice and the Role of Theory in Political Science." In *The Rational Choice Controversy*, edited by Jeffrey Friedman. New Haven: Yale University Press.

Downs, Anthony. 1957. *An Economic Theory of Democracy*. New York: Harper & Row.

Eckart, Carl and Gale Young. 1936. "The Approximation of One Matrix by Another of Lower Rank." *Psychometrika*, 1: 211–218.

Efron, Bradley. 1979. "Bootstrap Methods: Another Look at the Jackknife." *Annals of Statistics*, 7:1–26.

Efron, Bradley and Robert J. Tibshirani. 1993. *An Introduction to the Bootstrap*. New York: Chapman & Hall.

Ekman, Gosta. 1954. "Dimensions of Color Vision." *Journal of Psychology*, 38:467–474.

Ellenberg, Jordan. 2001. "Growing Apart: The Mathematical Evidence for Congress' Growing Polarization." *Slate,* 26 December 2001.

Elling, Richard C. 1982. "Ideological Change in the U.S. Senate: Time and Electoral Responsiveness." *Legislative Studies Quarterly*, 7(1):75–92.

Embretson, Susan and Steven P. Reise. 2000. *Item Response Theory for Psychologists*. Mahwah, NJ: Lawrence Erlbaum.

Enelow, James M. and Melvin Hinich. 1984. *The Spatial Theory of Voting*. New York: Cambridge University Press.

Ennis, Daniel M. 1988a. "Confusable and Discriminable Stimuli: Comment on Nosofsky (1986) and Shepard (1986)." *Journal of Experimental Psychology: General*, 117:408–411.

Ennis, Daniel M. 1988b. "Technical Comments: Toward a Universal Law of Generalization." *Science*, 242:944.

Ennis, Daniel M., Joseph J. Palen, and Kenneth Mullen. 1988. "A Multidimensional Stochastic Theory of Similarity." *Journal of Mathematical Psychology*, 32:449–465.

Feldman, Stanley and John Zaller. 1992. "Political Culture of Ambivalence: Ideological Responses to the Welfare State." *American Journal of Political Science*, 36:268–307.

Ferejohn, John and Debra Satz. 1996. "Unification, Universalism, and Rational Choice Theory." In *The Rational Choice Controversy*, edited by Jeffrey Friedman. New Haven: Yale University Press.

Ferejohn, John and Debra Satz. 2000. "Rational Choice Theory and Mental Models." Working Paper, Stanford University.

Feyerabend, Paul K. 1975. *Against Method*. London: New Left Press.

Fiorina, Morris P. 1996. "Rational Choice, Empirical Contributions, and the Scientific Enterprise." In *The Rational Choice Controversy*, edited by Jeffrey Friedman. New Haven: Yale University Press.

Firth, David and Arthur Spirling. 2003. "Divisions of the United Kingdom House of Commons, from 1992 to 2003 and Beyond." Working Paper, Nuffield College, Oxford.

Fischer, Gerhard H. and Ivo W. Molenaar. 1995. *Rasch Models: Foundations, Recent Developments, and Applications*. New York: Springer-Verlag.

Garner, Wendell R. 1974. *The Processing of Information and Structure*. New York: Wiley.

Gelfand, Alan E. and Adrian F. M. Smith. 1990. "Sampling-Based Approaches to Calculating Marginal Densities." *Journal of the American Statistical Association*, 85:398–409.

Gelman, Andrew. 1992. "Iterative and Non-iterative Simulation Algorithms." *Computing Science and Statistics*, 24:433–438.

Gelman, Andrew, John B. Carlin, Hal S. Stern, and Donald B. Rubin. 2000. *Bayesian Data Analysis*. New York: Chapman and Hall/CRC.

Geman, Donald and Stuart Geman. 1984. "Stochastic Relaxation, Gibbs Distributions, and the Bayesian Restoration of Images." *IEEE Transactions on Pattern Analysis and Machine Intelligence*, 6:721–741.

Gerber, Elizabeth R. and Jeffrey B. Lewis. 2002. "Beyond the Median: Voter Preferences, District Heterogeneity, and Representation." Working Paper, UCLA.

Gifi, Albert. 1990. *Nonlinear Multivariate Analysis*. Chicester, England: Wiley.

Gill, Jeff. 2002. *Bayesian Methods: A Social and Behavioral Sciences Approach*. Boca Raton, FL: Chapman & Hall/CRC.

Gleason, Terry C. and Richard Staelin. 1975. "A Proposal for Handling Missing Data." *Psychometrika*, 40:229–252.

Gluck, Mark A. 1991. "Stimulus Generalization and Representation in Adaptive Network Models of Category Learning." *Psychological Science*, 2:50–55.

Gombrich, Ernst Hans. 1978. *The Story of Art* (13th edition). New York: Phaidon Press.

Goodman, Craig. 2004. "Ideological Constraint in Congress: Experiments in Roll Call Voting." Ph.D. Dissertation, University of Houston.

Green, Donald P. and Ian Shapiro. 1994. *Pathologies of Rational Choice Theory: A Critique of Applications in Political Science.* New Haven: Yale University Press.

Greene, William H. 1993. *Econometric Analysis.* Englewood Cliffs, NJ: Prentice Hall.

Guttman, Louis L. 1944. "A Basis for Scaling Qualitative Data." *American Sociological Review*, 9:139–150.

Guttman, Louis L. 1954. "A New Approach to Factor Analysis." In *Mathematical Thinking in the Social Sciences,* edited by P. F. Lazarsfeld. Glencoe, IL: Free Press.

Haberman, Shelby J. 1977. "Maximum Likelihood Estimation in Exponential Response Models." *Annals of Statistics*, 5:815–841.

Hammond, Thomas H. and Jane M. Fraser. 1983. "Baselines for Evaluating Explanations of Coalition Behavior in Congress." *Journal of Politics*, 45:635–656.

Harrington, Joseph. 1992. "The Role of Party Reputation in the Formation of Policy." *Journal of Public Economics*, 49:107–121.

Hastings, W. Keith. 1970. "Monte Carlo Sampling Methods Using Markov Chains and Their Applications." *Biometrika*, 54:97–109.

Heckman, James J. and James M. Snyder. 1997. "Linear Probability Models of the Demand for Attributes with an Empirical Application to Estimating the Preferences of Legislators." *Rand Journal of Economics*, 28:142–189.

Heiser, Willem J. 1981. *Unfolding Analysis of Proximity Data.* Leiden: University of Leiden.

Hinich, Melvin J. and Michael Munger. 1994. *Ideology and the Theory of Political Choice.* Ann Arbor, MI: University of Michigan Press.

Hinich, Melvin J. and Michael Munger. 1997. *Analytical Politics.* New York: Cambridge University Press.

Hinich, Melvin J. and Walker Pollard. 1981. "A New Approach to the Spatial Theory of Electoral Competition." *American Journal of Political Science*, 25:323–341.

Hinich, Melvin J. and Richard Roll. 1981. "Measuring Nonstationarity in the Parameters of the Market Model." *Research in Finance*, 3:1–51.

Hitchcock, David B. 2003. "A History of the Metropolis–Hastings Algorithm." *The American Statistician*, 57:254–257.

Hoadley, John F. 1980. "The Emergence of Political Parties in Congress, 1789–1803." *American Political Science Review*, 74:757–779.

Hoffer, Eric. 1951. *The True Believer: Thoughts on the Nature of Mass Movements.* New York: Harper & Row (Perennial Library Edition, 1966, 1989).

Hojo, Hiroshi. 1994. "A New Method for Multidimensional Unfolding." *Behaviormetrika*, 21:131–147.

Horst, Paul. 1963. *Matrix Algebra for Social Scientists.* New York: Holt, Rinehart and Winston.

Hotelling, Harold. 1929. "Stability in Competition." *The Economic Journal*, 39:41–57.

Jackman, Simon D. 2000a. "Estimation and Inference via Bayesian Simulation: An Introduction to Markov Chain Monte Carlo." *American Journal of Political Science*, 44:375–404.

Jackman, Simon D. 2000b. "Estimation and Inference are 'Missing Data' Problems: Unifying Social Science Statistics via Bayesian Simulation." *Political Analysis*, 8:307–332.

Jackman, Simon D. 2001. "Multidimensional Analysis of Roll Call Data via Bayesian Simulation: Identification, Estimation, Inference and Model Checking." *Political Analysis*, 9:227–241.

Jenkins, Jeffery A. and Michael C. Munger. 2003. "Investigating the Incidence of Killer Amendments in Congress." *Journal of Politics* 65:498–517.

Jenkins, Jeffery A. and Brian R. Sala. 1998. "The Spatial Theory of Voting and the Presidential Election of 1824." *American Journal of Political Science*, 42:1157–1179.

Johnson, Richard M. 1963. "On a Theorem Stated by Eckart and Young." *Psychometrika*, 28:259–263.

Keller, Joseph B. 1962. "Factorization of Matrices by Least-Squares." *Biometrika*, 49:239–242.

Kiewiet, D. Roderick and Mathew D. McCubbins. 1991. *The Logic of Delegation: Congressional Parties and the Appropriation Process*. Chicago: University of Chicago Press.

King, Gary, James Honaker, Anne Joseph, and Kenneth Scheve. 2001. "Analyzing Incomplete Political Science Data: An Alternative Algorithm for Multiple Imputation." *American Political Science Review*, 95:49–69.

King, David. 1998. "Party Competition and Polarization in American Politics." Paper Prepared for the 1998 Annual Meeting of the Midwest Political Science Association.

Krehbiel, Keith. 1993. "Where's the Party?" *British Journal of Political Science*, 23(1):235–266.

Krehbiel, Keith. 1998. *Pivotal Politics: A Theory of U.S. Lawmaking*. Chicago: University of Chicago Press.

Kruskal, Joseph B. 1964a. "Multidimensional Scaling by Optimizing a Goodness of Fit to a Nonmetric Hypothesis." *Psychometrika*, 29:1–27.

Kruskal, Joseph B. 1964b. "Nonmetric Multidimensional Scaling: A Numerical Method." *Psychometrika*, 29:115–129.

Kruskal, Joseph B. and Myron Wish. 1978. *Multidimensional Scaling*. Beverly Hills, CA: Sage.

Kruskal, Joseph B., Forrest W. Young, and Judith B. Seery. 1973. "How to Use KYST: A Very Flexible Program to Do Multidimensional Scaling and Unfolding." Multidimensional Scaling Program Package of Bell Laboratories, Bell Laboratories, Murray Hill, NJ.

Kuhn, Thomas S. 1962/1996. *The Structure of Scientific Revolutions* (3rd edition). Chicago: University of Chicago Press.

Ladha, Krishna K. 1991. "A Spatial Model of Legislative Voting with Perceptual Error." *Public Choice*, 68:151–174.

Laudan, Larry. 1984. *Science and Values: The Aims of Science and Their Role in Scientific Debate*. Berkeley, CA: University of California Press.

Laudan, Larry. 1996. *Beyond Positivism and Relativism: Theory, Method and Evidence*. Boulder, CO: Westview Press.

Lawson, Charles L. and Richard J. Hanson. 1974. *Solving Least Squares Problems*. Englewood Cliffs, NJ: Prentice-Hall.

Lewis, Jeffrey B. and Gary King. 1999. "No Evidence on Directional vs. Proximity Voting." *Political Analysis*, 8:21–33.

Lewis, Jeffrey B. and Keith T. Poole. 2004. "Measuring Bias and Uncertainty in Ideal Point Estimates via the Parametric Bootstrap." *Political Analysis*, 12:105–127.

Livingstone, Margaret S. 2002. *Vision and Art: The Biology of Seeing*. New York: Harry N. Abrams.

Londregan, John B. 2000a. "Estimating Legislators' Preferred Points." *Political Analysis*, 8(1):35–56.

Londregan, John B. 2000b. *Legislative Institutions and Ideology in Chile*. New York: Cambridge University Press.

Londregan, John B. and James M. Snyder, Jr. 1994. "Comparing Committee and Floor Preferences." *Legislative Studies Quarterly*, 19:233–266.

Loomis, Michael. 1995. "Constituent Influences Outside the Spatial Structure of Legislative Voting." Doctoral Dissertation, Carnegie-Mellon University.

Lord, Frederic M. 1983. "Unbiased Estimates of Ability Parameters, of Their Variance, and of Their Parallel Forms Reliability." *Psychometrika*, 48:477–482.

Lott, John R., Jr. and Stephen G. Bronars. 1993. "Time Series Evidence on Shirking in the U.S. House of Representatives." *Public Choice*, 76:125–150.

Lublin, David (1997). *The Paradox of Representation: Racial Gerrymandering and Minority Representation in Congress*. Princeton, NJ: Princeton University Press.

Macdonald, Stuart, George Rabinowitz, and Ola Listhaug. 2001. "Sophistry versus Science: On Further Efforts to Rehabilitate the Proximity Model." *The Journal of Politics*, 63:482–500.

MacRae, Duncan, Jr. 1958. *Dimensions of Congressional Voting*. Berkeley: University of California Press.

MacRae, Duncan, Jr. 1970. *Issues and Parties in Legislative Voting*. New York: Harper and Row.

McCarty, Nolan M. 1997. "Presidential Reputation and the Veto." *Economics and Politics*, 9(1):1–26.

McCarty, Nolan M. 2000. "Proposal Rights, Veto Rights, and Political Bargaining." *American Journal of Political Science*, 44(3):506–522.

McCarty, Nolan M. and Keith T. Poole. 1995. "Veto Power and Legislation: An Empirical Analysis of Executive and Legislative Bargaining from 1961–1986." *Journal of Law, Economics, and Organization*, 11:.

McCarty, Nolan M., Keith T. Poole, and Howard Rosenthal. 1997. *Income Redistribution and the Realignment of American Politics*. Washington, DC: AEI Press.

McCarty, Nolan M., Keith T. Poole, and Howard Rosenthal. 2001. "The Hunt for Party Discipline in Congress." *American Political Science Review*, 95:673–687.

McCarty, Nolan M., Keith T. Poole, and Howard Rosenthal. 2003. "Political Polarization and Income Inequality." Manuscript, University of Houston.

McCarty, Nolan M. and Lawrence S. Rothenberg (1996). "Commitment and the Campaign Contribution Contract." *American Journal of Political Science*, 40:872–904.

McCarty, Nolan M. and Rose Razaghian. 1999. "Advice and Consent: Senate Response to Executive Branch Nominations 1885–1996." *American Journal of Political Science*, 43(3):1122–1143.

McFadden, Daniel. 1976. "Quantal Choice Analysis: A Survey." *Annals of Economic and Social Measurement*, 5:363–390.

Manski, Charles F. 1975. "Maximum Score Estimation of the Stochastic Utility Model of Choice." *Journal of Econometrics*, 3:205–228.

Manski, Charles F. 1985. "Semiparametric Analysis of Discrete Response: Asymptotic Properties of the Maximum Score Estimator." *Journal of Econometrics*, 27:313–333.

Manski, Charles F. and T. Scott Thompson. 1986. "Operational Characteristics of Maximum Score Estimation." *Journal of Econometrics*, 32:85–108.

Martin, Andrew D. 2003. "Bayesian Inference for Heterogeneous Event Counts." *Sociological Methods and Research*, 32:30–63.

Martin, Andrew D. and Kevin M. Quinn. 2001. "Bayesian Learning about Ideal Points of U. S. Supreme Court Justices, 1953–1999." Working Paper, Washington University, St. Louis.

Martin, Andrew D. and Kevin M. Quinn. 2002. "Dynamic Ideal Point Estimation via Markov Chain Monte Carlo for the U.S. Supreme Court, 1953–1999." *Political Analysis*, 10:134–153.

Merrill, Samuel III and Bernard Grofman. 1999. *A Unified Theory of Voting: Directional and Proximity Models*. New York: Cambridge University Press.

Metropolis, Nicholas C. and Stanislaw Ulam. 1949. "The Monte Carlo Method." *Journal of the American Statistical Association*, 44:335–341.

Miller, George A. 1956. "The Magical Number Seven, Plus Minus One: Some Limits on our Capacity for Processing Information." *Psychological Review*, 63:81–97.

Morgenstern, Scott. 2004. *Patterns of Legislative Politics: Roll-Call Voting in Latin America and the United States*. New York: Cambridge University Press.

Morrison, Richard J. 1972. "A Statistical Model for Legislative Roll Call Analysis." *Journal of Mathematical Sociology*, 2:235–247.

Morton, Rebecca B. 1987. "A Group Majority Voting Model of Public Good Provision." *Social Choice and Welfare*, 4:117–131.

Neyman, Jerzy and Elizabeth L. Scott. 1948. "Consistent Estimates Based on Partially Consistent Observations." *Econometrica*, 16:1–32.

Nie, Norman H., Sidney Verba, and John R. Petrocik. 1979. *The Changing American Voter*. New York: Replica Books.

Nokken, Timothy P. 2000. "Dynamics of Congressional Loyalty: Party Defection and Roll Call Behavior, 1947–1997." *Legislative Studies Quarterly*, 25:417–444.

Nokken, Timothy P. and Keith T. Poole. 2004. "Congressional Party Defection in American History." *Legislative Studies Quarterly*, forthcoming.

Nosofsky, Robert M. 1984. "Choice, Similarity, and the Context Theory of Classification." *Journal of Experimental Psychology: Learning, Memory and Cognition*, 10:104–114.

Nosofsky, Robert M. 1986. "Attention, Similarity, and the Identification–Categorization Relationship." *Journal of Experimental Psychology: General*, 115:39–57.

Nosofsky, Robert M. 1988. "On Exemplar-Based Exemplar Representations: Reply to Ennis (1988)." *Journal of Experimental Psychology: General*, 117:412–414.

Nosofsky, Robert M. 1991. "Stimulus Bias, Asymmetric Similarity, and Classification." *Cognitive Psychology*, 23:94–140.

Nosofsky, Robert M. 1992. "Similarity Scaling and Cognitive Process Models." *Annual Review of Psychology*, 43:25–53.

Oppenheimer, Bruce I. 2000. "The Roll Call Behavior of Members Who Switch Parties, 1900–99: The Effect of Variations in Party Strength." Paper Presented at the Annual Meeting of the Midwest Political Science Association, Chicago.

Ordeshook, Peter C. 1976. "The Spatial Theory of Elections: A Review and a Critique." In *Party Identification and Beyond,* edited by Ian Budge, Ivor Crewe, and Dennis Farlie. New York: Wiley.

Ordeshook, Peter C. 1996. "Engineering or Science: What is the Study of Politics?" In *The Rational Choice Controversy,* edited by Jeffrey Friedman. New Haven: Yale University Press.

Palfrey, Thomas R. 1984. "Spatial Equilibrium with Entry." *Review of Economic Studies,* 51:139–157.

Perlstein, Rick. 2001. *Before the Storm: Barry Goldwater and the Unmaking of the American Consensus.* New York: Hill and Wang.

Platt, Glenn, Keith T. Poole, and Howard Rosenthal. 1992. "Directional and Euclidean Theories of Voting Behavior: A Legislative Comparison." *Legislative Studies Quarterly,* 17:561–572.

Poole, Keith T. 1981. "Dimensions of Interest Group Evaluations of the U.S. Senate, 1969–1978." *American Journal of Political Science,* 25(1):49–67.

Poole, Keith T. 1984. "Least Squares Metric, Unidimensional Unfolding." *Psychometrika,* 49:311–323.

Poole, Keith T. 1988. "Recent Developments in Analytical Models of Voting in the U.S. Congress." *Legislative Studies Quarterly,* 13:117–133.

Poole, Keith T. 1990. "Least Squares Metric, Unidimensional Scaling of Multivariate Linear Models." *Psychometrika,* 55:123–149.

Poole, Keith T. 1997. "Non-parametric Analysis of Binary Choice Data." Manuscript, University of Houston.

Poole, Keith T. 1998. "Recovering a Basic Space From a Set of Issue Scales." *American Journal of Political Science,* 42:954–993.

Poole, Keith T. 1999. "NOMINATE: A Short Intellectual History." *The Political Methodologist,* 9:1–6.

Poole, Keith T. 2000a. "Non-parametric Unfolding of Binary Choice Data." *Political Analysis,* 8(3):211–237.

Poole, Keith T. 2000b. "Appendix to Non-parametric Unfolding of Binary Choice Data." Manuscript, University of Houston.

Poole, Keith T. 2001. "The Geometry of Multidimensional Quadratic Utility in Models of Parliamentary Roll Call Voting." *Political Analysis,* 9(3):211–226.

Poole, Keith T. 2003. "Changing Minds? Not in Congress!" Manuscript, University of Houston.

Poole, Keith T. and Thomas Romer. 1993. "Ideology, Shirking and Representation." *Public Choice,* 77:185–196.

Poole, Keith T. and Howard Rosenthal. 1984a. "U.S. Presidential Elections 1968–1980: A Spatial Analysis." *American Journal of Political Science,* 28:282–312.

Poole, Keith T. and Howard Rosenthal. 1984b. "The Polarization of American Politics." *Journal of Politics,* 46:1061–1079.

Poole, Keith T. and Howard Rosenthal. 1985. "A Spatial Model for Legislative Roll Call Analysis." *American Journal of Political Science,* 29:357–384.

Poole, Keith T. and Howard Rosenthal. 1987. "Analysis of Congressional Coalition Patterns: A Unidimensional Spatial Model." *Legislative Studies Quarterly,* 12:55–75.

Poole, Keith T. and Howard Rosenthal. 1991. "Patterns of Congressional Voting." *American Journal of Political Science,* 35:228–278.

Poole, Keith T. and Howard Rosenthal. 1997. *Congress: A Political–Economic History of Roll Call Voting.* New York: Oxford University Press.

Poole, Keith T. and Howard Rosenthal. 2001. "D-NOMINATE After 10 Years: A Comparative Update to *Congress: A Political–Economic History of Roll Call Voting.*" *Legislative Studies Quarterly*, 26:5–26.

Poole, Keith T., Fallaw B. Sowell, and Stephen E. Spear. 1992. "Evaluating Dimensionality in Spatial Voting Models." *Mathematical and Computer Modeling*, 16: 85–101.

Quinn, Kevin M. 2004. "Bayesian Factor Analysis for Mixed Ordinal and Continuous Responses." *Political Analysis*, 12:338–353.

Quinn, Kevin M. and Andrew D. Martin. 2002. "An Integrated Computational Model of Multiparty Electoral Competition." *Statistical Science*, 17:405–419.

Quinn, Kevin M., Andrew D. Martin, and Andrew B. Whitford. 1999. "Voter Choice in Multi-party Democracies: A Test of Competing Theories and Models." *American Journal of Political Science*, 43:1231–1247.

Rabinowitz, George. 1976. "A Procedure for Ordering Object Pairs Consistent with the Multidimensional Unfolding Model." *Psychometrika*, 45:349–373.

Rabinowitz, George and Stuart Macdonald. 1989. "A Directional Theory of Issue Voting." *American Political Science Review*, 83:93–121.

Rasch, Georg. 1961. "On General Laws and the Meaning of Measurement in Psychology." In *Proceedings of the IV Berkeley Symposium on Mathematical Statistics and Probability*, vol. 4, pp. 321–333.

Riker, William H. 1982/1988. *Liberalism Against Populism: A Confrontation Between the Theory of Democracy and the Theory of Social Choice*. Prospect Heights, IL: Waveland Press.

Rivers, Douglas. 2004. "Identification of Multidimensional Spatial Voting Models." Manuscript, Stanford University.

Romano, Roberta. 1997. "The Political Dynamics of Derivative Securities Regulation." *Yale Journal on Regulation*, 14:279–406.

Rosenberg, Seymour, Carnot Nelson, and P. S. Vivekananthan. 1968. "A Multidimensional Approach to the Structure of Personality Impressions." *Journal of Personality and Social Psychology*, 9:283–294.

Rosenthal, Howard and Erik Voeten. 2004. "Analyzing Roll Calls with Perfect Spatial Voting: France 1946–1958." *American Journal of Political Science*, 48:620–632.

Ross, John and Norman Cliff. 1964. "A Generalization of the Interpoint Distance Model." *Psychometrika*, 29:167–176.

Rothenberg, Lawrence S. and Mitchell S. Sanders. 2000. "Severing the Electoral Connection: Shirking in the Contemporary Congress." *American Journal of Political Science*, 44:316–325.

Rothkopf, Ernst Z. 1957. "A Measure of Stimulus Similarity and Errors in Some Paired-Associate Learning Tasks." *Journal of Experimental Psychology*, 53:94–101.

Ruger, Theodore W., Pauline T. Kim, Andrew D. Martin, and Kevin M. Quinn. 2004. "The Supreme Court Forecasting Project: Legal and Political Science Approaches to Predicting Supreme Court Decision-Making." *Columbia Law Review*, 104:1150–1209.

Schofield, Norman. 1996. "Rational Choice Theory and Political Economy." In *The Rational Choice Controversy*, edited by Jeffrey Friedman. New Haven: Yale University Press.

Schofield, Norman, Andrew D. Martin, Kevin M. Quinn, and Andrew B. Whitford. 1998. "Multiparty Electoral Competition in the Netherlands and Germany: A Model Based on Multinomial Probit." *Public Choice*, 97:257–293.

Schonemann, Peter H. 1966. "A Generalized Solution of the Orthogonal Procrustes Problem." *Psychometrika*, 31:1–10.

Schonemann, Peter H. 1970. "Fitting a Simplex Symmetrically." *Psychometrika*, 35: 1–21.

Schonemann, Peter H. and Robert M. Carroll. 1970. "Fitting One Matrix to Another Under Choice of a Central Dilation and Rigid Motion." *Psychometrika*, 35:245–256.

Schonhardt-Bailey, Cheryl. 2003. "Ideology, Party and Interests in the British Parliament of 1841–1847," *British Journal of Political Science*, 33:581–605.

Schonhardt-Bailey, Cheryl. 2004. *Interests, Ideas and Institutions: Repeal of the Corn Laws Re-told*. Manuscript, London School of Economics and Political Science.

Sen, Amartya K. 1970. *Collective Choice and Social Welfare*. San Francisco, CA: Holden-Day.

Shepard, Roger N. 1962a. "The Analysis of Proximities: Multidimensional Scaling with an Unknown Distance Function. I." *Psychometrika*, 27:125–139.

Shepard, Roger N. 1962b. "The Analysis of Proximities: Multidimensional Scaling with an Unknown Distance Function. II." *Psychometrika*, 27: 219–246.

Shepard, Roger N. 1963. "Analysis of Proximities as a Technique for the Study of Information Processing in Man." *Human Factors*, 5:33–48.

Shepard, Roger N. 1986. "Discrimination and Generalization in Identification and Classification: Comment on Nosofsky." *Journal of Experimental Psychology: General*, 115:58–61.

Shepard, Roger N. 1987. "Toward a Universal Law of Generalization for Psychological Science." *Science*, 237:1317–1323.

Shepard, Roger N. 1988a. "Technical Comments: Toward a Universal Law of Generalization." *Science*, 242:944.

Shepard, Roger N. 1988b. "Time and Distance in Generalization and Discrimination: Reply to Ennis (1988)." *Journal of Experimental Psychology: General*, 117:415–416.

Shepard, Roger N. 1991. "Integrality Versus Separability of Stimulus Dimensions: Evolution of the Distinction and a Proposed Theoretical Basis." In *Perception of Structure*, edited by James R. Pomerantz and Gregory Lockhead. Washington, DC: APA.

Shepsle, Kenneth A. 1996. "Statistical Political Philosophy and Positive Political Theory." In *The Rational Choice Controversy*, edited by Jeffrey Friedman. New Haven: Yale University Press.

Shipan, Charles R. and Bryon Moraski. 1999. "The Politics of Supreme Court Nominations: A Theory of Institutional Constraints and Choices." *American Journal of Political Science*, 43:1069–1095.

Silvapulle, Mervyn J. 1981. "On the Existence of Maximum Likelihood Estimators for the Binomial Response Models." *Journal of the Royal Statistical Society Series B*, 43(3):310–313.

Simmons, George F. 1972. *Differential Equations with Applications and Historical Notes*. New York: McGraw-Hill.

Smithies, Arthur. 1941. "Optimum Location in Spatial Competition." *The Journal of Political Economy*, 49:423–439.

Snyder, James M., Jr. 1992. "Artificial Extremism in Interest Group Ratings." *Legislative Studies Quarterly*, 17:319–345.

Snyder, James M., Jr., and Timothy Groseclose. 2000. "Estimating Party Influence in Congressional Roll-Call Voting." *American Journal of Political Science*, 44(2):193–211.

Sowell, Thomas. 1987. *A Conflict of Visions: Ideological Origins of Political Struggles.* New York: Quill.

Spector, David. 2000. "Rational Debate and One-Dimensional Conflict." *Quarterly Journal of Economics*, 115:181–200.

Stratmann, Thomas. 2000. "Congressional Voting Over Legislative Careers: Shifting Positions and Changing Constraints." *The American Political Science Review*, 94:665–676.

Tajfel, Henri. 1981. *Human Groups and Social Categories.* London: Cambridge University Press.

Thomas, Martin. 1985. "Election Proximity and Senatorial Roll Call Voting." *American Journal of Political Science*, 29(1):96–111.

Torgerson, Warren S. 1952. "Multidimensional Scaling: I. Theory and Method." *Psychometrika*, 17:401–419.

Treier, Shawn and Simon Jackman. 2003. "Democracy as a Latent Variable." Manuscript, Stanford University.

Tucker, Ledyard R. 1960. "Intra-individual and Inter-individual Multidimensionality." In *Psychological Scaling: Theory and Applications,* edited by Harold Gulliksen and Samuel Messick. New York: Wiley.

Tversky, Amos. 1977. "Features of Similarity." *Psychological Review*, 84:327–352.

Voeten, Erik. 2000. "Clashes in the Assembly." *International Organization*, 54:185–215.

Voeten, Erik. 2001. "Outside Options and the Logic of Security Council Action." *The American Political Science Review*, 95:845–858.

Voeten, Erik. 2004. "Resisting the Lonely Superpower: Responses of States in the U.N. to U.S. Dominance." *Journal of Politics*, 66:729–754.

Wang, Ming-Mei, Peter H. Schonemann, and Jerrold G. Rusk. 1975. "A Conjugate Gradient Algorithm for the Multidimensional Analysis of Preference Data." *Multivariate Behavioral Research*, 10:45–80.

Weisberg, Herbert F. 1968. *Dimensional Analysis of Legislative Roll Calls.* Doctoral Dissertation, University of Michigan.

Weisberg, Herbert F. 1978. "Evaluating Theories of Congressional Roll-Call Voting." *American Journal of Political Science*, 22:551–577.

Weisberg, Herbert F. 1983. "Alternative Baseline Models and Their Implications for Understanding Coalition Behavior in Congress." *Journal of Politics*, 45:657–671.

Weisberg, Herbert F. and Jerrold G. Rusk. 1970. "Dimensions of Candidate Evaluation." *American Political Science Review*, 64:1167–1185.

Wills, Garry. 1982. *The Federalist Papers by Alexander Hamilton, James Madison, and John Jay.* New York: Bantam Books.

Wish, Myron. 1971. "Individual Differences in Perceptions and Preferences Among Nations." In *Attitude Research Reaches New Heights,* edited by Charles W. King and Douglas J. Tigert. Chicago: American Marketing Association.

Wish, Myron and J. Douglas Carroll. 1974. "Applications of Individual Differences Scaling to Studies of Human Perception and Judgment." In *Handbook of Perception*, vol. 2, edited by Edward C. Carterette and Morton P. Friedman. New York: Academic Press.

Wittman, Donald A. 1977. "Candidates with Policy Preferences: A Dynamic Model." *Journal of Economic Theory*, 14:180–189.

Wittman, Donald A. 1983. "Candidate Motivations: A Synthesis of Alternatives." *American Political Science Review*, 77:142–157.

Wright, Gerald C. and Michael B. Berkman. 1986. "Candidates and Policy in United States Senate Elections." *American Political Science Review*, 80(2):567–588.

Wright, Gerald C. and Brian F. Schaffner. 2002. "The Influence of Party: Evidence from the State Legislatures." *American Political Science Review*, 96:367–379.

Young, Gale and A. S. Householder. 1938. "Discussion of a Set of Points in Terms of their Mutual Distances." *Psychometrika*, 3:19–22.

Index

Made in the USA
Las Vegas, NV
02 October 2021